Rational Emotive Behavior Therapy
A Training Manual

Windy Dryden, PhD, is Professor of Counseling at Goldsmith's College, University of London. He authored and edited more than 100 books, numerous book chapters and articles, and he has edited 12 book series. Among those books published by Springer is *The Practice of Rational-Emotive Therapy, The Essential Albert Ellis: Seminal Writings on Psychotherapy, Overcoming Resistance: Rational-Emotive Therapy With Difficult Clients*, and *Doing RET: Albert Ellis in Action*. He is a Fellow of the Albert Ellis Institute of Rational-Emotive Behavior Therapy, the British Psychological Society, the British Association for Association for Counseling, and is Consulting Editor of the *Journal of Cognitive Psychotherapy: An International Quarterly* (Springer Publishing).

Rational Emotive Behavior Therapy

A Training Manual

Windy Dryden, PhD

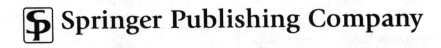

Springer Publishing Company

Springer Publishing Company, Inc.
536 Broadway
New York, NY 10012-3955

Cover design by Janet Joachim
Acquisitions Editor: Bill Tucker
Production Editor: Helen Song

99 00 01 02 03 / 5 4 3 2 1

Library of Congress Cata;oging-in-Publication Data

Dryden, Windy.
    Rational emotive behavior therapy : a training manual / Windy Dryden.
        p.   cm.
    Includes bibliographical references and index.
    ISBN 0-8261-1249-8 (hardcover)
    1. Rational-emotive psychotherapy—Study and teaching—Handbooks, manuals, etc.   I. Title.
    RC489.R3D7887   1999
    616.89'14—dc21   98-48400
                                                    CIP

Contents

96673

Module 22

Introduction

Having given numerous introductory certificate courses in rational emo-tive behavior therapy (REBT) in Britain, Ireland, South Africa, Holland, Israel, and the USA, it seemed to me that it would be valuable to write a very practical book on REBT in which I recreate the atmosphere of these training courses. In particular, because REBT is a simple approach that is difficult to practice well, I wanted to alert trainees to areas of difficulty that they are likely to experience while attempting to use the approach and show them how they can deal constructively with the problems that they will doubtless encounter along the way.

To do this I will use constructed verbatim transcript material between trainees and myself as trainer. What this means is that to highlight trainee difficulty and trainer response, I have constructed dia-logues that approximate those that have occurred between me and my trainees over the years. None of these dialogues have actually taken place, however. As I do not tape record my training sessions, I do not have access to actual trainer—trainee dialogues that have occurred. Nevertheless, the constructed dialogues illustrate common misconceptions that trainees have of REBT and typical errors they make in its practice. In addition, I will make extensive use of actual and constructed dialogue between myself as therapist and my clients. Where the dialogue was actual, I have obtained permission from clients to use our therapeutic work for educational purposes. In these cases, I have changed all names, some clients' gender and all identifying material.

Please note that on introductory training programs in REBT, peer counseling is used extensively as a training vehicle. This means that trainees form a pair and take turns counseling one another on real emotional problems and concerns using REBT. In my experience this is a far more effective way of learning how to use REBT and what it feels like to be an REBT client than the use of role plays. To preserve confidentiality, any dialogue that appears in this book between trainees in peer counseling has also been constructed. However, these dialogues are typical of the emotional problems that are raised in this part of the course by trainees in the client role. The performance of REBT trainees in these interchanges approximates the level of skill beginning trainees tend to demonstrate on introductory training courses.

It is important for me to stress that no book on Rational Emotive Behavior Therapy, however practical, can substitute for proper training and supervision in the approach. Thus, this book is best used as an adjunct to these educational activities. I have provided information on where to get training and supervision in REBT in Appendix 3, should you be interested in pursuing your interest in this therapeutic approach. Indeed, I hope that this book might encourage you to attend an initial training course in REBT so that you can learn for yourself what it has to offer you and your clients.

Module 1
What You Need To Know About the Theory of Rational Emotive Behavior Therapy To Get Started

Most books on counseling and psychotherapy begin by an introduction to the theory and practice of the approach in question. This is obviously a sensible way to start such a book because otherwise how are you to understand the practical techniques described by the author? However, in my experience as a reader of such books, I am often given more information than I need about an approach to begin to practice it, at least in the context of a training setting. As I explained in the introduction, my aim in this book is to recreate the atmosphere of a beginning training seminar in REBT. In such seminars the emphasis is on the acquisition of practical skills and, consequently, theory is kept to a minimum. What I aim to do in such seminars and what I will do in this opening module is to introduce the information you will need to know about the theory of REBT so that you can begin to practice it in a training seminar setting. In the following module, I will cover what you need to know about the *practice* of REBT to get started.

Let me reiterate a point that I made in the introduction. When learn-ing any approach to counseling and psychotherapy, you will need to be trained by a competent trainer in the approach you are learning and supervised in your work with clients by a competent supervisor in that approach. To do otherwise is bad and, some would say, unethical practice. Certainly, when learning to practice REBT you will need to be trained and supervised by people competent not only in the practice of REBT, but also in educating others how to use it (see Appendix 3).

REBT

Rational Emotive Behavior Therapy is one of the cognitive-behavioral approaches to psychotherapy. This means that it pays particular attention to the role that cognitions and behavior play in the development and maintenance of people's emotional problems. However, as I will show in Unit 2,

3

REBT argues that at the core of emotional disturbance lies a set of irrational beliefs that people hold about themselves, other people and the world.

When assessing their clients' psychological problems, REBT therapists employ an ABC framework and I will now discuss each element of this framework in turn. In doing so, I will first consider a client's healthy responses to life events and then discuss her unhealthy responses to these same events.

Unit 1: As

As are events which you as a person are potentially able to discern and attend to and which can trigger your beliefs at B. Whilst you are potentially able to focus on different As at any moment, in an ABC episode A represents that actual or psychological event in your life which activates, at that moment, the beliefs that you hold (at B) and which lead to your emotional and behavioral responses (at C). As have a number of features that I will explain below.

As can be actual events

While Susan was in therapy, her mother died. She felt very sad about this event and grieved appropriately. Using the ABC framework to understand this we can say that the death of her mother represented an actual event at A which activated a set of beliefs that underpinned Susan's grief. When actual events serve as belief-triggering As they do not contain any inferences that the person adds to the event.

As can be inferred events

When Wendy was in therapy, her mother died. Like Susan she felt very sad about this and as such we can say that the death was an actual A which triggered her sadness-related beliefs. However, unlike Susan, Wendy also felt guilty in relation to her mother's death. How can we explain this?

According to REBT, people make interpretations and inferences about the events in their lives. I regard interpretations and inferences as hunches about reality that go beyond observable data which may be correct or incorrect, but need to be tested out. Whilst most REBT therapists regard interpretations and inferences to be synonymous I make the following distinction between them. Interpretations are hunches about reality that go beyond observable data, but are not personally significant to the person making them. They are, thus, not implicated in the person's emotional experience.

For example, imagine that I am standing with my face to a window and I ask you to describe what I am doing. If you say, 'You are looking out of the window', you are making an interpretation in that you are going beyond the data at hand (e.g. I could have my eyes closed) in an area that is probably insignificant to you (i.e. it probably doesn't matter to you whether I have my eyes open or not) and thus you will not have an emotional response while making the interpretation.

However, imagine that in response to my request for you to describe what I was doing in this example, you said, 'You are ridiculing me'. This, then, is an inference in that you are going beyond the data available to you in an area that is probably significant to you (i.e. it probably matters to you whether or not I am ridiculing you) and thus you will have an emotional response while making the inference. Whether this emotional response is healthy or not, however, depends on the type of belief you make about the inferred ridicule (as I will show in Unit 2).

Returning to the example of Wendy who felt guilty about the death of her mother, I hope you can now see that she is guilty not about the death itself, but about some inferred aspect of the death that is significant to her. In this case it emerged that Wendy felt guilty about hurting her mother's feelings when she was alive. This, then, is an inferred A—it points to something beyond the data available to Wendy; it is personally significant to her and it triggered her guilt-producing belief.

As can be external or internal

So far I have discussed As that have related to events that have actually happened (e.g. the death of Susan's mother) or were deemed to have happened (e.g. Wendy's inference that she hurt her mother's feelings when she was alive). In REBT, these are known as external events in that they are external to the person concerned. Thus, the death of Susan's mother is an actual external A and Wendy's statement that she hurt her mother's feelings is an inferred external A.

However, As can also refer to events that are *internal* to the person. Such events can actually occur or their existence can be inferred. An example of an actual internal event is when I experience a pain in my throat. An example of an inferred internal event is when I think that this pain means that I have throat cancer. As well as bodily sensations, internal As can refer to such phenomena as a person's thoughts, images, fantasies, emotions and memories. Again with these internal As it is important to distinguish between actual and inferred As as demonstrated in Figure 1.1.

It is important to remember that, as with external As, internal As have their emotional impact by triggering beliefs at B.

As can refer to past, present and future events

Just as As can be actual or inferred and external or internal, they can also refer to past, present or future events. When your A in an ABC

Actual Internal A	*Inferred Internal A*
Thought 'Why do people stare at me'	'I'm going mad'
Image 'A pink lobster cooking a man'	'I'm a creative genius'
Fantasy 'Becoming a great singer'	'I'm wasting my time'
Emotion 'Jealousy'	'This is a sign of immaturity'
Memory 'Specific memory of time at university'	'Things were better then than now'

Figure 1.1 Examples of actual internal As and inferences about these As.

episode is a past actual event, then you do not bring any inferential meaning to this event. Thus, if your father died when you were a teenager, this very event can serve as an A. However, more frequently, particularly in therapy, you will find that your clients will bring inferential meaning to past events. Thus, you may infer that your father's death meant that you were deprived in some way or you may infer that his passing away was a punishment for some misdeed that you were responsible for as a child. It is important to remember that it is the inferences that you make now about a past event that trigger your beliefs at B. Such inferences may relate to the past, present and future. An example of a future-related inference that you might make about an actual past event is as follows: 'Because my father died when I was a teenager, I will continually look for a father figure to replace him'.

I have already discussed present As. However, I do want to stress that you can make past-, present- or future-related inferences about present events. For example, if you are angry about your son coming home late (present actual A), you may make the following time-related inferences about this event that trigger anger-provoking beliefs:

1. Past-related inference: 'He reminds me of the rough kids at school who used to bully me when I was a teenager.'
2. Present-related inference: 'He broke our agreement.'
3. Future-related inference: 'If he does this now he will turn into a criminal.'

The importance of assuming temporarily that the critical A is true

As I will show in greater detail in module 8, in order to assess a client's beliefs accurately, you will need to do two things. First, you will need to help your client to identify the A which triggered these beliefs. Because there are many potential As that are in your client's perceptual field, it takes a lot of care and skill to do this accurately. To distinguish between the A that triggered the client's beliefs and the other As in his perceptual field, in this book I will follow the lead of Don Beal (personal communication) and call the former the critical A and the latter non-critical As. Second, it is important that you encourage your client to assume temporarily that the critical A is true, when it is an inferred A. The reason for doing this is to help your client to identify the beliefs that the critical A triggered. You may be tempted to help your client to challenge the inferred critical A if it is obviously distorted, but it is important for you to resist this temptation if you are to proceed to assess B accurately.

Unit 2: Bs

A major difference between REBT and other approaches to cognitive-behavior therapy is in the emphasis REBT gives to beliefs. In REBT, beliefs are fully and explicitly evaluative and are at the core of a person's emotions and significant behaviors. Such beliefs are the only cognitions that constitute the B in the ABC framework. Thus, whilst other approaches which use an ABC framework lump all cognitive activity under B, REBT reserves B for evaluative beliefs and places inferences, for example, under A. It does so because it recognizes that the same inferred As can be evaluated in two different ways at B. It is the type of evaluative belief that determines the nature of the person's emotional response at C.

Rational beliefs

REBT keenly distinguishes between rational and irrational beliefs. In this section I will discuss rational beliefs. When applied to beliefs, the term 'rational' has four defining characteristics as shown in Figure 1.2.

Rational beliefs are:

Flexible

Consistent with reality

Logical

Helpful to the individual in pursuing his basic goals and purposes

Figure 1.2 Defining characteristics of rational beliefs.

Human beings do not only proceed in life by making descriptions of what they perceive, nor do they just make interpretations and inferences of their perceptions. Rather, humans engage in the fundamentally important activity of evaluating what they perceive. In REBT, when these evaluations point to a person's preferences, on the one hand, and demands, on the other, they are known as beliefs. REBT theory posits that people have four types of rational beliefs as shown in Figure 1.3.

Preferences

Anti-awfulizing

High frustration tolerance

Self-acceptance/Other-acceptance

Figure 1.3 Four types of rational beliefs.

Preferences

As humans we often express our flexible evaluations in the form of preferences, wishes, desires, wants, etc. According to REBT, our non-dogmatic preferences are at the core of psychological health. In their full form, they are often expressed thus:

'I want to do well in my forthcoming test, but I do not have to do so.'

If only the first part of this rational belief was expressed: 'I want to do well in my forthcoming test', then the person could, implicitly, change this to an irrational belief: 'I want to do well in my forthcoming test... (and therefore I have to do so)'. So, it is important to help your clients to express their rational beliefs in their full form and this involves negating the irrational belief (i.e. 'but I do not have to do so').

This belief is rational for the following reasons:

1. It is flexible in that the person allows for the fact that he might not do well.
2. It is consistent with reality in that the person really does want to do well in the forthcoming test, but acknowledges that there is no universal law that decrees that he has to do so.
3. It is logical in that this specific belief makes sense in the context of the person's general desire to do well at things that are important to him.
4. It will help him to do well in the sense that the belief will motivate him to focus on what he is doing as opposed to how well he is doing it.

According to Albert Ellis, a preference is a primary rational belief and three other rational beliefs are derived from it. These beliefs are anti-awfulizing, high frustration tolerance and self- and other-acceptance. I will deal with each in turn. In doing so I will emphasize and illustrate the importance of negating the irrational belief in formulating a rational belief in each of these derivatives.

Anti-awfulizing

When a person does not get his preference met, then it is rational for him to conclude that it is bad, but not awful that he has failed to get what he wanted. The more important the person's preference, then the more unfortunate is his failure to get it. Evaluations of badness can be placed on a continuum from 0%–99.99% badness. However, it is not possible to get to 100% badness. The words of the mother of pop singer Smokey Robinson capture this concept quite nicely: 'From the day you are born till you ride in the hearse, there's nothing so bad that it couldn't be worse.' This should not be thought of as minimising the badness of a very negative event, rather to show that 'nothing is truly awful in the universe.'

Taking our example of the person whose primary rational belief is: 'I want to do well in my forthcoming test, but I do not have to do so', his full anti-awfulizing belief is:

'It will be bad if I fail to do well in my forthcoming test, but it is not awful if I don't do well.'

This belief is rational for the following reasons:

1. It is flexible in that the person allows for the fact that there are things that can be worse than not doing well on the test.
2. It is consistent with reality in that the person really can prove i) that it would be bad for him not to do well, and ii) that it is not awful if he does not do well.
3. It is logical in that this specific belief makes sense in the context of the person's general tendency to view not doing well at things that are important to him as bad, but not awful.
4. It will help the person to do well in that it will encourage him to focus on what he needs to do in order to perform well on the test rather than on how well he is doing while he is doing it.

High frustration tolerance

When a person does not get his preference met, then it is rational for him to conclude that this is difficult to bear, but it is not intolerable. Adhering to a philosophy of high frustration tolerance (HFT) enables the person to put up with the frustration of having his goals blocked and in doing so he is more likely to deal with or circumvent these obstacles so that he can get back on track. REBT holds that the importance of developing a philosophy of HFT is that it helps people to pursue their goals, not because tolerating frustration is in itself good for people.

Applying this to our example when he believes: 'I want to do well in my forthcoming test, but I do not have to do so', the person's HFT belief will be:

'If I don't do well in my forthcoming test, that will be difficult to bear, but I can stand it. It will not be intolerable.'

This belief is rational for the following reasons:

1. It is flexible in that the person allows for the fact that not doing well is tolerable as opposed to the rigid position that it is unbearable.
2. It is consistent with reality in that the person really can bear that which is difficult to tolerate.
3. It is logical in that this specific belief makes sense in the context of the person's general tendency to tolerate with difficulty things that go against his important desire.
4. It will help him to do well in the sense that it will lead him to focus on what he needs to do to avoid the difficult to tolerate situation of not doing well rather than on the 'intolerable' aspects of doing poorly.

Self- and other-acceptance

When a person does not get his preference met and this failure can be attributed either to himself or to the blocking efforts of another person, then it is rational for him not to like his or the other person's behavior, but to accept himself or the other person as a fallible human being who has acted poorly. Adopting a philosophy of self- and other-acceptance will encourage the person to focus on what needs to be done to correct his own behavior or to deal with the frustrating efforts of the other person

In our example, if the person who believes: 'I want to do well in my forthcoming test, but I do not have to do so', fails to do well on this test because of his own failings, then his self-accepting belief will be:

'I don't like the fact that I messed up on the test, but I can accept myself as a fallible human being for this. I am not less worthy for my poor performance.'

This belief is rational for the following reasons:

1. It is flexible in that the person sees that he is able to do well as well as poorly.
2. It is consistent with reality in that whilst he can prove that he did not do well on the test (remember that at this point we have assumed temporarily that his inferred A is true), he can also prove that he is a fallible human being.
3. It is logical in that the person's conclusion that he is a fallible human

being logically follows from the observation that he did poorly on the test.
4. It will help him to do well in the future in the sense that he will be motivated to learn from his previous errors and translate this learning to plan what he needs to do to improve his performance on the next test rather than dwell unfruitfully on his past poor performance.

However, if the person failed to do well owing to the behavior of another person, then his other-accepting belief will be:

'I dislike the fact that this person kept stopping me from revising for my test. However, he is not a bad person for doing so. Rather, he is a fallible human being who acted selfishly. Now, what am I going to do to prevent him from acting in that way next time?'

This belief is again rational for the following reasons:

1. It is flexible in that the person sees that the other person is able to act well as well as poorly.
2. It is consistent with reality in that the person can prove that the other person has acted poorly (remember that at this point we have assumed temporarily that his inferred A is true), but that he is a fallible human being.
3. It is logical in that the person's conclusion that the other person is a fallible human being logically follows from the observation that he acted poorly.
4. It will help him to do well in the future in the sense that he will focus on what he needs to do to correct the situation rather than on what the other person did to prevent him from doing well in the first place.

Irrational beliefs

As I mentioned above, REBT keenly distinguishes between rational and irrational beliefs. Having discussed rational beliefs, I will now turn my attention to irrational beliefs which are, according to REBT theory, the core of psychological problems. When applied to beliefs, the term 'irrational' has four defining characteristics as shown in Figure 1.4.

Irrational beliefs are:

Rigid

Inconsistent with reality

Illogical

Detrimental to the individual in pursuing his basic goals and purposes

Figure 1.4 Defining characteristics of irrational beliefs.

I explained earlier in this chapter that people can have four types of rational beliefs. According to REBT theory, people easily transmute or change these rational beliefs into four types of irrational beliefs (see Figure 1.5).

Musts

Awfulizing

Low frustration tolerance

Self-downing/Other-downing

Figure 1.5 Four types of irrational beliefs.

Musts

As humans we often express our rigid evaluations in the form of musts, absolute shoulds, have to's, got to's, etc. According to REBT, our dogmatic musts or demands are at the core of psychological disturbance. Taking the example which I introduced above they are expressed thus:

'I must do well in my forthcoming test.'

Dogmatic demands are often based on healthy preferences. According to Dryden, (1990a), it is difficult for human beings only to think rationally when their desires are strong. Thus, in our example, if the person's preference is strong it is easy for him to change it into a must: 'Because I really want to do well in my forthcoming test, therefore I absolutely have to do so'.

This belief is irrational for the following reasons:

1. It is rigid in that the person does not allow for the fact that he might not do well.
2. It is inconsistent with reality in that if there was a law of the universe that decreed that the person must do well in his forthcoming test, then there could be no possibility that he would not perform well in it. Obviously, no such law exists
3. It is illogical in that there is no logical connection between his healthy desire and his unhealthy must. In general, musts do not follow logically from preference.
4. It will interfere with him doing well in the sense that the belief will motivate him to focus on how well he is doing rather than on what he is doing.

According to Albert Ellis, a must is the primary irrational belief and three other irrational beliefs are derived from it. These beliefs are awfulizing, low frustration tolerance and self- and other-downing. I will deal with each in turn.

Awfulizing

When a person does not get what he believes he must get, then he will tend to conclude that it is awful that he has failed to get what he considers essential. Awfulizing, according to REBT theory, can be placed on a continuum from 101%–infinity and means worse than it absolutely should be.

Taking our example of the person whose primary irrational belief is

'Because I really want to do well in my forthcoming test, therefore I absolutely have to do so', his full awfulizing belief is

'It will be awful if I fail to do well in my forthcoming test.'

This belief is irrational for the following reasons:

1. It is rigid in that the person does not allow for the fact that there are things that can be worse than not doing well on the test.
2. It is inconsistent with reality in that the person really cannot prove that it would be awful if he does not do well. Whilst there is evidence that it would be bad for him not to do well, there is no evidence that it would be more than 100% bad.
3. It is illogical in the sense that the idea that it would be awful if he does not do well does not logically follow from the idea that it would be bad if this occurred.
4. It will not help him to do well in that it will discourage him from focusing on what he needs to do in order to perform well on the test; rather it will draw him to focus on how poorly he is doing while he is doing it.

Low frustration tolerance

When a person does not get what he believes he must get, then he will tend to conclude that this situation is intolerable and that he can't stand it. In REBT theory 'I can't stand it' either means that the person will disintegrate or that he will never experience any happiness again if the 'dreaded' event occurs. Adhering to a philosophy of low frustration tolerance (LFT) discourages the person from putting up with the frustration of having his goals blocked and thus he will tend to back away from dealing with these obstacles

Applying this to our example when he believes: 'Because I really want to do well in my forthcoming test, therefore I absolutely have to do so', the person's LFT belief will be:

'If I don't do well in my forthcoming test, that will be intolerable. I won't be able to stand it.'

This belief is irrational for the following reasons:

1. It is rigid in that the person does not allow for the fact that not doing well is tolerable

2. It is inconsistent with reality in that if there was a law of the universe which stated that the person couldn't bear not doing well, then he couldn't bear it no matter what attitude he held. This means that he would literally disintegrate or would never experience any happiness again if he failed to do well in the test. Hardly likely!
3. It is illogical in that the belief that not doing well on a test is unbearable does not logically follow from the belief that it is difficult to tolerate, but bearable.
4. It will interfere with him doing well in the sense that it will lead him to focus on the 'intolerable' aspects of doing poorly rather than on what he needs to do to circumvent the obstacles in his way.

Self- and other-downing

When a person does not get what he believes he must get and this failure can be attributed either to himself or to the blocking efforts of another person, then he will tend to dislike himself or the other person as well as his own or the other person's poor behavior. Adopting a philosophy of self- and other-downing will discourage the person from focusing on what needs to be done to correct his own behavior or to deal with the frustrating efforts of the other person.

In our example, if the person who believes: 'Because I really want to do well in my forthcoming test, therefore I absolutely have to do so', fails to do well because of his own failings, then his self-downing belief will be

'I am a failure because I failed to do well on the test.'

This belief is irrational for the following reasons:

1. It is rigid in that the person only sees himself as a reflection of his behavior, rather than a complex person with many different facets
2. It is inconsistent with reality in that whilst he can prove that he did not do well on the test (remember that at this point we have assumed temporarily that his inferred A is true), he cannot prove that he is a failure. Indeed if he was a failure then he could only and ever fail in life. Again this is hardly likely!
3. It is illogical in that the person's conclusion that he is a failure does not logically follow from the observation that he did poorly on the test.
4. It will prevent him from doing well in the future in the sense that he will be preoccupied with his own worthlessness rather than motivated to learn from his previous errors.

However, if the person failed to do well owing to the behavior of another person, then his other-downing belief will be:

'The other person is rotten for stopping me from revising for my test.'

This belief is irrational for the following reasons:

1. It is rigid in that the person only sees the other person in terms of that person's bad behavior, rather than as a person with many facets
2. It is inconsistent with reality in that whilst he can prove that the other person acted poorly by stopping him from revising for his test (remember again that at this point we have assumed temporarily that his inferred A is true), he cannot prove that the other person is rotten. Indeed if the other person was rotten then he could only and ever act badly in life. Once again this is very unlikely!
3. It is illogical in that the person's conclusion that the other person is rotten does not logically follow from his observation that the latter acted poorly by disrupting his studies.
4. It will prevent him from doing well in the future in the sense that he will be preoccupied with the other person's badness rather than motivated to think of a plan to avoid a similar situation in the future.

Unit 3: Cs

Healthy and unhealthy negative emotions

In REBT Cs mainly represent the emotional and behavioral consequences of holding a set of beliefs at B about the critical A. As I will discuss in detail in Module 5, REBT theory holds that people experience healthy negative emotions when their preferences are not met. These negative emotions (which are listed in Figure 1.6) are healthy because they encourage people to change what can be changed or make a constructive adjustment when the situations that they face cannot be changed.

Alternatively, people experience unhealthy negative emotions when they get what they demand they must not get or when they do not get what they demand they must get. These negative emotions (which are again listed in Figure 1.6 and discussed in detail in Module 5) are unhealthy in that they tend to discourage people from changing what can be changed and from adjusting constructively when they cannot change the situations that they encounter. In short, healthy negative emotions stem from rational beliefs about negative As, whilst unhealthy negative emotions stem from irrational beliefs about negative As.

As I have explained elsewhere (Dryden, 1991), it is important for you to understand that your clients may use feeling words very differently from the way they are used in REBT theory. As such you will need to explain very carefully the distinctions between healthy and unhealthy negative emotions and adopt a shared vocabulary when working with your clients. I will discuss this issue fully in Module 5.

Healthy Negative Emotions	*Unhealthy Negative Emotions*
Concern	Anxiety
Sadness	Depression
Remorse	Guilt
Sorrow	Hurt
Disappointment	Shame
Healthy anger	Unhealthy anger
Healthy jealousy	Unhealthy jealousy
Healthy envy	Unhealthy envy

Figure 1.6: Types of healthy and unhealthy negative emotions.

Mixed Emotions

As I will discuss in Module 6, Unit 18, when you and your client select a problem to work on this problem is called a target problem. While assessing a target problem, you will ask for a concrete example of its occurrence. You need to realize at this point that it is likely that your client will have a mixture of emotions about the situation in which his or her problem occurred, thus, perhaps not having a single, unalloyed emotion. For example, let's suppose that your client has difficulty expressing her negative feelings to her friends when she considers that they take advantage of her. Thus, she keeps her feelings to herself with the result that her friends continue to use him or her. When you come to assess a specific example of this problem you may well find that your client experiences a mixture of the following emotions: unhealthy anger, hurt, anxiety and shame. Now, it is important to appreciate that each of these emotions has its own critical A, which as you know may be an actual event or an inferred event. Thus, your client was angry when focusing on the selfish aspects of friends' behavior, hurt when focusing on the uncaring aspects of their behavior, anxious when thinking about the possible rejection that might follow any assertion and ashamed when focusing on his or her own weakness for not having the courage to speak up. I argue that if you want to deal with all these issues, then it is helpful to do an ABC analysis for each of the four unhealthy emotions that your client experienced. If you try to do one ABC for the entire experience, you will become confused and so, undoubtedly, will your client

Meta-emotions

As human beings we have the ability to reflect on our experiences and think about our thoughts, feelings and behaviors. Thus, our own emotions can serve as a critical A in an ABC episode in which our beliefs determine what subsequent emotions we will have about our prior emotions. I call these emotions about emotions, 'meta-emotions'. As is the case with negative emotions, negative meta-emotions can be healthy or unhealthy. Thus, as Figure 1.7 shows, we may have healthy negative meta-emotions about both healthy and unhealthy negative emotions and we may also experience unhealthy negative meta-emotions about both healthy and unhealthy negative emotions. The term I use to describe the latter situation, where we have emotional problems about our emotional problems is 'meta-emotional problems'. As you will see in Module 10, the identification and analysis of meta-emotional problems plays a particularly important role in the overall REBT assessment process

	Healthy negative emotion	Unhealthy negative emotion
Healthy negative meta-emotion	Disappointment about being healthily angry	Disappointment about being unhealthily angry
Unhealthy negative meta-emotion	Ashamed about being healthily angry	Ashamed about being unhealthily angry [Meta-emotional Problem]

Figure 1.7 Negative emotion and meta-emotion matrix.

Action tendencies and behavior

According to REBT theory, whenever a person experiences a negative emotion then he or she has a tendency to act in a certain way. Whether or not the person actualises that tendency and goes on to execute a behavior consistent with it depends mainly on whether or not he or she makes a conscious decision to go against the tendency. One major task that you have as an REBT therapist is to help your client to see the purpose of going against the action tendencies that are based on unhealthy negative emotions and to develop alternative behaviors that are consistent with action tendencies based on the corresponding healthy negative emotions. Before you can do this you need to help your client to identify and dispute irrational beliefs and to develop and strengthen alternative rational beliefs. I will discuss more fully in Module 5, Unit 15, the action tendencies associated with each of the major healthy and unhealthy negative emotions listed in Figure 1.6 above.

Unit 4: ABCs Interact in Complex Ways: The Principle of Psychological Interactionism

So far in this module I have discussed the ABCs of REBT as if they were separate processes, distinct from one another. However, while in therapy it is important to deal with the ABCs as if they were separate components – because otherwise your clients will end up confused – in reality, REBT theory has, right from the outset, advocated the principle of psychological interactionism. This principle states that the events that we choose to focus on, our interpretations and inferences, the beliefs that we hold, the emotions that we experience and the behaviors that we enact are all interrelated and reciprocally influence one another in often complex ways. It is beyond the scope of this book for me to discuss fully and in detail these complex interactions. Those of you who are interested to learn more about the principle of psychological interactionism should consult Ellis (1991) and Dryden (1994b).

However, to illustrate this principle, let me discuss one such interrelationship. In keeping with the practical nature of this book, I will consider the impact of holding beliefs at B on the inferences that your clients may make at A because an understanding of this influence has direct relevance for the practice of REBT.

The influence of beliefs on inferences

You will recall that earlier I discussed the differences between actual events and inferred events. I argued that although inferences are cognitions, they are best considered as As in that when critical, they trigger a person's beliefs at B. In this straightforward case the A triggers the B. We can denote this by the following formula:

$A \rightarrow B$.

However, the beliefs that a person holds can influence the subsequent inferences that he makes at C. In this more complicated case, we can denote this influence by the following formula:

$B \rightarrow InfA$.

Let me illustrate the influence of beliefs on inferences in two ways. The first concerns a series of experiments that I conducted with my colleagues in the late 1980s. In one of these studies (Dryden, Ferguson and Clark,

1989), we asked one group of subjects to imagine that they held a rational belief about giving a class presentation and another group to imagine that they held an irrational belief about the class presentation. Then we asked them to make a number of judgements on a series of inferential measures related to giving a class presentation, while maintaining the belief that they were asked to hold. We found that the type of beliefs subjects held had a profound influence on the inferences that they made. In general, subjects holding the irrational belief made more negatively distorted inferences about their performance in the class presentation and about other people's reactions to it than did subjects who held the rational belief.

The second illustration of the effect of beliefs on inferences is a clinical one. Sarah, a 34 year old woman, came into therapy because she was depressed about her facial appearance. At the beginning of therapy she held the following irrational belief: 'I must be more attractive than I am and I am worthless because I am less attractive than I must be.' At this point she thought that everybody that she met would consider her ugly and that no man would want to go out with her. You will note that these latter statements are her inferences about the reactions of people in general and men in particular. During therapy I worked predominantly at the belief level and at no time did I target her distorted inferences for change. As a result of my interventions, Sarah came to hold the following rational belief:

'I would like to be more attractive than I am, but there is no reason why I must be. I don't like the fact that I am less attractive than I would like to be, but I can accept myself as a fallible, complex human being with this lack. I am not worthless and my looks are just one part of me, not the total whole.'

As a result of this belief change, Sarah reduced markedly her inferences that others would consider her ugly and that men would not want to go out with her. In fact, soon her after therapy ended she started dating a man whom she later married. This clinical vignette shows quite clearly, I believe, the influence of beliefs on inferences.

Having introduced you to the theoretical fundamentals of REBT in this module, in the next I will cover what you need to know about the practice of REBT to begin to practice it in a training seminar setting.

Module 2
What You Need To Know About the Practice of Rational Emotive Behavior Therapy To Get Started

In this module, I will outline aspects of the practice of REBT that you need to know before beginning to practice it. In particular, I will discuss (a) the REBT perspective on the so-called 'core conditions'; (b) the active-directive therapeutic style adopted by REBT therapists and the skills involved in the implementation of this style;(c) the goals of REBT; and (d) the tasks that both therapist and client need to accomplish in the REBT therapy process.

Unit 5: The "Core Conditions"

In the late 1950s Carl Rogers (1957) wrote a highly influential paper on what has come to be known as the 'core conditions'. These represent the qualities which therapists need to communicate to clients who in turn need to perceive their presence for their therapeutic effect to be realized. Before I present the REBT perspective on these 'core conditions', I want to address one point that Rogers made with which REBT therapists fundamentally disagree. Rogers argued that the 'core conditions' that he posited were necessary and sufficient for therapeutic change to occur. In contrast REBT theory claims that certain therapist qualities are desirable conditions for therapeutic change to occur, but that these qualities are neither necessary nor sufficient conditions for the occurrence of client change. REBT holds this view as therapeutic change can take place in the absence of such therapist qualities, although such change is more likely to occur when these 'core conditions' are present. What are the 'core conditions' in REBT?

Empathy

REBT therapists agree with our person-centred colleagues in regarding empathy as an important therapist quality. However, we distinguish between two different types of empathy. First, there is affective empathy whereby we communicate to our clients that we understand how they feel. Here, we need to clarify for ourselves and for our clients whether they have experienced healthy or unhealthy negative emotions (see Modules 1 and 5). This is an important pre-condition for the second type of empathy delineated in REBT, i.e. philosophic empathy. In this type of empathy, we communicate to our clients that we understand the rational or irrational beliefs that underpin their emotional experience. When we are accurate in communicating such philosophic empathy, clients often exclaim that they truly 'feel' understood.

Unlike our person-centred colleagues, however, we not do not see either type of empathy as curative. Rather, we consider that both types of empathy serve to strengthen the therapeutic bond between therapist and client and that philosophic empathy, in particular, has an educational effect in that it helps clients to understand the link between their emotions and the beliefs that underpin them.

Unconditional acceptance

The second 'core condition' put forward by Rogers has been variously called unconditional positive regard, prizing, non-possessive warmth and respect. From an REBT perspective these terms are problematic in that they imply that the therapist is giving her client a global positive evaluation. As such, REBT therapists prefer to offer their clients unconditional acceptance. This term means that the therapist demonstrates that she regards the client as a fallible human being, too complex to merit any kind of global evaluation, who has many different aspects, positive, negative and neutral.

In an interview with me (Dryden, 1985), Ellis cautioned REBT therapists against being overly warm with their clients. He feared that undue therapist warmth would sidetrack the therapeutic process, lead the client to become involved with the therapist at the expense of involving himself in self-change methods outside the consulting room, inhibit the therapist from confronting the client and reinforce the client's need for approval. Interestingly, in a recent research study (DiGiuseppe et al., 1993), Ellis was rated low on warmth by his clients, a finding consistent with his ideas on the dubious value of this variable.

Genuineness

The third 'core condition' advocated by Rogers again has been described differently. It has variously been called genuineness, congruence and open-ness. From an REBT perspective genuineness means that the ther-apist does not hide behind a facade and answers clients' questions hon-estly, even at times those directed to her personal life, as long as she does not consider that the client will disturb himself about what the therapist may say. With this caveat, the REBT therapist will, for example, point out to the client his self-defeating or anti-social behavior. In order to do this therapeutically, the therapist needs to show the client that she accepts him unconditionally and the client needs to perceive the presence of this acceptance.

Humor

Rogers did not write about therapist humor, but I consider this to be a desirable therapist quality in REBT. Ellis has argued that one way of looking at psychological disturbance is that it involves taking oneself, other people and life conditions, not just seriously, but too seriously (Dryden, 1990a). As such, if the REBT therapist can help her client not to take anything too seriously, then this is considered therapeutic in REBT. It is important that the therapist does not poke fun at the client himself; but, given this, then the judicious use of humor through the use of jokes, witticisms and even rational humorous songs (see Dryden, 1990a) can provoke constructive belief change in those clients who will accept such unorthodox behavior in therapists.

Unit 6: Therapeutic Style

Although it is possible to practice REBT in a variety of different styles, the style adopted by most REBT therapists and that advocated by Albert Ellis is active-directive in nature. In my experience as a trainer of REBT therapists for over twenty years, it is this aspect of the therapy with which most trainees struggle. This is especially the case with trainees who have had prior training in person-centred therapy or psychodynamic therapy. Therapists from these approaches have been schooled in the philosophy that it is therapeutic to give clients as much time and 'space' as they need and that the therapist should not interrupt or direct the flow of the client's exploration or experiencing.

In contrast, REBT therapists believe that it is beneficial to provide a structure to therapy and to be active in directing their clients' attention to salient points that will help them to understand their problems more clearly and that will enable them to do something productive to help themselves. Let me make an important point at this juncture. REBT represents ONE perspective and not THE perspective in psychotherapy. It is my practice to explain this to my clients and to men-tion that there do exist other approaches to psychotherapy that may be equally or more useful to them. I then explain that I will be using the REBT structure for understanding and dealing with their psychological problems and encourage them to sample this to determine whether or not it could be helpful to them. I have found that this approach has been more successful in engaging clients in REBT than a messianic approach which lauds

REBT as the only worthwhile approach to therapy and denigrates other therapeutic approaches.

Having thus explained to my clients that I will be using a structured approach to therapy, I then get down straightaway to demonstrate this approach in action. Whilst REBT is structured, it is important to stress, however, that this therapeutic structure is used flexibly by REBT therapists. At times, the structure is loose, particularly when clients are given an extended opportunity to talk about their concerns in their own way, while at other times a tight structure is employed, as when therapists teach the ABCs of REBT (see Module 4).

Therapist directiveness in REBT

Let me deal more explicitly with the issue of REBT's active-directive therapeutic style. If we break down this style into its constituent parts, we have therapist directiveness and therapist activity. Taking directiveness first, it is important for you to understand towards what issues therapists direct their own and, more particularly, their clients' attention towards. As REBT is a problem-solving approach to psychotherapy, its practitioners tend, at the outset, to direct their clients to their emotional problems and to help them to describe these problems as concretely as possible. Then, clients are asked directly to select a problem that they want to tackle first (this is called a target problem in REBT) and they are asked, again directly, to provide a specific example of this target problem which is then assessed using the ABC framework discussed in Module 1 and expanded on in Modules 7–10.

During this assessment, REBT therapists are highly directive. They direct the assessment process because they know what they are looking for, whilst their clients do not. Clients, therefore, need help to provide their therapists with the kind of information that the latter need in order to help the former. I will deal with the practical skills needed to carry out an effective ABC assessment in Modules 7–10. For the present, let me outline the direction that such an assessment tends to take.

In general, when a client starts to describe a specific example of her target problem, the REBT therapist directs her attention to her feelings and helps her to identify whether she has experienced a healthy negative emotion or an unhealthy negative emotion. If her negative emotion is unhealthy then the REBT therapist directs her attention to the critical A, which is the aspect of the A that she is most disturbed about (see Module 1, Unit 1). Once that has been identified, the direction of the therapeutic discussion turns to the client's constructive goals for change.

Here, the REBT therapist will direct the client to the argument that given the existence of the critical A, it would be in the client's best interests to aim for a healthy, albeit negative emotional response to this A.

Doing so will, in fact, make it more likely that she will be able to change this A if it can be shown to exist or to correct any inferential distortions that she has been making in viewing the A than if she retains an unhealthy negative emotional response to the critical A.

Once the client's goals for change have been elicited, the therapist directs her attention to an assessment of the irrational beliefs that underpin her unhealthy negative emotion at C. Once these have been identified, the REBT therapist directs the client to the irrational belief–emotion link and ensures that she understands what is known colloquially as the iB–C connection. This is an important stage in the therapeutic process in that it not only forms a bridge between assessment and intervention, it also provides a rationale for the disputing that follows.

As I will show later in the book, while disputing the client's irrational beliefs, the therapist directs the client to three kinds of arguments: empirical, logical and pragmatic. In empirical disputing of irrational beliefs, the client is asked to find empirical evidence to support these beliefs. In logical disputing of irrational beliefs, the client is asked for logical justification for these beliefs and in pragmatic disputing of irrational beliefs the client is asked to reflect on the consequences of holding these beliefs. If the therapist has been successful at this stage, he will have helped his client to see that her irrational beliefs are: (i) inconsistent with reality; (ii) illogical and (iii) largely disruptive to her basic goals and purposes and that her alternative rational beliefs are: (i) consistent with reality, (ii) logical and (iii) largely enhancing of her basic goals and purposes.

The client's insight into the above is likely to be 'intellectual' at this point, which means that she may understand the points that the therapist has helped her to see and agree with them, but her strength of conviction in these points will be low, i.e. she will not have so-called emotional insight. As such, the therapist will need to direct her to consider what she needs to do to gain emotional insight into her rational beliefs. Again if the therapist has done his job well at this point, the client is able to see that weakening her conviction in her irrational beliefs and strengthening her conviction in her rational beliefs so that the latter influence, in a significant way, how she feels and acts takes a lot of what Ellis calls 'work and practice'. Much of this work is undertaken by the client in the form of homework assignments which the therapist negotiates with the client and checks in the following session .

I hope you can see from this brief overview, the extent of therapist directiveness in this approach to psychotherapy. Effective REBT therapists are skilled not only in varying the amount of structure in therapy sessions, but also in being flexible concerning how much direction to provide at any point in the therapeutic process (see Dryden, 1994d, for a fuller discussion of this latter point).

Therapist activity

I have considered the directive constituent of the REBT therapist's active-directive therapeutic style, but what does she do while being directive? In other words, what comprises the active component of this style of doing therapy?

Advancing hypotheses

As Ray DiGiuseppe (1991a) has shown, REBT therapists follow the hypothetical-deductive approach to knowledge and this is especially true when assessing clients' problems. This means that we use a body of knowledge to form hypotheses about, for example, what our clients may be feeling based on the inferences they make about the world and what their beliefs may be based on these inferences and the feelings they have about these inferred As. Rather than collect a great deal of information before advancing these hypotheses we apply our knowledge of REBT theory to the discrete information provided by our clients about their inferences, in the first case, and their feelings, in the second case, to generate hypotheses about their feelings and beliefs respectively. We particularly use hypothesis testing when clients do not respond to open-ended enquiry regarding the information we are seeking. In doing so we ask such questions as:

* Could it be that you were feeling hurt when your partner ignored you and thus in your eyes showed that he did not care about you? (hypothesis about a feeling based on a disclosure of an inferred A).
* When you were feeling hurt when your partner, in your view, demonstrated that he didn't care that much about you, I wonder if you were telling yourself something like: 'He must care about me. If he does not, it proves that I'm not worth caring about?' (hypothesis about an irrational belief based on an inference and a feeling).

When advancing such hypotheses, it is very important for you to do two things. First, make it clear to your client that you are testing a hunch (i.e. hypothesis) and that you could be wrong. Emphasize to your client that it is very helpful for him to give you honest feedback about your hunch and that he can help you in the assessment process by correcting or refining your hunches. In this way your client becomes an active participant in the assessment process and not a passive recipient of your clinical wisdom (or otherwise!). Second, pay particular attention to the way in which your client responds to your hypothesis. There is a world of difference between a client saying to you: 'That's exactly right. How did you know?' and 'Well, er...I guess...I suppose you could be right.' In the latter case, it is advisable for you to say something like: 'You seem quite hesitant. That tells me that my hunch is off target. Can you help me to correct it?'

Asking questions

Many people who are trained in person-centred therapy and other so-called non-directive approaches to therapy and then seek training in Rational Emotive Behavior Therapy are shocked to discover the extent to which REBT therapists employ questions. Whilst they were initially trained to use questions sparingly, if at all, they are now asked to make liberal use of questions.

What are our purposes in asking questions? In addition to the questions that are a central part of hypothesis testing discussed above, we ask questions for the following reasons. First, we ask questions to gather general information about the client and his life situation.

Second, we ask questions to obtain specific information in the assessment phase of therapy. These questions are directed towards the salient aspect of the ABC framework that the therapist is currently assessing (see Modules 7 and 10). Third, we ask questions as part of the disputing phase of therapy, i.e. to help us to challenge our clients' irrational beliefs. As I will discuss in greater detail later, we ask questions directed towards the empirical status, the logical status and the pragmatic status of both our clients' irrational beliefs and the alternative rational beliefs that we encourage our clients to acquire and strengthen.

Fourth, we ask Socratic questions to encourage client understanding of rational principles. While educating his pupils, Socrates would ask them questions to involve them actively in the educational process. Rather than tell them the answers, Socrates asked questions to encourage them to think for themselves as he gently guided them towards the answers. Whenever we can, REBT therapists use the same type of orienting questions. Thus, for example, if we want our clients to understand why self-rating is a pernicious concept, rather than tell them why this is so, we ask questions designed to encourage them to think actively about this issue. In response to their incorrect answers, we ask further questions based on their replies to guide them towards the correct answer. In reality, a combination of Socratic questioning and brief didactic explanations (see below) are employed in concert to get the teaching points across because few clients respond readily to the sole use of Socratic questioning.

Finally, we ask questions to ensure that our clients have understood any teaching points that we have made using didactic explanations (see below). REBT can be viewed as an educational approach to therapy. As such, its impact lies not in the information imparted, but in the information received and digested. Given this fact, it is important for the therapist to gauge whether or not the client comprehends and agrees with the point being made. First, then, the therapist asks the client to put into his own words his understanding of the point that the thera-pist has made.

Once the therapist is satisfied that the client has understood the point in question, then she asks the client for his views on that point.

Two matters should be noted about the use of questions in REBT. First, it is important to avoid asking too many questions, particularly when these are directed to the same target. For example, when seeking information about the client's irrational beliefs, it is important to ask one question at a time. Second, when asking a question that is directed to a particular target, e.g. the client's feelings, it is important for the therapist to monitor closely the client's response to determine whether or not he has answered the question satisfactorily. If not, and the information is important, then the therapist should ask the question again, using a different form of words if necessary.

Providing didactic explanations

The second major class of therapist activity involves the use of didactic explanations. As I have already mentioned, REBT can be viewed as an educational approach to therapy. As such, one way of presenting educational points is to provide explanations of these points in a didactic manner. Didactic explanations are generally used in REBT when a client has not understood a teaching point that the therapist has tried to convey by the use of Socratic questioning (see above). Such explanations involve the deliberate imparting of information concerning, for example:

1. The ABCs of REBT;
2. How REBT theory may help the client to understand his problems;
3. What is likely to happen in REBT;
4. How the therapist construes her role in the therapeutic process and what tasks she needs to carry out during therapy;
5. How the therapist construes the client's role in the therapeutic process and what tasks he needs to carry out during therapy; and
6. The importance of homework.

This illustrative list shows the range of issues that REBT therapists need to be prepared to explain to their clients. A full list would be much longer. Given this range of issues, it is important for the therapist to have a lot of information at her fingertips and be able to explain a variety of concepts in ways that are meaningful to different clients. I will briefly consider the main teaching methods used by REBT therapists in the next section. Before I do so, let me discuss a number of points that you need to bear in mind while using didactic explanations.

1. It is important for you to explain relevant information clearly and succinctly. Avoid long-winded, rambling expositions.
2. Explain only one concept at a time.
3. As discussed in the section on questioning, check out your client's grasp of the point you are making by encouraging him to put his under-

standing into his own words. This is a particularly important point. It is all too easy for REBT therapists to think that clients have understood rational principles because they indicate understanding non-verbally. This is no substitute for the active attempt on the part of clients to convey understanding by representing their comprehension in their own words.

4. Elicit his view on the material you have presented, correct any misconceptions and engage him in a dialogue on any matters arising.

Using other methods in teaching rational principles

In addition to Socratic questioning and didactic explanations, REBT therapists employ a variety of other active methods to teach clients rational principles. As my goal here is to give you a 'feel' of the active constituent of the active-directive therapeutic style, I will briefly mention some of these methods.

1. Use of visual aids. Here the REBT therapist uses posters and flipcharts to present rational principles in visual form.
2. Self-disclosure. Here the therapist tells the client how she has used REBT to overcome her emotional problems. Therapist self-disclosure can be tailored to highlight different rational principles with different clients
3. Hypothetical teaching examples. Here the therapist uses hypothetical examples to teach the client salient aspects of REBT. The $11–$10 example of teaching the ABCs of REBT presented in Module 4 is a good illustration of this
4. Stories, aphorisms and metaphors. The therapist employs these methods to teach rational principles when she wants to do so in a vivid and memorable way.
5. Flamboyant therapist actions. These are active examples of the use of humor in REBT. For instance, the therapist may bark like a dog to demonstrate the point that he is not a fool even though he acts foolishly at times.

Unit 7: The Goals of REBT

In the late 1960s, Alvin Mahrer (1967) edited a book entitled *The Goals of Psychotherapy*. In his summary chapter, Mahrer reviewed the ideas of his contributors and argued that the goals of psychotherapy can fall into one of two major categories: (1) relief of psychological problems and (2) promotion of psychological health. REBT therapists would basically concur with this view and extend it. First, we need to help our clients over their psychological disturbances, then we need to help them to address their life dissatisfactions and finally we can help them to become more psychologically healthy and strive towards self-actualisation.

This is fine as an ideal, but the actual world of the consulting room can be very different. As such, as I will show you, REBT therapists are often called to make compromises with their preferred goals (Dryden, 1991).

Philosophic change

Ideally, REB therapists like to help their clients to achieve philosophic change. This means that clients relinquish their irrational beliefs and adopt rational beliefs. Clients may achieve philosophic change in specific situations, in one or more broad areas of their lives or generally. According to REBT theory, the more clients acquire and implement a general rational philosophy, the more psychologically healthy they are deemed to be. It needs to be stressed, however, that only a minority of clients will achieve general philosophic change. In my experience, a larger number will achieve philosophic change in one or more broad areas of life and most clients who achieve philosophic change will do so in specific situations.

When clients achieve a philosophic change, their inferences tend to be accurate representations of reality and they tend to behave more constructively. The point I want to make here is that achieving a philosophic change does not mean that person only changing her beliefs. Rather, such change facilitates other constructive changes in the ABC framework. However, not all clients are willing or able to change their irrational beliefs and when this is the case then REBT therapists are called upon to make compromises with their preferred goals and help clients in other ways. There are three kinds of change other than philosophic change that REBT therapists attempt to effect when promoting philosophic change. I will now discuss each in turn.

Inferential change

If REBT therapists cannot help their clients to achieve philosophic change, they will often attempt to help them to achieve inferential change.

An example of a therapist helping a client to effect inferential change without accompanying philosophic change occurred when a colleague of mine failed to help his client to think rationally about her husband's presumed uncaring behavior, but succeeded in helping her to correct her inference that he did not care for her. As such inferential change involves clients identifying and correcting distorted inferences and thus viewing situations more accurately. As with philosophic change, clients may achieve inferential change in specific situations, in one or more broad areas of life or more generally. Given the REBT view that inferential distortions stem largely from underlying irrational beliefs, inferential change is deemed to be unstable as clients are more likely to form distorted inferences about themselves, other people and the world if their irrational beliefs remain unchecked than if they hold rational beliefs.

Behavioral change

Sometimes when REBT therapists fail to help their clients achieve a philosophic change, they can assist them by encouraging them to change their behavior. Thus, if a client is anxious about being rejected by women, the therapist may help him to minimise rejection by helping him to improve his social skills. If successful, this may be very therapeutic for the client. However, even sophisticated social skills do not guarantee that the client will never be rejected and thus he remains vulnerable to anxiety in this area because his underlying irrational beliefs remain.

Changing actual As

Sometimes when clients are unable or unwilling to think rationally about negative life events, change their inferences about these events or change their own behavior in the hope of modifying these events, then REBT therapists may best help them by encouraging them to leave the relevant situation. In REBT, this is known as changing the A. Whilst such environmental change is fine in the overall context of other psychological changes that clients are making (especially philosophic change), on its own it leaves clients particularly vulnerable. Because they have not effected any philosophic change, such clients take their tendency to disturb themselves from situation to situation. Also, if solely relied upon, opting for environmental change teaches clients that the only way that they can help themselves is by changing or leaving aversive situations. They will therefore not even be motivated to attempt other, more psychologically based changes.

Different types of change within a case

It is important to stress that a given client may make different types of change on different issues. In the following example please note the point that I have previously made: namely, when a person makes a philosophic change she will also make other relevant kinds of changes, but this principle does not necessarily apply when that person makes an inferential, behavioral or environmental change.

    For example, one of my clients, Sarah, came to therapy with the following problems: approval anxiety, coping with pressure from her mother, dealing with her boyfriend's lateness and a fear of spiders. At the end of therapy Sarah had made a philosophic change on the broad issue of approval anxiety, a philosophic change on the specific problem of dealing with her mother's pressure, an inferential change on the specific problem of her boyfriend's lack of punctuality and a change of A on the specific issue of spiders.

Clients' goals for change

So far, I have dealt with the goals that REBT therapists have for their clients. Whilst we have preferred goals for client change which we are explicit about, we are flexible and, as noted above, are prepared to compromise and accept less preferred goals when it becomes clear that it is very unlikely that certain clients will achieve philosophic change.

It is also crucial to note that clients come to therapy with ideas about what they want to achieve from the therapeutic process. These goals can be explicitly stated or implicit in what clients say. Sometimes a client's true goals may be contrary to his stated goals and can only be inferred from his behavior later in therapy. The point I want to stress here is that clients' goals may well be at variance with their therapists' goals and this may be a source of conflict in the therapeutic process. One way to minimise such conflict is for the therapist to encourage his client to make a problem list (which is updated throughout therapy) and to set goals for each problem. I will discuss this issue further later. For now I want to reiterate that REBT therapists believe that they can be most helpful to their clients by encouraging them to set goals which involve philosophic change. However, as noted above, his is not always possible.

Unit 8: Tasks in REBT I: The Therapist's Tasks

When I write of therapeutic tasks I mean specific or general activity that a person carries out in psychotherapy. As Bordin (1979) noted in a seminal paper on the therapeutic alliance, both therapists and clients have tasks to accomplish in therapy. Some of these tasks are common across therapies, whilst others are specific to a given approach. In Units 8 and 9, I will focus mainly on the tasks that are characteristic of REBT, but in doing so I will consider tasks that are general in nature. As such, I will not consider specific techniques here because I want to give an overall picture of task-related activity in REBT.

In this unit, I will mainly concentrate on the therapist's tasks that are characteristic of REBT and in the following unit I will consider the client's tasks in this approach to therapy. Figure 2.1 summarizes the REBT therapist's major tasks across the therapeutic process.

The beginning phase

The initial task of the REBT therapist is to establish a therapeutic alliance with her client. At this stage, this primarily involves encouraging the client to talk about her concerns, communicating affective empathy, helping the client to develop a problem list and outlining REBT and how it may apply to the problems on this list.

The Beginning Stage
> Establish a therapeutic alliance
> Socialise the client into REBT
> Begin to assess and intervene on the client's target problem
> Teach the ABCs of REBT
> Deal with your client's doubts

The Middle Stage
> Follow through on the client's target problem
> Encourage your client to engage in relevant tasks
> Work on the client's other problems
> Identify core irrational beliefs
> Deal with obstacles to change
> Encourage your client to maintain and enhance his gains
> Undertake relapse prevention and deal with vulnerability factors
> Encourage your client to become his own counselor

The Ending Stage
> Decide on how and when to end
> Encourage your client to summarize what has been learned
> Attribute improvement to the client's efforts
> Deal with obstacles to ending
> Agree on criteria for follow-ups and resuming therapy

Figure 2.1 The therapist's tasks in REBT.

Once the client has indicated that REBT could be useful to him, then the REBT therapist begins to outline what her own tasks are in therapy and what is expected of the client. Whilst it is important to stress to the client that he needs to be active in the therapeutic process, this needs to be done without presenting an overwhelming picture of what the client needs to do. I will presently discuss client tasks in REBT.

At this point the therapist encourages the client to choose a problem on which to work (known as a target problem), initiates an ABC assessment of this problem and begins to intervene to help the client to overcome the problem. At a salient point in this assessment process, the therapist will endeavour to teach the client the ABCs of REBT. There are a number of ways of doing this and I will illustrate some of these in Module 4. Because REBT has a definite standpoint on people's problems and its practitioners are prepared to be explicit about this standpoint and the approach to therapy that follows from it, it is likely that a client may have certain doubts or questions about REBT. It is an important task for the REBT therapist to be aware of the possible existence of such doubts and questions and to help the client to express these. Indeed, I think that the therapist needs to indicate that she welcomes questions and the expression of doubts in that it is important that she demonstrate an open, nondefensive approach so that the client can see that his doubts will be taken seriously. Once the client has, for example, expressed a reservation about some aspect of the therapy so far, the therapist needs to respond respectfully to this communication, but correct any misconceptions that may underpin the client's reservation. This should be done with tact and, if necessary, the counselor needs to make clear that even though she is correcting a misconception of REBT, she is accepting of the client.

The middle phase

As the therapist and client get to grips with the latter's target problem, they begin to move into the middle phase of therapy. It is here that the disputing process that may have been initiated in the beginning phase takes hold and here that the client is called upon to undertake a number of tasks which are designed to help him (i) to develop his own disputing skills and (ii) to go from an intellectual understanding of rational principles to being able to act on them and for them to make a difference to the way he feels.

As therapist and client make progress on the client's target problem, the therapist helps the client to apply his learning to other similar problems. In addition, work proceeds on the client's other problems. As client and therapist gain a detailed understanding of the client's problems and the irrational beliefs that underpin these problems, they are in a position to identify and work on the client's core irrational beliefs. These are usually few in number and account for the existence of the problems on his problem list. As such they are expressed in general terms (e.g. 'I must have the love of significant people in my life').

It is in the middle phase of therapy that most of the obstacles to client change occur. Whilst a detailed consideration of such obstacles is beyond the scope of this introductory text, it is important to bear in mind that an investigation of these obstacles is best done when the therapist accepts herself and her client as fallible human beings who have tendencies to block the development of therapeutic progress. In brief, obstacles to client change can be attributed to client factors, therapist factors, the interaction between these two sets of factors or environmental factors (see Dryden and Trower, 1989, and Ellis, 1985, for a more detailed discussion of obstacles to client change).

As the client makes progress, the REBT therapist encourages him to maintain and enhance his gains. At this point, when he is feeling better, the client may be tempted to stop working on himself. However, this would be a mistake because there is a distinction between 'feeling better' and 'getting better'. The former involves a cessation of symptoms whilst the latter involves a philosophic change either at a specific level or more generally. In order to achieve a philosophic change that is robust, the client needs to be encouraged to continue to work to maintain his therapeutic gains in the first instance and later to extend these gains to other areas of his life that may not have featured in the therapeutic dialogue.

As part of the process of maintaining and extending therapeutic progress, the therapist needs to raise the issue of relapse prevention. In particular, this involves the identification of vulnerability factors, i.e. As which if encountered would trigger the client's core and other irrational beliefs. These critical As may have not yet been discussed in therapy or, if they have, discussion may have been only cursory. Now is the time for thoroughgoing work on these issues.

Throughout the process of REBT, the therapist is looking for ways of encouraging her client to take responsibility for his self-change. Realistically, this comes to the fore during the latter stages of therapy. Here, when the client discusses his problems, the therapist encourages him to take the lead in assessing his underlying beliefs and in coming up with suggestions for how he might challenge and change these beliefs. At this point, the therapist acts more as a consultant prompting the client to use skills that he has been taught previously, but which he may not think of applying to his own problems, hoping that the therapist may continue to take the lead as she did in the beginning and early-middle phases of therapy. Now the therapist explicitly states that the client has the necessary tools to take the major responsibility for ongoing therapeutic change and that this will be her major task in the time that they have together. It is often at this point that the issue of ending therapy is first raised and discussed.

The ending phase

The first task of the therapist in the ending phase of REBT is to agree with the client the best way to end therapy. There are a number of ways of bringing therapy to a suitable conclusion. The approach that I personally favour is to increase gradually the time between sessions so that clients can increasingly rely on their resources as they work towards becoming their own therapists.

Whenever I carry out an initial assessment session with new clients who have had previous experience of being in therapy, I ask what they have learned from that experience. I am frequently struck by how little they claim to have learned. Whether this means that they have, in fact, learned little or that they cannot articulate their learning is not clear. If the latter, one remedy is for therapists to encourage their clients to summarize what they have learned. In my view, being able to articulate their learning makes it more likely that clients will retain and apply it after therapy has ended. Consequently, encouraging clients to summarize and keep a written record of what they have learned from therapy is a key therapist task in the end phase of therapy.

As the therapist reviews her client's progress and helps him to summarize his learning, it is important that she encourages him to attribute his progress to his own efforts. The way I tend to do this is take some credit for helping my client to understand her problems and for showing her what she can do about them, but to encourage her to take credit for putting this learning into practice in her own life. If clients attribute their progress mainly to their therapists' efforts, thus minimising their own efforts, they will be less likely to work to maintain and enhance their gains than if they take full responsibility for their contribution to their own progress.

Although REBT therapists do not strive to form and maintain close relationships with their clients, the latter do perceive their therapists to be empathic, respectful and genuine (DiGiuseppe et al., 1993). As such, this relationship is likely to be a significant one for them and its end may well constitute a critical A. Thus, REBT therapists are advised to elicit their clients' feelings about the end of the therapeutic relationship and to uncover, challenge and help clients' change their irrational beliefs if these feelings are negative and unhealthy and constitute obstacles to a productive end to therapy.

REBT therapists do not take an absolutistic view on the ending of therapy. As such they are prepared to resume therapy with their clients should the latter be in need of further therapeutic assistance. My own practice is to encourage my clients to use their REBT self-help skills when they encounter the recurrence of old problems or the appearance of new problems. I encourage them to deal with such problems even though they may have to struggle to do so, but tell them to contact me for booster sessions if their struggles fail. What I want to avoid is clients contacting me for extra sessions as soon as they encounter problems before even attempting to use their self-help skills to overcome these problems. What I advocate, then, is that REBT therapists set agreed criteria with their clients concerning the resumption of therapy. I also suggest that therapists and clients agree on the timing and purpose of relevant follow-up sessions.

Unit 9: Tasks in REBT II: The Client's Tasks

As Bordin (1979) has pointed out, clients have tasks to carry out in psychotherapy. Shortly, I shall discuss the specific tasks that clients are called upon to implement in REBT, but first I shall say a few general words about tasks, from the client's point of view. First, it is important that clients understand the tasks they are called upon to carry out in REBT. If they do not understand what these tasks are, they can hardly be expected to execute them. Second, they need to see the relevance of carrying out their tasks. In particular, they need to see the link between their tasks and their goals for change. If they do not understand the goal-directed nature of their tasks, they may well be reluctant to carry them out. Third, it is important that clients understand the tasks that their therapists are executing and see the relevance of these tasks to their goals. Again, unless clients see this task-goal connection, they may well be puzzled and uncomfortable about their therapist's behavior. Fourth, clients need to understand the relationship between their tasks and the tasks of their therapists. Therapy is more likely to go smoothly when clients see that their tasks complement the tasks carried out by their therapists than when they lack such understanding. Figure 2.2 reviews the client tasks that I will consider in this module.

Specify problems

Be open to the therapist's REBT framework

Apply the specific principle of emotional responsibility

Apply the principle of therapeutic responsibility

Disclose doubts, difficulties and blocks to change

Figure 2.2 The client's tasks in REBT.

Specify problems

The first client task that I will discuss concerns his ability and preparedness to be specific about problems. REBT is a problem-solving approach to psychotherapy and as such it calls upon the client to focus on his problems and discuss them in a specific manner, giving typical, explicit examples of these problems to enable the therapist to carry out a proper ABC assessment. If the client cannot be specific about his problems, he will probably derive less benefit from REBT than if he can talk specifically about his concerns. In addition, lack of client specificity means that the therapist will have greater difficulty in carrying out her tasks. These tasks are themselves specific in nature and if the therapist is to perform them effectively, she needs specific information from the client.

Be open to the therapist's REBT framework

The second client task that I will discuss involves a willingness to listen to the therapist's explanations of his problems and to be open-minded about the REBT viewpoint on the nature of his problems, how he perpetuates these problems and what he needs to do to overcome these problems. If the client has a fixed idea about these issues and his idea is markedly at variance with the REBT perspective, then therapy will quickly stall. Now I am not suggesting that the client accepts what the therapist has to say about the above issues in an unthinking way. Indeed, Ellis (1985) has argued that suggestibility and gullibility are hallmarks of emotional disturbance. What I am advocating is that the client is open-minded enough to consider the merit of the therapist's ideas and is sceptical (in the healthy sense) about these ideas. The therapist can encourage the client to think for himself about these matters by encouraging him to express his doubts and concerns about REBT principles so that they can have an open dialogue on these ideas where the therapist corrects the client's misconceptions in a respectful manner. If the therapist is dogmatic about REBT theory, she not only serves as a poor role model of flexibility, she is also likely to create a situation where polarisation of viewpoints occurs with the result that the client defends his irrational position and cannot thereby benefit from therapy.

Apply the specific principle of emotional responsibility

The third client task that I wish to address involves applying the specific principle of emotional responsibility. This principle states that the client largely makes himself disturbed by the irrational beliefs that he holds about the adversities in his life. Applying this principle means that the client actively looks for these beliefs whenever he experiences an unhealthy negative emotion and countering any tendency that he has to blame other people and situations for causing these emotions. Whilst this principle places the responsibility for his psychological problems fairly and squarely on the client, it does not preclude the client from acknowledging that negative events contribute to these problems. And because responsibility is a different concept from blame this principle does not advocate blaming the client for making himself disturbed.

Apply the principle of therapeutic responsibility

The fourth client task that I will consider involves the client applying the principle of therapeutic responsibility. This principle logically follows on from the specific principle of emotional responsibility. It involves the client acknowledging that in order to overcome his emotional problems he needs to put into practice the REBT theory of therapeutic change (in this case, philosophic change) which I discuss more fully in the second volume in the series (Dryden, 1995). Albert Ellis and I have summarized this in our book, *The Practice of Rational Emotive Behavior Therapy* (Ellis and Dryden, 1997, p. 24). To effect a philosophic change clients are advised to:

1. First, realize that they create, to a large degree, their own psychological disturbances and that whilst environmental conditions can contribute to their problems they are in general of secondary consideration in the change process.
2. Fully recognize that they do have the ability to significantly change these disturbances.
3. Understand that emotional and behavioral disturbances stem largely from irrational, absolutistic beliefs.
4. Detect their irrational beliefs and discriminate them from their rational alternatives.
5. Dispute these irrational beliefs using the logical-empirical methods of science.
6. Work toward the internalization of their new rational beliefs by employing cognitive, emotive, and behavioral methods of change.
7. Continue this process of challenging irrational beliefs and using multimodal methods of change...

Disclose doubts, difficulties and blocks to change

The final client task that I will consider involves the client disclosing to the therapist his doubts about REBT principles, the difficulties that he experiences in implementing REBT and any blocks to psychological change that he encounters. If the client keeps these doubts, difficulties or blocks to himself or worse, if he dissimulates by actively stating that he agrees with REBT principles, that he is able to implement its techniques without difficulty and that he encounters no blocks to change, then he will not derive benefit from therapy. Now, whether he discloses his doubts etc. will depend, in part, upon the therapist providing the kind of therapeutic climate that encourages such disclosure. Assuming that the therapist succeeds in providing this climate and asks the client for this information, then the client has responsibility for providing it.

I have now presented the basic information that you need to know about the theory and practice of REBT to begin to practice this approach to therapy. This is the information that I present to trainees on first-level training courses on REBT. Having presented this information I give trainees an opportunity to ask questions about the points I have made. Many of the questions that trainees ask reveal basic misunderstandings about REBT. In the next module, I will discuss these misconceptions and how they can be corrected.

Module 3
Correcting Misconceptions
Aabout Rational Emotive
Behavior Therapy

As I mentioned at the end of Module 2, after presenting basic information about the theory and practice of REBT on initial training courses, I pause to take questions and reactions from trainees. These questions and reactions often reveal important misunderstandings about the theoretical underpinnings of REBT and how it is practiced. Dealing with these misunderstandings is an important part of the training process. If these misconceptions are left uncorrected then trainees will not get as much out of the training practicum as they will if I elicit their doubts and reservations and respond to the misunderstandings implicit in their questions and reactions. I attempt to respond to trainee misconceptions about REBT in the same way as I attempt to respond to client misconceptions about the therapy and the ideas upon which its practice is based, i.e. with tact, sensitivity and respect. I will now consider fifteen major misconceptions that trainees have about REBT at this point of the training process. I compiled this list of misconceptions from my own experience as a trainer, the experiences of other REBT trainers and the REBT literature (e.g. Gandy, 1985; Saltzberg and Elkins, 1980; Young, 1979). In presenting these reservations that trainees have about REBT, I will put them in the form of typical questions that trainees ask.

Question 1: REBT states that activating events don't cause emotions. I can see that this is the case when negative events are mild or moderate, but don't very negative events like being raped or losing a loved one cause disturbed emotions?

Answer: Your question directly impinges on the distinction that REBT makes between healthy and unhealthy negative emotions (see Module 5). Let me take the example of rape that you mentioned. There is no doubt that being raped is a tragic event for both women and men. As such, it is healthy for the person who has been raped to experience a lot of distress. However, REBT conceptualises this distress as healthy even though it is intense. Other approaches to cognitive-behavior therapy have as their goal the reduction of the intensity of negative emotions. They take this position because they do not keenly differentiate between healthy negative emotions (distress) and unhealthy negative emotions (disturbance).

Now, as I have explained to you, REBT does keenly distinguish between healthy distress and unhealthy disturbance (see Module 1, Unit 3). If you recall, distress stems from a person's rational beliefs about a negative activating event, whilst disturbance stems her irrational beliefs about the same event. I now have to introduce you to one of the complexities of REBT theory (see Dryden, 1994b) and as I do you will see that REBT is not always as simple as ABC!

REBT theory holds that the intensity of a person's healthy distress increases in proportion to the negativity of the encountered activating event (A) and to the strength of increase in her rational beliefs. Now, when a person has been raped, her intense distress stems from her strongly held rational beliefs about this very negative A. As virtually everyone who has been raped will have strongly held rational beliefs about this event, we could almost say that being raped 'causes' intense healthy distress.

Now let me introduce irrational beliefs into the picture. REBT theory argues that people easily transmute their rational beliefs into irrational beliefs especially when the As that they encounter are very negative. However, and this is a crucial and controversial point, the specific principle of emotional responsibility states that people are responsible for their emotional disturbance because they are responsible for transmuting their rational beliefs into irrational beliefs. They retain this responsibility even when they encounter tragic adversities such as rape. So REBT theory holds that when a person has been raped, she is responsible for transmuting her strongly held rational beliefs into irrational beliefs, even though it is very understandable that she should do this.

Actually, if we look at the typical irrational beliefs that people have about being raped we will see that these beliefs are not an integral part of the rape experience, but reflect what people bring to the experience. Examples of irrational beliefs are:

'I absolutely should have stopped this from happening.'
'This has completely ruined my life.'
'Being raped means that I am a worthless person.'

Whilst it is understandable that people who have been raped should think this way, this does not detract from the fact that they are responsible for bringing these irrational beliefs to the experience. It is for this reason that REBT theory holds that very negative As do not 'cause' emotional disturbance. This is actually an optimistic position. If very negative events did cause emotional disturbance then people would have a much harder time overcoming their disturbed feelings than they do now when we make the assumption that these feelings stem largely from their irrational beliefs.

One more point. Some REBT therapists distinguish between disturbed emotions that are experienced when a very negative event occurs and disturbed feelings that persist well after the event has happened. These therapists would argue that being raped does 'cause' disturbed feelings when the event occurs and for a short period after it has happened, but if the person's disturbed feelings persist well after the event then the person who has been raped is responsible for the perpetuation of her disturbances via the creation and perpetuation of her irrational beliefs. These therapists argue that time-limited irrationalities in response to very negative activating events are not unhealthy reactions, but the perpetuation of these irrationalities is unhealthy. Thus, for these REBT therapists a very negative event like rape does 'cause' emotional disturbance in the short term, but not in the long term (for a fuller discussion of time-limited irrationalities see Dryden, 1994d).

Question 2: I'm worried about the principle of emotional responsibility. Doesn't it lead to blaming the victim?

Answer: You have raised one of two criticisms that make up the principle of emotional responsibility which is so central to REBT theory, the other one being the cop-out criticism. I will deal with each in turn.

As I showed you in my previous answer, when someone is raped, it is possible to argue that this very negative A 'causes' the intense healthy distress that the person almost invariably experiences. However, if she experiences emotional disturbance, particularly well after the event happened, REBT theory holds that she is responsible for her disturbed feelings through the irrational beliefs that she brings to the event. However, there is a world of difference between being responsible for one's disturbance and being blamed for having these feelings. The con-cept of responsibility in this situation means that the person largely disturbs herself about the event because of the irrational beliefs she brings to that event. The concept of blame here means that someone believes that the person absolutely should not experience such disturbed feelings and is something of a bad person for having these feelings. This is obviously nonsense for two reasons. First, if the person disturbs herself about being raped then all the conditions are in place for her to do so. In other words, if she holds a set of irrational beliefs about the event, then empirically she should disturb herself about it. It is obviously inconsistent with reality for someone to demand that the person absolutely should not disturb herself in this way. Second, even if we can say that it is bad for her to do so (and this is a big if) there is no reason to conclude that she is a bad person for doing so. There is, of course, evidence that she is a fallible human being who understandably holds a set of irrational beliefs about a tragic event. Rather than being blamed for her disturbance, she should preferably be helped to overcome it.

The concept of blame in this situation also tends to mean, at least in some people's eyes, that she is responsible for being raped and therefore should be blamed for it happening. This is again nonsense. Let me be quite clear about this. Rape inevitably involves coercion. Even if the woman is responsible for 'leading the man on', he is responsible for raping her. Nothing, including whether the woman experiences distressing or disturbed feelings, absolves him from this responsibility. So, if a woman has been raped nothing that she did or failed to do detracts from the fact that the rapist is solely responsible for committing the rape. As such, the woman cannot be held responsible for being raped. She can be held responsible for 'leading the man on' if this can be shown to be the case; but, I repeat, she cannot be held responsible for being raped.

Thus, the principle of emotional responsibility means in this situation that the woman is responsible for her disturbed feelings only. She is not to be blamed for this, nor is she to be held responsible for being raped no matter how she has behaved in the situation

Let me now deal with the cop-out criticism of the principle of emotional responsibility.

The cop-out criticism can be stated thus. If a person is largely responsible for her own disturbed feelings, then if you act nastily towards her all you have to say is that because she largely disturbs herself about your bad behavior then her feelings have nothing to do with you.

Earlier on in this answer, I pointed out that a rapist is responsible for carrying out a rape regardless of how the person who has been raped feels and regardless of any so-called mitigating circumstances. Now if I act nastily towards you I am responsible for my behavior regardless of how you feel about my behavior. If my behavior is nasty then I cannot be absolved of responsibility for my action just because you are largely responsible for your making yourself disturbed about the way I have treated you. Don't forget, if my behavior is that bad it is healthy for you to hold strongly a set of rational beliefs about it and, whereas I cannot be held responsible for your disturbance, I can be said to be responsible for your distress. Thus, I cannot 'cop-out' of my responsibility for my own behavior nor for 'distressing' you.

The cop-out criticism is also made of the REBT position on guilt. As I have shown in my book, *Overcoming Guilt* (Dryden, 1994c), guilt is an unhealthy emotion that stems from a set of irrational self-blaming beliefs about breaking one's moral code, for example. The healthy alternative to guilt is remorse which stems from a set of rational self-accepting beliefs about a moral code violation. The important point to note about remorse

is that it does not absolve the person from taking responsibility for breaking his moral code. It does not, in short, encourage the person in 'copping
out' of assuming responsibility from what he did. Now this is apparently a
difficult point for people to grasp.

For example, Marje Proops, a famous agony aunt, claimed to have
read my book on guilt – in which I continually reiterate the non' cop-out'
position of remorse – but said in response to a letter from a reader who
sought help to stop feeling guilty about sleeping with her best friend's
husband that the reader SHOULD feel guilty. Proops feared that remorse
and even guilt (which she clearly failed to differentiate) would provide
the person with a 'cop-out' or an excuse for continuing to act immorally.
The truth is, however, very different. Remorse is based on the rational
belief, 'I wish I hadn't broken my moral code, but there is no reason why
I absolutely should not have broken it. I broke it because of what I was
telling myself at the time. Now let me accept myself and think how I can
learn from my past behavior so that I can act morally in the future.' As
you see, in remorse the person takes responsibility for her behavior, is
motivated to act better next time by her rational belief which also
enables her to learn from her moral code violation. By contrast, guilt is
based on an irrational belief which will either encourage her to deny
responsibility for her past action or interfere with her attempt to learn
from it. So far from encouraging the person to 'cop-out' of her responsibility, the principle of emotional responsibility encourages the person to
take responsibility for her actions and for her disturbed guilt feelings. It
further encourages the person to challenge her irrational, guilt-producing beliefs and adopt a rational, remorse-invoking philosophy so that she
can learn from her past behavior, make appropriate amends and take
responsibility for her future behavior.

Question 3: You have discussed the ABCs of REBT, but I find this overly
simplistic. Isn't the theory of REBT too simple?

Answer:

First, let me say in answer to your question that I have presented
enough of the theory of REBT to help you get started with its practice.
Don't forget that you are on a first-level training course on REBT. If I presented the full complexity of the ABCs of REBT, then I would run the risk
of overwhelming you with too much information too soon. In reality, as
Albert Ellis (1991) has recently shown and as I have myself demonstrated
(Dryden, 1994b) the ABCs interact in often complex ways. Let me give
you a few examples of this complexity. So far, as you have rightly
observed, I have introduced the simple version of the ABCs where A
occurs first, and is then evaluated at B to produce an emotional and/or
behavioral consequence at C. This is the version of the ABCs that is usually taught on first-level training courses and that we, as practitioners,
teach our clients.

Now let's introduce some complexity into the picture. If a person holds an irrational belief about an event, then he will tend to create further distorted inferences about this A. For example, if you believe that you must be loved by your partner (iB) and he shouts at you (A1) then you will more likely think that he doesn't love you and is thinking of leaving you (A2) than if you he have an alternative rational belief (rB). So, instead of the usual formula: $A \to B \to C$, we have $A1 \to iB \to A2$.

Second, if a person is already experiencing an unhealthy negative emotion then this will lead him to attend to certain aspects in a situation. Thus, if you are already anxious then you are more likely to focus on threatening aspects of a situation than if you are concerned, but not anxious. Putting this into a formula, we have $C \to A$.

I hope these two examples have given you a flavor of the complexity of the ABCs of REBT and have helped you to see that whilst in its rudimentary form the ABC model is simple, its full version is neither too simple nor simplistic

Question 4: I get the impression that REBT neglects the past. Am I right?

Answer: As I have shown, REBT states that people disturb themselves (C) by the beliefs (B) that they hold about the negative activating events in their lives (A). Now As can be present events, future events and past events. Thus, if a client is disturbed now about certain aspects of her past, then an REBT therapist would certainly deal with this using the ABC framework where A is the past event (or events).

What REBT questions, however, is the position that a client's past has MADE him disturbed now. This, you will recall is an example of 'A causes C' thinking to which REBT objects. Now, even if we assume temporarily that the client was made disturbed as a child by a past event, or more usually by an ongoing series of events, REBT theory argues that the reason that the person is disturbed now about his past is because in the present he holds a set of irrational beliefs that he has actively kept alive or perpetuated from the past. Actually, the situation is more complex than this because REBT holds that we are not, as children, made disturbed by events; rather, we bring our tendencies to disturb ourselves to these events. Thus, REBT adheres to a constructivist position even about the origins of psychological disturbance.

I have stressed that the REBT therapist certainly works with the past mainly by looking at the client's presently-held irrational beliefs about his past. In addition, the therapist can consider the client's past disturbed feelings about specific or ongoing historical situations and help him to see what irrational beliefs he was holding then to create those disturbed feelings. I have also found it useful to make the past present by, for example, encouraging the client to have a two-chair dialogue with figures from the past to identify, challenge and change the client's present irrational beliefs about these figures. This technique has to be used sensitively as it often provokes strong affect.

To summarize, REBT does not ignore a client's past, but works with past material either by disputing currently held irrational beliefs about historical events or by challenging the past irrational beliefs that the client may have held about these same events. However, REBT guards against A → C thinking by making it clear that it does not think that past events cause present disturbance.

Question 5: Doesn't the REBT concept of acceptance encourage complacency?

Answer: The REBT concept of acceptance certainly gives rise to a lot of confusion in people's minds. Some, like you, consider that it leads to complacency, others think it means indifference; yet others judge it to mean that we should condone negative events. Actually it means none of these things. Let me carefully spell out what REBT theory does mean by the term 'acceptance'.

The first point to stress is that acceptance means acknowledging the existence of an event, for example, and that all the conditions were in place for an event to occur. However, it does not mean that it is good that the event happened, nor that there is nothing one can do to rectify the situation. Let's suppose that I betray your trust. By accepting this event, you would acknowledge that I did in fact betray you, that unfortunately all the conditions were in place for this betrayal to occur, namely that I had a set of thoughts which led me to act in the way that I did. Accepting my betrayal also means that you actively dislike my betrayal (i.e. you don't condone the way I treated you), but that you do not condemn me as a person. Furthermore, acceptance certainly does not preclude you from taking constructive action to rectify the situation. Acceptance, in short, is based on a set of rational beliefs that leads you to feel healthily negative about my behavior, rather than emotionally disturbed about what I did.

The same argument applies to the concept of self-acceptance. When I accept myself for breaking my moral code, I regard myself as a fallible human being for my wrongdoing. I do not condone my behavior; rather, I take responsibility for it, strive to understand why I acted in the way that I did, learn from the experience, make appropriate amends and resolve to apply my learning so that, in similar circumstances, I can act morally.

So rather than encouraging complacency, acceptance is the springboard for constructive change.

Question 6: Doesn't REBT neglect clients' emotions?

Answer: The short answer to this question is no. Your question focuses on the meaning of the term 'rational'. Many people think that the term 'rational' means devoid of emotion. They think that the model of psychological health advocated by REBT is epitomised by Mr Spock in *Star Trek* or the android, Data, in *Star Trek: The Next Generation*, who were both incapable of experiencing human emotion. This is far from the case. The term 'rational' in REBT means, amongst other things, experiencing healthy emotions, i.e. emotions which aid and abet the person as she strives to pursue her basic constructive goals and purposes.

The REBT therapist is particularly interested in helping her client to identify his unhealthy negative emotions about negative activating events as a prelude to identifying his irrational beliefs which are deemed to underpin these emotions. As a first step in therapy, the therapist helps her client to challenge and change these irrational beliefs so that he can think rationally about these events and feel healthily negative about them.

In addition, unlike other cognitive-behavior therapists, REBT therapists encourage their clients to feel intense healthy negative emotions about very negative events. As they keenly differentiate between healthy and unhealthy negative emotions, a distinction that other CBT therapists tend not to make, REBT therapists are able on theoretical grounds to help their clients feel healthily distressed without feeling emotionally disturbed.

On the other hand, REBT therapists do not believe that emotional catharsis is therapeutic *per se*, nor do they actively encourage their clients to explore the subtle nuances of their emotions. Rather, they encourage their clients to acknowledge their feelings, to feel their feelings, but thence to detect and dispute the irrational beliefs that underlie these feelings when they are unhealthily negative. So whereas REBT therapists certainly do not neglect their clients' emotions, they do adopt a particular stance towards these emotions as outlined above.

Question 7: My previous counselor training taught me that the most important ingredient in counseling is the relationship between client and counselor. Doesn't REBT neglect the therapeutic relationship?

Answer: As I pointed out in Module 2, Unit 5, Carl Rogers (1957) wrote a seminal paper on the therapeutic relationship which for many set the standard against which other approaches should be judged. Rogers argued that there were a set of necessary and sufficient core conditions that the therapist had to provide and the client had to perceive the therapist as having provided these conditions for therapeutic change to occur. Two years later Ellis (1959) published a reply in which he acknowledged that these conditions were important and frequently desirable, but they were hardly necessary and sufficient. This has been the REBT position ever since.

Thus, REBT therapists do not neglect the therapeutic relationship. However, they do not regard the relationship as the *sine qua non* of therapeutic change. Some REBT therapists regard the development of a good therapeutic relationship as setting the ground for the 'real therapy' to take place, i.e. the application of REBT techniques. My own position is somewhat different. I regard the application of REBT techniques and so-called relationship factors as interdependent therapeutic variables. The one set of variables depend for their therapeutic effect on the presence of the other set.

Finally, as I mentioned in Module 2, Unit 5, DiGiuseppe *et al.* (1993) found that REBT therapists scored as highly as therapists from other schools on measures of the 'core conditions' provided by clients. If we are neglecting the therapeutic relationship, our clients don't seem to think so!

Question 8: REBT therapists may not neglect the therapeutic relationship with their clients, but isn't this relationship unequal?

Answer: It depends on what you mean by unequal. REBT therapists consider themselves to be equal to their clients as humans. The therapist is not more worthy than the client, nor vice versa. However, on different aspects of themselves there are likely to be inequalities. The client may know more about gardening or be more sociable than the therapist, for example. They are equal in humanity, but unequal in certain areas.

Now, the purpose of therapy is to help the client to overcome his psychological problems and live more resourcefully. In this area, the REBT therapist claims to know more about the dynamics of emotional problems and facilitating personal change than the client, at least from an REBT perspective, and this does constitute an inequality as do the ones mentioned earlier that are in the client's favour. REBT therapists openly acknowledge this real inequality, but stress that it needs to be placed in the context of a relationship between two equally fallible human beings.

Question 9 How do you respond to the criticism that REBT therapists brainwash their clients?

Answer: First, let me be clear what I mean by brainwashing. Brainwashing is a process where the person to be brainwashed is isolated from her normal environment and from people whom she knows, is deprived of food, water and sleep and when judged to be in a susceptible state is provided with information and beliefs which are usually counter to the information and beliefs she would normally hold. Obviously, by this definition REBT therapists do not brainwash their clients.

However, I think you mean something more subtle than this. I think you mean that REBT therapists tell their clients what to think without due regard to their current views and press them hard to believe the REBT 'line'. If this is what you mean then I would deny that well-trained, ethical REBT therapists would do this (I cannot speak for untrained individuals who pass themselves off as REBT practitioners).

REBT holds that one of the hallmarks of mental health is the ability to think for oneself and to be sceptical of new ideas (Dryden, 1994a). It regards gullibility, suggestibility and uncriticalness as breeding grounds for emotional disturbance. So, in presenting rational principles, skilled REBT therapists elicit both their clients' understanding of these concepts and their views of these ideas. There usually follows a healthy debate between client and therapist where the therapist aims to correct the client's misconceptions of these rational principles in a respectful manner (as I hope I am demonstrating with you now). At no time does the therapist insist that the client must believe the rational concepts he is being taught. If the therapist does so insist, this is evidence of a therapist's irrationality such as: 'I have to get my client to think rationally and if I fail in this respect this proves that I am a lousy therapist and a less worthy person as a result.'

Also, you will recall from the previous chapter that I stressed that REBT therapists encourage their clients to voice their doubts and reservations about REBT and take these seriously. This is almost the antithesis of brainwashing. Now, it is true that REBT therapists do have a definite viewpoint concerning the nature of psychological disturbance and which conditions best facilitate therapeutic change. It is also true that REBT therapists are open with their clients concerning these views and strive to present them as clearly as they can. However, just because REBT therapists teach REBT principles to their clients, it does not follow that they are attempting to brainwash their clients or impose their views on them. My own practice is to make clear (a) that I will be offering a specific approach to therapy based on a particular framework; (b) that there are other approaches to therapy that offer different frameworks; and (c) that I am happy to make a referral if it transpires that the client is better served by a different therapeutic approach. I believe that many REBT therapists act similarly with their clients. This, I hope you will agree, is a long way from brainwashing.

As I mentioned in Module 2, Unit 7, REBT therapists have preferred therapeutic goals, but are prepared to make compromises if it becomes clear that the client is unwilling or unable to work towards philosophic change. I have yet to hear of a brainwasher who is prepared to make compromises!

Question 10: But don't REBT therapists tell their clients what to feel and what to do?

Answer: My answer to this question is similar to my reply above. As I mentioned in Module 1, Unit 3, and as I will cover in greater detail in Module 5, REBT therapists keenly discriminate between healthy and unhealthy negative emotions. Their initial goal is to help clients minimise their disturbance about negative As, while encouraging them to acknowledge, experience and channel their healthy distress about these As. However, REBT therapists make clear that their clients have a choice concerning their feelings and behavior. Just because REBT theory advocates that clients minimize their disturbed feelings, but not their distressed feelings, it does not follow that clients have to agree with this view. The same is true of behavior. An REBT therapist may well point out to her client the self-defeating nature of his behavior, but she does not insist that the client follow her lead. As with the issue of beliefs, REBT therapists have preferences concerning how clients feel and behave in relation to the issue of psychological health and disturbance and they may well articulate these preferences during therapy. After all, they genuinely want to help their clients live psychologically healthy lives and they believe that they have a good theory to help their clients do this. However REBT therapists firmly respect their clients' freedom and do not transmute their preferences into musts on this issue, even if this means that a particular client may continue to perpetuate her psychological problems. Her REBT therapist will, of course, explore the reasons for this, but will not in the final analysis insist that the client do the healthy thing.

Incidentally, in areas not related to the issue of psychological health and disturbance, REBT therapists are quite *laissez-faire* about their clients' feelings and behavior. For example, whether a client pursues stamp-collecting or body building is not the therapist's concern assuming that both of these activities are based on preferences and are not harmful to others or to the environment.

Question 11: From what you have been saying, it seems to me that REBT therapists prevent clients from finding their own solutions to their problems. Am I right about this?

Answer: In answering this question, I need to distinguish between two types of solutions: psychological solutions and practical solutions. In REBT, a psychological solution to the client's problems in the main involves the client identifying, challenging and changing his irrational beliefs. Whereas a practical solution involves, amongst other things, responding behaviorally to negative As in functional ways. In this analysis, achieving a psychological solution facilitates the client applying the practical solution and, therefore, preferably should be achieved first.

Now, the REBT therapist assumes that the client will not achieve a philosophically-based psychological change on his own. She further assumes that she needs to help the client in active ways to understand what this psychological solution involves and how he can apply it. Once she has helped the client to do this then the client is generally able to choose the best practical solution to his problem. If not, the REBT therapist helps him to specify different practical solutions to his problem, encourages him to list the advantages and disadvantages of each course of action and to select and implement the best practical solution.

So, in summary, REBT therapists actively encourage their clients to understand and implement REBT-orientated psychological solutions to their problems and assume that once this has been done then clients will often be able to see for themselves which practical solutions to implement. When the therapist does intervene in the practical problem-solving phase of therapy, it is to help the client weigh up the pros and cons of his own generated solutions and to select the most effective course of action.

Question 12: Isn't REBT too confrontational?

Answer: As you know from Module 2, Unit 6, REBT is basically an active-directive approach to psychotherapy where the therapist intervenes actively and directs the client to the attitudinal core of his problems and helps him to develop a plan to challenge his self-defeating beliefs which constitute this core. In disputing the client's irrational beliefs, the therapist does take the lead in questioning the client concerning the empirical, logical and pragmatic nature of these beliefs. The disputing techniques of the therapist often seem overly confrontational to therapists who advocate less directive counseling methods. It is the contrast between these methods and the active-directive methods of REBT that lead these therapists to conclude that REBT is TOO confrontational.

If the REBT therapist prepares the client adequately for her active-directive methods, particularly her challenging disputing techniques, then in general the client will not consider the therapist to be TOO confrontational, although the observing less directive therapist who does not fully understand what the REBT therapist is trying to do might consider this therapist to be overly confrontational. However, if the therapist fails to give a satisfactory rationale for her challenging behavior then she may well be experienced as TOO confrontational.

Question 13: You say that REBT is a structured therapy, but doesn't it 'straitjacket' clients?

Answer: This is often a criticism levelled against REBT by therapists who prefer to give their clients a lot of 'space' to explore themselves and their concerns. Whilst it is true that REBT is a structured approach to psychotherapy, it is also the case that skilled REBT therapists vary the amount of structure according to what is happening in the session. Thus, at times an REBT therapist may be quite unstructured, for example when her client has started to talk about a newly discovered problem or she may use session structure rather loosely, for example in the ending phase when prompting the client to assess a problem using the ABC framework. Of course, at other times the REBT therapist will be quite structured, particularly when disputing her client's irrational beliefs. Again, if the therapist provides a rationale for the use of a tight structure and the client understands and assents to this, then the client won't consider that he has been 'straitjacketed' by the therapist although the observer might make such a conclusion.

Question 14: Isn't it the case that REBT is only concerned with changing beliefs?

Answer: REBT therapists are primarily concerned with helping clients to pursue their basic goals and purposes. In order to facilitate this process, the therapist encourages the client to experience healthy rather than unhealthy negative emotions about negative As and to act functionally in the face of these negative events. Now, REBT therapists do hold the view that a central way of helping clients to achieve all this is to encourage them to change their irrational beliefs, but this is not their sole goal. So, REBT therapists are interested in helping clients to change their beliefs, their feelings, their behavior, their images, their interpersonal relationships and the aversive events in their lives. As such REBT is a multimodal rather than a unimodal approach to therapy.

A similar issue relates to how REBT is often portrayed in therapeutic outcome studies. In these studies REBT is deemed to be synonymous with its cognitive restructuring methods rather than a multimodal approach which also employs emotive, behavioral, imaginal and relationship-enhancement techniques. As such, some psychotherapy researchers have also wrongly concluded that REBT therapists are ONLY interested in helping their clients to change the latter's beliefs.

Question 15: REBT relies heavily on verbal interchange between therapist and client. It also advocates concepts that are difficult to grasp. Doesn't this mean that REBT only works with highly verbal, intelligent clients?

Answer: This is a common criticism of REBT and I can understand why you have made it. I have presented REBT to you in its complex sophisticated form. I have used a lot of words and explained its concepts in a way that reflects this complexity. After all, everyone here in the training group is highly verbal and intelligent; otherwise we wouldn't have let you onto the course...(General laughter). However, skilled REBT therapists can also tailor the way they explain REBT concepts to match the verbal and intellectual capacities of their clients. Because this issue is beyond the scope of this book I refer you, in particular, to the work of Knaus and Haberstroh (1993) and Howard Young (see Dryden, 1989) who have written about the application of REBT to clients who are neither particularly verbal nor intelligent.

I hope that I have dealt satisfactorily and respectfully with the fifteen most common misconceptions of REBT. I am now in a position to deal with a particularly important REBT skill, i.e. teaching the ABCs of REBT.

Module 4
Teaching the ABCs of REBT

As I have stressed so far in this book, the ABC framework is at the heart of the REBT theory of psychological disturbance. It provides both the therapist and the client with a way of assessing the client's problems. As an accurate assessment of the client's problems is a prerequisite for effective intervention, the ability to teach the ABCs of REBT clearly and succinctly to clients is an important skill in which all aspiring REBT therapists need to develop competence. There are a number of ways in which you can teach your clients the ABCs and in this module, I will demonstrate several of these methods.

Unit 10: The Money Example

Let me go through the money example by providing a typical example of how I demonstrate it with a trainee (in this case, Robin) on a first-level training course in REBT. In this role play, I ask Robin to play the role of a client, while I play the role of REBT therapist.

Windy: OK, Robin. I'd like to teach you a model which explains the factors that account for people's emotional problems. Now this is not the only explanation in the field of counseling, but it is the one that I use in my work. Are you interested in learning about this explanation?

Robin: Yes, I am.

Windy: Good. Now there are four parts to this model. Here's part one. I want you to imagine that you have $10 in your pocket and that you believe the following: 'I would prefer to have a minimum of $11 on me at all times, but it's not essential that I do so. It would be bad to have less than my preferred $11, but it would not be the end of the world.' Now, if you really believed this, how would you feel about only having $10 when you want, but don't demand a minimum of $11?

Robin: I'd feel concerned.

Windy: Right. Or you'd feel healthily angry or disappointed. But you wouldn't kill yourself.

Robin: Certainly not.

Windy: Right. Now, here's part two of the model. This time you hold a different belief. You believe the following: 'I absolutely must have a minimum of $11 on me at all times. I must! I must! I must! And it would be the end of the world if I had less.' Now, with this belief you look in your pocket and again find that you only have $10. Now, how would you feel this time about having $10 when you demand that you must have a minimum of $11?

Robin: I'd feel quite panicky.

Windy: That's exactly right. Now, note something really important. Faced with the same situation, different beliefs lead to different feelings. Now, the third part of the model. This time you still have the same belief as you did in the last scenario, namely: 'I absolutely must have a minimum of $11 on me at all times. I must! I must! I must! And it would be the end of the world if I had less.' This time, however, in checking the contents of your pocket you discover four fifty-cent pieces nestling under the $10 bill. How would you feel about now having $12 when you believe that you have to have a minimum of $11 at all times?

Robin: ... I'd feel very relieved.

Windy: Right. Now, here is the fourth and final part of the model. With that same $12 in your pocket and that same belief, namely: 'I absolutely must have a minimum of $11 on me at all times. I must! I must! I must! And it would be the end of the world if I had less', one thing would occur to you that would lead you to be panicky again. What do you think that might be?

Robin: Let me think... I believe that I must have a minimum of $11 at all times, I've got more than the minimum and yet I'm anxious. Oh I see I'm now saying 'I must have a minimum of $13.'

Windy: No. You are sticking with the same belief as before namely: 'I must have a minimum of $11 on me at all times. I NOW have $12...'

Robin: Oh! I see... I NOW have the $12. Right, so I'm scared I might lose $2.

Windy: Or you might spend $2 or you might get mugged. Right. Now the point of this model is this. All humans, black or white, rich or poor, male or female make themselves disturbed when they don't get what they believe they must get. And they are also vulnerable to making themselves disturbed when they do get what they believe they must get, because they could always lose it. But when humans stick rigorously (but not rigidly) to their non-dogmatic preferences and don't change these into musts then they will feel healthily concerned when they don't have what they prefer and will be able to take constructive action under these conditions to prevent something undesirable happening in the future. Now in our work together we will pay close attention to the differences between absolute musts and non-dogmatic preferences. Is that clear?

Robin: Yes.

Windy: Well, I'm not sure I've made my point clearly enough. Can you put it into your own words...?

Let me now briefly summarize the steps here. As I do so, go back to the dialogue and see if you can follow the steps.

Step 1. Ask the client if he is interested in an explanation of emotional problems.

Step 2. Present part 1 of the model. Stress that the client has less money than he prefers (rational belief). Inquire about his feeling. If he does not give you a healthy negative emotion, explain why this would be his emotional response.

Step 3. Present part 2 of the model. Stress that the client has less money than he demands (irrational belief). Inquire about his feeling. If he does not give you an unhealthy negative emotion, explain why this would be his emotional response. Prompt if necessary.

Step 4. Emphasize that different beliefs about the same situation lead to different feelings.

Step 5. Present part 3 of the model. Stress that the client has more money than he demands (irrational belief). Inquire about his feeling. If he doesn't reply that he would feel relieved or pleased, explain why this would be his emotional response.

Step 6. Present part 4 of the model. Stress that he still has more money than he demands (irrational belief), but that he has a thought that leads him to feel disturbed again. Inquire about the nature of this thought. Encourage him to identify possible thoughts by himself, but give suggestions if he is stuck.

Step 7. Summarize all the information emphasising the importance of distinguishing between rational and irrational beliefs and showing their differential effects.

Correct your client's errors

One of the important points to note when you present this model to your clients is that you will have to both correct the errors that they make in responding to your questions and explain the nature of these errors. For example, when you present the first part of the model the client may say that he would experience an unhealthy negative emotion rather than a healthy negative emotion. Unless you correct this error and explain why it is an error then your client may take away erroneous information. Here is an example of what I mean.

Windy: There are four parts to this model. Here's part one. I want you to imagine that you have $10 in your pocket and that you believe the following: 'I would prefer to have a minimum of $11 on me at all times, but it's not essential that I do so. It would be bad to have less than my preferred $11, but it would not be the end of the world'. Now, if you really believed this, how would you feel about only having $10 when you want, but don't demand, $11?

Sarah: I'd be very anxious.

Windy: I don't think you would. Don't forget that your belief is that it would be undesirable not having the $11, not that it is an absolute, dire necessity to have that sum. Also you don't believe it would be the end of the world if you did not have the $11, rather that it would be unfortunate not to have this amount. Think carefully about this. Now how do you think you would feel?

Sarah: Oh, I see. I'd be concerned.

Common trainee errors in teaching the money example

The money example, when presented correctly, is a potent way of teaching the ABC model. However, it is difficult to master and trainees do experience difficulty in learning it. When they first practice it, they tend to make a number of errors. In discussing the following errors, I will use illustrative dialogue from training situations.

1. Failure to distinguish fully between rational and irrational beliefs

Mary (in the role of counselor):...Now there are four parts to this model. Here's part one. I want you to imagine that you have $10 in your pocket and that you believe the following: 'I would prefer to have a minimum of $11 on me at all times.' Now, if you really believed this, how would you feel about only having $10 when you want a minimum of $11?

Windy (as trainer): Well. It was good that you began by stressing that there are four parts to the model and you started the model correctly with a rational belief. However, it is important that you present the client with the full version of the rational belief which is in two parts. The first part of the rational belief involves asserting the person's preference which is, as you said correctly: 'I would prefer to have a minimum of $11 on me at all times.'

However, REBT theory that people can easily change their preferences to demands and the major way of guarding against this when teaching the money example is to negate the person's demand as well as asserting his preference. You do this by saying: 'I would prefer to have a minimum of $11 on me at all times, but it's not essential that I do so.'

You will recall that REBT theory states that preferences are primary rational beliefs and three other rational beliefs are derived from these preferences, namely: anti-awfulizing, high frustration tolerance and self/other-acceptance. To reinforce the rational belief here, I recommend that you add the anti-awfulizing derivative. When you do this, it is once again to assert the rational belief and negate the irrational belief. Thus the full rational derivative is: 'It would be bad to have less than my preferred $11, but it would not be the end of the world.'

If we put together the primary rational belief (i.e. the preference) and its anti-awfulizing derivative remembering to assert the rational beliefs and negate the irrational beliefs we have: 'I would prefer to have a minimum of $11 on me at all times, but it's not essential that I do so. It would be bad to have less than my preferred $11, but it would not be the end of the world.'

2. Failure to clarify vague emotional statements thus not distinguishing between healthy and unhealthy negative emotions

REBT therapists place great emphasis on encouraging clients to be clear rather than vague about their emotions. Thus, if a client describes a vague emotion in the money example, the therapist needs to help him clarify its precise nature.

Windy: OK, Mary. Why not back up and then continue?

Mary: Now there are four parts to this model. Here's part one. I want you to imagine that you have $10 in your pocket and that you believe the following: 'I would prefer to have a minimum of $11 on me at all times, but it's not essential that I do so. It would be bad to have less than my preferred $11, but it would not be the end of the world'. Now, if you really believed this, how would you feel about only having $10 when you want, but don't demand a minimum of $11?

Arthur (in the role of client): Upset.

Mary: Right. Now here's part two of the model.

Windy: OK. Let's stop there. A very important part of REBT theory states that when a person faces a negative A, like having $1 less than her goal, her unhealthy negative emotions about this A stem largely from irrational beliefs, whilst her healthy negative emotions stem largely from rational beliefs. In order clearly to teach the client the difference between rational and irrational beliefs in the money example, it is very important that you help her to differentiate clearly her healthy from her unhealthy negative emotions. One way of doing this is to be precise about emotional terms. Now, when your client used the word 'upset' just then, we do not know whether this refers to a healthy negative emotion like concern, disappointment and annoyance or to an unhealthy negative emotion like anxiety, feelings of self-pity or anger. If you accept the word 'upset' uncritically here, then you are making life more difficult for yourself later in the model when you come to show that irrational beliefs lead primarily to disturbed emotions. If by the word 'upset' here your client means a disturbed negative emotion then he will later be confused. He'll say something to himself like: 'Wait a minute. The therapist is now showing me that irrational beliefs lead to disturbed negative emotions. But she also accepted my point that my 'upset' feelings – which I also see as disturbed – stem from rational beliefs. I'm very confused.'

So instead of accepting the term 'upset' uncritically, you need to clarify what your client means by it and proceed accordingly. Let me demonstrate how to do this. In doing so I want Arthur in the first instance to construe 'upset' as a healthy negative emotion and in the second instance as an unhealthy negative emotion and I'll show you what to do in each case.

Instance 1

Windy: So you say that you would feel upset if you have $10 when you want, but don't demand a minimum of $11. I'm not quite sure what you mean by 'upset'. Do you mean upset in a healthy concerned way, for example, or upset in an unhealthy anxious way?

Arthur: Put that way, I'd be concerned rather than anxious.

Instance 2

Windy: So you say that you would feel upset if you have $10 when you want, but don't demand a minimum of $11. I'm not quite sure what you mean by 'upset'. Do you mean upset in a healthy concerned way, for example, or upset in an unhealthy anxious way?

Arthur: Put that way, I'd be anxious rather than concerned.

Windy: Now I may be wrong here, but I don't think you would. Don't forget you believe that whilst you would like to have a minimum of $11 at all times, it is not essential. Can you see the difference between believing that having $11 at all times is desirable, but not essential and believing that having $11 at all times is absolutely essential?

Arthur: Yes. In the first case, I believe that it is necessary for me to have $11 and in the second case, I believe that it would be nice to have it, but that it is not a necessity.

Windy: That's right. Now which belief would lead to unanxious concern and which to anxious overconcern?

Arthur: I see what you mean. I'd feel concerned about not having the $10 if I believed that having the $11 at all times is desirable, but not necessary.

3. Failure to emphasize the irrationality of the client's irrational belief in part two of the model

When going over part two of the model, it is important to emphasize the irrationality of the client's irrational belief. If this is not done, the client may not understand its full implications. Let's go back to Mary and Arthur.

Mary: Right. Now, here's part two of the model. This time you hold a different belief. You believe the following: 'I must have a minimum of $11 on me at all times.' With this belief you look in your pocket and again find that you only have $10. Now, how would you feel this time about having $10?

Windy: Let's stop there, Mary. Now, at this point, it's really important to emphasize the irrationality of the irrational beliefs you are asking Arthur to hold in his mind. Just mentioning the must with little or no emphasis is usually insufficient. Listen carefully to what I usually say and see if you can see the difference between this and what you said.

OK, Arthur, here's part two of the model. This time you hold a different belief. You believe the following: "I absolutely must have a minimum of $11 on me at all times. I must! I must! I must! And it would be the end of the world if I had less." Now, with this belief you look in your pocket and again find that you only have $10. Now, how would you feel this time about having $10 when you demand that you must have a minimum of $11?

Mary: Well first, you used the phrase 'absolute must' where I just used the word 'must'. Second, you repeated the phrase 'I must' three times with a considerable degree of emphasis. Then you provided an awfulizing belief...(pause)....

Windy: Why do you think I did that?

Mary: I'm not sure.

Windy: I did that to emphasize the irrationality of the irrational belief.

Mary: I see. Then you asked Arthur how he would feel about having $10 when he demanded that he must have a minimum of $11? So once again you emphasized the irrational belief when I did not.

4. Failure to summarize accurately all the points in the money example

One of the most difficult parts of the money example is the summary. To summarize all the points effectively, the therapist needs to have a full understanding of the these points and the sequence in which they need to be presented. Let's consider Mary's summary.

Mary: Now the point of this model is this. All humans, black or white, rich or poor, male or female are upset (1) when they don't get what they demand. And they are also vulnerable to becoming upset (1) when they do get what they demand because they could always lose it. But when people stick with their desires (2) they won't get upset (1) (3).

Windy: That was a pretty good first attempt, Mary. You were able to show Arthur some key parts of the model such as the difference between musts and desires. There are three points that you need to consider in order to improve this summary. [The following numbers correspond to the bracketed numbers shown in Mary's summary.]

(1) First, you used the word 'upset' throughout. This is problematic for two reasons. First, as discussed before 'upset' is a vague word and therefore you are helping the client neither to be precise about his own emotions nor to differentiate between healthy and unhealthy negative emotions. Second, in using 'upset' throughout the summary, you have unwittingly taught your client that emotional upset stems from both rational beliefs an irrational beliefs. This is obviously going to be confusing for him. So, what could you do differently next time?

Mary: I'll be precise in my use of emotional language and use words that clearly reflect healthy negative emotions like concern and healthy anger and words that clearly reflect unhealthy negative emotions such as anxiety and unhealthy anger.

Windy: Excellent. My second piece of feedback is as follows.

(2) At the end you said, 'But when people stick with their desires they won't get upset'. Compare this with what I generally say at this point: 'But when humans stick rigorously (but not rigidly) to their non-dogmatic preferences and don't change these into musts then they will feel healthily concerned.' Can you see the difference between these two statements?

Mary: Well, I just stated the rational belief, whilst you stressed that holding this belief precludes people from implicitly changing it to an irrational belief. Also you stress that people can rigorously hold a rational belief without it being rigid. I didn't mention that. Finally, whilst I used the vague term 'upset' you were explicit in stressing that a specific healthy negative emotion stems from a rational belief.

Windy: Again that is a full and excellent answer. Now, here is my third and final piece of feedback.

(3) At the very end you mention, albeit vaguely, that a negative emotional state stems from a rational belief, whereas I also stress that holding a rational belief also leads to people being able to take constructive action to prevent something undesirable happening in the future.

The summary is difficult to master, so let me break it down point by point.

Point 1. Irrational beliefs lead to disturbance when the A is negative.

'All humans, black or white, rich or poor, male or female make themselves disturbed when they don't get what they believe they must get...'

Point 2. Irrational beliefs leave people vulnerable to disturbance when the A is positive because the A could become negative in the future.

'...And they are also vulnerable to making themselves disturbed when they do get what they believe they must get, because they could always lose it...'

Point 3. Rational beliefs lead to healthy negative emotions and constructive behavior when the A is negative.

'...But when humans stick rigorously (but not rigidly) to their non-dogmatic preferences and don't change these into musts then they will feel healthily concerned when they don't have what they prefer and will be able to take constructive action under these conditions and to prevent something undesirable happening in the future...'

Summary

In order to master this important method of teaching the ABCs of REBT, let me suggest the following steps.

1. Rewrite my version on pp. 53–5, using your own words, ensuring that you don't change any of the meaning or any of the teaching steps.
2. Learn it off by heart, being careful to focus on the meaning of your words. Don't do this parrot fashion, though.
3. Test yourself by putting the model on audiotape. Play both yourself and a very cooperative client. If you get stuck, consult your written script. Do this until you can teach the model smoothly without self-prompting.
4. Pair up with a fellow trainee and teach him or her the model, ensuring that your colleague plays a cooperative client.
5. Repeat step 4, but this time encourage the client to make minor errors of understanding in the client role. Correct these errors until the 'client' understands the model fully.

6. Repeat step 4, but this time encourage the client to make major errors of understanding in the client role. Again, correct these errors until the 'client' understands the model fully.
7. Teach the model to several people who are unfamiliar with REBT.
8. Bring any problems in teaching the model to your REBT trainer or supervisor.

Unit 11: The Lateness Example

Certain clients cannot relate easily to the money example. For this reason it is useful to be able to use different teaching examples. Remember, though, that you need to teach the same points in the same order. I will demonstrate this now by teaching the 'Lateness Example'.

Windy: OK, Jane. I'd like to teach you a model which explains the factors that account for people's emotional problems. Now this is not the only explanation in the field of counseling, but it is the one that I use in my work. Are you interested in learning about this explanation?

Jane (trainee in the role of client): Yes, I am.

Windy: Good. Now there are four parts to this model. Here's part one. I want you to imagine that you are ten minutes late for an appointment and that you believe the following: 'I would prefer to be on time for all my appointments, but it's not essential that I do so. It would be bad to be late, but it would not be the end of the world.' Now, if you really believed this, how would you feel about being ten minutes late for your meeting when you want, but don't demand that you be punctual?

Jane: I'd feel concerned.

Windy: Right. Or you'd feel healthily angry or disappointed. But you wouldn't kill yourself.

Jane: That's right.

Windy: Right. Now, here's part two of the model. This time you hold a different belief. You believe the following: 'I absolutely must be on time for all my appointments. I must! I must! I must! And it would be the end of the world if I was late.' Now, with this belief you check your watch and again you realize that you are ten minutes late for your appointment. Now, how would you feel this time about being ten minutes late when you demand that you must be on time?

Jane: I'd feel quite panicky.

Windy: That's exactly right. Now, note something really important. Faced with the same situation, different beliefs lead to different feelings. Now, the third part of the model. This time you still have the same belief as you did in the last scenario, namely: 'I absolutely must be on time for all my appointments. I must! I must! I must! And it would be the end of the world if I was late.' This time, however, you see a clock in the street which shows that your watch is twenty minutes fast and you are, in fact, ten minutes early. How would you feel about now being ten minutes early when you believe that you have to be on time for all your appointments?

Jane: ... I'd feel very relieved.

Windy: Right. Now, here is the fourth and final part of the model. Knowing that you are ten minutes early and with that same belief, namely: 'I absolutely must be on time for all my appointments. I must! I must! I must! And it would be the end of the world if I was late', one thing would occur to you that would lead you to be panicky again. What do you think that might be?

Jane: That something might delay me.

Windy: Or that you may have got the time of the meeting wrong and in fact you are late rather than early. Now the point of this model is this. All humans, black or white, rich or poor, male or female make themselves disturbed when they don't get what they believe they must get. And they are also vulnerable to making themselves disturbed when they do get what they believe they must get, because they could always lose it. But when humans stick rigorously (but not rigidly) to their non-dogmatic preferences and don't change these into musts then they will feel healthily concerned when they don't have what they prefer and will be able to take constructive action under these conditions and to prevent something undesirable happening in the future. Now in our work together we will pay close attention to the differences between absolute musts and non-dogmatic preferences. Is that clear?

Jane: Yes.

Windy: Well, I'm not sure I've made my point clearly enough. Can you put it into your own words...?

Having discussed the money example in detail, and shown you the lateness example, I will now discuss one other related method. It is called 'The Four Surgeon Example' and stresses the dysfunctional consequences of irrational beliefs in a vivid manner. I will present this method without discussing the typical mistakes that trainees make in implementing it and suggest that you follow the eight steps presented on p. 61 if you wish to use it skilfully.

Unit 12: The Four Surgeon Example

The 'Four Surgeon Example' is best used with clients who think that musts have pragmatic value in motivating them towards excellence and that without these musts, they would lapse into apathy. Here is an example of how I generally use it with clients.

Windy: So, if I understand you correctly, Richard, your point is that having a dogmatic must helps you to do well and without it, you would have little or no motivation to excel. Have I understood you correctly?

Richard: That's about the size of it.

Windy: Would you be interested in hearing a teaching vignette which puts a different point of view?

Richard: If you want.

[This reply does not give me sufficient strength of permission, so I don't proceed quite yet.]

Windy: I thought that as you seem like an open-minded man, you would judge the case on its merits.

Richard: Yeah. I consider myself open-minded.

Windy: So would you like to go through the teaching vignette with me and then come to your own conclusion?

Richard: Yes. I would.

[By appealing to his open-mindedness, I have elicited from Richard an agreement to listen to my argument which is much stronger than his previous statement: 'If you want'.]

Windy: OK. Now this involves your participation too. OK?

Richard: OK.

Windy: Now I want you to imagine that you have to have surgery. You have a condition which is painful, but not life-threatening, and which requires a skilled surgeon. Luckily, you work for a company that has a top of the range private insurance plan and you can have the operation immediately. Because the insurance cover is top class, it offers an additional benefit. You get to choose your own surgeon. They assemble four top surgeons and you are allowed to interview each one before making your selection. They are all equally skilful as technicians, but each one has a different attitude towards surgery, so you can only choose among them on the basis of attitude, not technical competence. Is that clear?

Bill: As a bell.

Windy: OK. Surgeon number one comes in and tells you his philosophy of surgery. He says the following:

'My philosophy of surgery is this: If I make a mistake during surgery, I don't care a fig. I might cut an artery and you'd bleed to death and I wouldn't

give a damn. That's my philosophy of surgery.'
Windy: Would he be on your short list?

Bill: Are you crazy! The guy is a disgrace to his profession. He's obviously never heard of the Hippocratic Oath. I wouldn't let him near me.

Windy: Now, surgeon number two comes in and says the following:

'My philosophy of surgery is this: I'm good and I can guarantee you that I won't make any mistakes during the operation. This procedure is a piece of cake. I could do it with my eyes closed....In fact, I will do it with my eyes closed. But, don't worry. I'll guarantee total success.'

Windy: Would she be a likely candidate?

Bill: Over my dead body, if you'll pardon the pun. I've heard of overconfidence, but this woman wins the gold medal. Again, I wouldn't let her near me.

Windy: OK, here is surgeon number three who says the following:

'My philosophy of surgery is as follows: I believe that it is absolutely imperative that I don't make any mistakes. I mustn't make a mistake! I mustn't make a mistake! I mustn't make a mistake! I've got to do a good job! I've got to do a good job!'

[While saying this, my hands are shaking furiously.]
Would you choose this man?

Bill: Only if I want to be chopped salami! No way!

Windy: But I thought you said earlier that musts motivate people to do well. This man certainly has musts, so why don't you want him?

Bill: OK. I'm beginning to see that perhaps musts are not such a good idea after all.

Windy: Good. But keep your mind open until you've heard the last surgeon. She comes in and says:

'My philosophy of surgery is this: I can't guarantee you that I won't make a mistake and I don't believe that I mustn't make one. I'm human after all. I will say this; although I'm not perfectionistic, I really do take pride in my work and really want to do the best job that I can. I don't have to do so, but I really want to. I find that this attitude helps me to focus on what I'm doing rather than how well I am doing it.'
Would you choose her, Bill?

Bill: I sure would. She's realistic and not a basket case like the others. I'd trust my body to her.

Windy: But she doesn't have a must. Surely, she won't be motivated to do a good job.

Bill: Well, she sure sounds motivated. Maybe you don't need a must to do a good job. You've persuaded me, doc.

Windy: From where I'm sitting one open-minded fellow persuaded himself!

[It is important to attribute belief change to the client's own endeavours whenever possible. In this case I had no hesitation to point out to Bill that, in truth, he really did persuade himself. I just issued the invitation.]

In reviewing this technique, it is important to be clear which belief each surgeon portrayed. Figure 4.1 presents this in visual form. Read the summary in this figure and go over the text so that you are clear what is being conveyed in the 'Four Surgeon Example'. Then use the training sequence presented on p. 61 to develop your skills at teaching this method. The point of this technique is, of course to demonstrate the pragmatic value of healthy preferences and the negative consequences that stem from demandingness, indifference and Pollyannaism.

Surgeon No. 1: Indifference

Surgeon No. 2: Overconfidence/Pollyannaism

Surgeon No. 3: Demandingness

Surgeon No. 4: Non-dogmatic preference

Figure 4.1 Beliefs portrayed by each surgeon in the 'Four Surgeon Example'.

Unit 13: The Blind Man Example

It sometimes happens on first-level REBT training courses that trainees have been previously exposed to a method known as 'The Blind Man Example' which purports to demonstrate the ABCs of REBT. Because it is a commonly taught example, but one that DOES NOT represent the true position of REBT on the ABCs, I will first accurately present it and then explain why it does not accurately represent REBT.

Therapist: Would you be interested in a model that explains the factors that account for people's emotional problems?

Client: Yes.

Therapist: Well, imagine that you are standing on an up escalator and someone behind you keeps digging something sharp into the small of your back. How would you feel?

Client: After the first dig, I'd feel mad.

Therapist: What would be going through your mind when you were feeling mad?

Client: This person is deliberately poking me in the back.

Therapist: Can you see the relationship between that thought and your angry feeling?

Client: I would have said that the poke in the back made me angry.

Therapist: Well let's see. Because you would be feeling angry, what would you do?

Client: I'd turn around and give the person a piece of my mind.

Therapist: But imagine as you did so, you discovered that the person behind you was blind. Would you still feel angry?

Client: No, of course not.

Therapist: Even though the poke in the back was the same?

Client: I see what you mean.

Therapist: What would you be thinking differently to allow you to calm down?

Client: It's a blind man and he couldn't help poking me in the back.

Therapist: Right. What this model tells us is that it is not so much situations that cause our feelings, but the way we think about them. The poke in the back was the same, but first you were angry because you were thinking...?

Client: This person is deliberately poking me in the back.

Therapist: And when you turned, you calmed down because you changed your thought to...?

Client: It's a blind man and he couldn't help poking me in the back.

Therapist: So, how would you sum up what we've gone over today?

Client: It's not so much the situation that causes my feeling, but the way I think about it.

Therapist: That's exactly it.

From an REBT perspective, this example is problematic in that it does not teach that emotions are determined largely by beliefs at B. It teach-es that the way we feel is determined largely by the inferences that we make at A. In the first part of the scenario the person is unhealthily angry because he is thinking:'This person is deliberately poking me in the back'. According to REBT theory, this is an inference and does not, by itself, explain the person's unhealthy anger. In order to account for his unhealthy anger, we need his irrational belief which would be something like: 'He must not deliberately poke me in the back.' Now when the person turned round to confront the individual behind him, his feelings of unhealthy anger dissipated. Why? Because he thought the following: 'It's a blind man and he couldn't help poking me in the back.' From an REBT perspective, this change of emotion has been brought about by an inference change not a change of belief. Indeed, REBT theory predicts that the person would remain unhealthily angry when he saw the blind man if he believed something like: 'Even a blind man must take care not to poke me in the back!' Whilst REBT acknowledges that a person may change her emotion in many ways, e.g. by changing her inferences, by withdrawing from a situation or by influencing another person to change his behavior, the most healthy and resilient form of change involves belief change. It is in this respect that the 'Blind Man Example' fails, in that it teaches clients that they can change their feelings by changing their inferences. It therefore does not teach the REBT position that clients can change their unhealthy negative emotions to healthy negative emotions by changing their irrational beliefs to rational beliefs. This latter message is better portrayed in the 'Money' or 'Lateness' examples discussed earlier.

I have once again mentioned the important distinction that REBT therapists make between healthy and unhealthy emotions. As it is very useful to address this distinction early in the therapeutic process, I will discuss this distinction and how to raise it with clients more fully in the following module.

Module 5
Distinguishing Between Healthy and Unhealthy Negative Emotions

I first trained in REBT (or RET as it was known in those days) in 1977. At that time the distinction between healthy and unhealthy negative emotions was present in REBT theory, but was not particularly emphasized. Since that time I have come to realize the central place this distinction occupies in the theory and practice of REBT and how important it is to teach it to clients early in the therapeutic process. In this module, I will provide a diagrammatic summary of the eight major unhealthy emotions and their healthy counterparts (see Figure 5.1). In doing so I will review the inferences, beliefs, cognitive consequences and action tendencies that are associated with each healthy and unhealthy pairing. It is crucial that you understand the factors that help differentiate between healthy and unhealthy negative emotions before explaining these distinctions to your clients. After providing the diagrammatic summary and reviewing briefly each component I will demonstrate how to introduce some of these distinctions to clients by using illustrative therapist–client dialogue. Finally, I will suggest an exercise that you can do in small training groups to become personally and professionally more familiar about the distinctions between healthy and unhealthy negative emotions. This exercise will also help you to practice assessing the emotional problems of your fellow trainees before you do so with your clients. But first, let me say a word about terminology.

Unit 14: Terminology ("Healthy–Unhealthy" vs "Appropriate–Inappropriate" Negative Emotions)

You will have noted that I use the words 'healthy' and 'unhealthy' to distinguish between two types of negative emotions. Until recently, Albert Ellis has preferred using the terms 'appropriate' and 'inappropriate' in making this distinction and you will find numerous references to these terms in his voluminous writings. Following the lead of Gilmore (1986), I consider the use of the terms 'appropriate' negative emotions and 'inappropriate' neg-

Emotion	Healthy or unhealthy	Inference[1] in relation to personal domain[2]	Type of belief	Cognitive consequences	Action tendencies
Anxiety (ego or discomfort)	Unhealthy	* Threat or danger	Irrational	* Overestimates negative features of the threat * Underestimates ability to cope with the threat * Creates an even more negative threat in one's mind * Has more task-irrelevant thoughts than in concern	* To withdraw physically from the threat * To withdraw mentally from the threat * To ward off the threat (eg. by superstitious behavior * To tranquilise feelings * To seek reassurance
Concern	Healthy	* Threat or danger	Rational	* Views the threat realistically * Realistic appraisal of ability to cope with the threat * Does not create an even more negative threat in one's mind * Has more task-relevant thoughts than in anxiety	* To face up to the threat * To deal with the threat constructively
Depression (ego or discomfort)	Unhealthy	* Loss (with implications for future) * Failure	Irrational	* Only sees negative aspects of the loss or failure * Thinks of other losses and failures that one has experienced * Thinks one is unable to help self (helplessness) * Only sees pain and blackness in the future (hopelessness)	* To withdraw from reinforcements * To withdraw into oneself * To create an environment consistent with feelings * To attempt to terminate feelings of depression in self-destructive ways
Sadness	Healthy * Failure	* Loss (with implications for future)	Rational	* Able to see both negative and positive aspects of the loss or failure * Less likely to think of other losses and failures than when depressed * Able to help self * Able to look into the future with hope	* To express feelings about the loss or failure and talk about these to significant others * To seek out reinforcements after a period of mourning

Emotion	Triggers		Cognitive consequences	Behaviors
Unhealthy anger	* Frustration * Self or other transgresses personal rule * Threat to self-esteem	Irrational	* Overestimates the extent to which the other person acted deliberately * Sees malicious intent in the motives of others * Self seen as definitely right; other(s) seen as definitely wrong * Unable to see the other person's point of view * Plots to exact revenge	* To attack the other physically * To attack the other verbally * To attack the other passive-aggressively * To displace the attack onto another person, animal or object * To withdraw aggressively * To recruit allies against the other
Healthy anger	* Frustration * Self or other transgresses personal rule * Threat to self-esteem	Rational	* Does not overestimate the extent to which the other person acted deliberately * Does not see malicious intent in the motives of the other * Does not see self as definitely right and the other as definitely wrong * Able to see the other's point of view * Does not plot to exact revenge	* To assert self with the other * To request, but not demand behavioral change from the other
Guilt	* Violation of moral code (sin of commission) * Failure to live up to moral code (sin of omission) * Hurts the feelings of a significant other	Irrational	* Assumes that one has definitely committed the sin * Assumes more personal responsibility than the situation warrants * Assigns far less responsibility to others than is warranted * Does not think of mitigating factors * Thinks that one will receive retribution	* To escape from the unhealthy pain of guilt in self-defeating ways * To beg forgiveness from the person wronged * To promise unrealistically that she will not 'sin' again * To punish self physically or by deprivation * To disclaim responsibility for wrong doing
Remorse	* Violation of moral code (sin of commission) * Failure to live up to moral code (sin of omission) * Hurts the feelings of a significant other	Rational	* Considers behavior in context and with understanding in making a final judgement concerning whether one has "sinned" * Assumes appropriate level of personal responsibility * Assigns appropriate level of responsibility to others * Takes into account mitigating factors * Does not think one will receive retribution	* To face up to the healthy pain that accompanies the realization that one has sinned * To ask, but not beg for forgiveness * To understand reasons for wrongdoing and act on one's understanding * To atone for the sin by taking a penalty * To make appropriate amends * No tendency to make excuses for one's behavior or enact other defensive behavior

Emotion	Healthy/Unhealthy	Theme	Rational/Irrational	Cognitions	Behaviours/action tendencies
Shame	Unhealthy	* Something shameful has been revealed about self (or group with whom one identifies) by self or others * Others will look down or shun self (or group with whom one identifies)	Irrational	* Overestimates the 'shamefulness' of the information revealed * Overestimates the likelihood that the judging group will notice or be interested in the information * Overestimates the degree of disapproval self (or reference group) will receive * Overestimates the length of time any disapproval will last	* To remove self from the 'gaze' of others * To isolate self from others * To save face by attacking other(s) who have 'shamed' self * To defend threatened self-esteem in self-defeating ways * To ignore attempts by others to restore social equilibrium
Disappoint-ment	Healthy	* Something shameful has been revealed about self (or group with whom one identifies) by self or others * Others will look down or shun self (or group with whom one identifies)	Rational	* See information revealed in a compassionate self-accepting context * Is realistic about the likelihood that the judging group will notice or be interested in the information * Is realistic about the degree of disapproval self (or reference group) will receive * Is realistic about the length of time any disapproval will last	* To continue to participate actively in social interaction * To respond to attempts of others to restore social equilibrium
Hurt	Unhealthy	* Other treats self badly (self undeserving)	Irrational	* Overestimates the unfairness of the other person's behavior * Other perceived as showing lack of care or indifference * Self seen as alone, uncared for or misunderstood * Tends to think of past 'hurts' * Thinks that the other has to put things right of own accord first	* To shut down communication channel with the other * To criticise the other without disclosing what one feels hurt about
Sorrow	Healthy	* Other treats self badly (self undeserving)	Rational	* Is realistic about the degree of unfairness of the other person's behavior * Other perceived as acting badly rather than as uncaring or indifferent * Self not seen as alone, uncared for or misunderstood * Less likely to think of past hurts than when hurt * Doesn't think that the other has to make the first move	*To communicate one's feelings to the other directly * To influence the other person to act in a fairer manner
Unhealthy jealousy	Unhealthy	* Threat to relationship with partner from other person	Irrational	*Tends to see threats to one's relationship when none really exists * Thinks the loss of one's relationship is imminent * Misconstrues one's partner's ordinary conversations as having romantic or sexual connotations * Constructs visual images of partner's infidelity	*To seek constant reassurance that one is loved *To monitor the actions and feelings of one's partner * To search for evidence that one's partner is involved with someone else

Emotion	Health	Inference	Rational/Irrational	Thinking	Action tendencies
		* If partner admits to finding another attractive, believes that the other is seen as more attractive than self and that one's partner will leave self for this other person			* To attempt to restrict the movements or activities of one's partner * To set tests which partner has to pass * To retaliate for partner's presumed infidelity * To sulk
Healthy jealousy	Healthy	* Threat to relationship with partner from another person	Rational	* Tends not to see threats to one's relationship when none exists * Does not misconstrue ordinary conversations between partner and other men/women * Does not construct visual images of partner's infidelity * Accepts that partner will find others attractive but does not see this as a threat	* To allow partner to express love without seeking reassurance * To allow partner freedom without monitoring his/her feelings, actions and whereabouts * To allow him/her to show natural interest in members of the opposite sex without setting tests
Unhealthy envy	Unhealthy	* Another person possesses and enjoys something desirable that the person does not have	Irrational	* Tends to denigrate the value of the desired possession * Tries to convince self that one is happy with one's possessions (although one is not) * Thinks about how to acquire the desired possession regardless of its usefulness * Thinks about how to deprive the other person of the desired possession	* To disparage verbally the person who has the desired possession * To disparage verbally the desired possession * To take away the desired possession from the other person (either so that one will have it or the other is deprived of it) * To spoil or destroy the desired possession so that the other person does not have it
Healthy envy	Healthy	* Another person possesses and enjoys something desirable that the person does not have	Rational	* Honestly admits to oneself that one desires the desired possession * Does not try to convince self that one is happy with one's possession when one is not * Thinks about how to obtain the desired possession because one desires it for healthy reasons * Can allow the person to have and enjoy the desired possession without denigrating the person or the possession	* To obtain the desired possession if it is truly what one wants

Figure 5.1 A diagrammatic summary of healthy and unhealthy negative emotions

Notes:
[1] Inference = Personally significant hunch that goes beyond observable reality and which gives meaning to it; may be accurate or inaccurate
[2] Personal domain = The objects - tangible and intangible - in which a person has an involvement (Beck, 1976). REBT theory distinguishes between ego and comfort aspects of the personal domain although those aspects frequently interact

ative emotions problematic. I do so because it is not clear, especially to clients and beginning REBT trainees, to what the terms refer. It could be said that they refer to emotional responses to activating events at A. However, this view that events can determine the appropriateness of an emotion which implies a kind of 'A causes C' thinking that runs counter to REBT theory.

On the other hand, the terms 'appropriate' and 'inappropriate' can be construed as referring to the beliefs on which these emotions are based. In this case 'appropriate' negative emotions are deemed to stem from 'appropriate' (i.e. rational) beliefs and 'inappropriate' negative emotions from 'inappropriate' (i.e. irrational). However, the terms 'appropriate' and 'inappropriate' beliefs do not appear in the REBT literature and if terms were needed to stress the link between emotions and beliefs in this way, 'rational' negative emotions and 'irrational' negative emotions would make this connection clearer. Indeed, for a time, I experimented with the use of just these terms.

In addition, there is a problem with using the terms 'appropriate' and 'inappropriate' when pointing to the relationship between emotions and beliefs. It could be argued that given the REBT view that emotions stem largely (but not exclusively) from beliefs, an 'appropriate' negative emotion is one that is appropriate to the belief that the person holds irrespective of whether this belief is rational or irrational. Thus, an inappropriate negative emotion in REBT theory, according to this view, an appropriate negative emotion in that it is an appropriate response to an irrational belief.

To avoid these problems with the terms 'appropriate' and 'inappropriate' negative emotions, I suggest using terms such as 'healthy' and 'unhealthy' or 'constructive' and 'unconstructive' negative emotions. These terms make it clear that 'healthy' negative emotions stem from rational beliefs and have functional consequences and that 'unhealthy' negative emotions stem irrational beliefs and have dysfunctional consequences. As such they aid both trainee and client learning.

Unit 15: Healthy and Unhealthy Negative Emotions: A Diagrammatic Summary

Figure 5.1 presents a comprehensive diagrammatic summary of the major distinctions between healthy and unhealthy negative emotions. Looking at the columns from right to left, the first column provides the name of each emotion. You will note that there are eight pairs of unhealthy and healthy negative emotions, with the unhealthy negative emotion listed first. Please note that I have used the names of emotions as they are employed in REBT theory. As I will discuss in Module 5, Unit 16, clients bring to therapy their own emotional terminology and may well not understand the REBT distinctions just by being introduced to the REBT emotional terminology. Your tasks at this point are to discover your client's emotional terminology, to explain the REBT version and to negotiate a shared language which reflects the distinctions between healthy and unhealthy negative emotions as they are made in REBT theory. This does not necessarily involve using REBT terminology. I jokingly explain to trainees that it is acceptable to use the words 'fish' and 'chips' to distinguish between what REBT theory calls 'anxiety' and 'concern' as long as you and your client understand that 'fish' has the inferences, irrational beliefs, cognitive consequences and action tendencies that are associated with what REBT calls 'anxiety' and that the term 'chips' has the inferences, rational beliefs, cognitive consequences and action tendencies associated with what REBT theory calls 'concern'.

The second column from the left in Figure 5.1 shows whether the emotion listed in the first column is an unhealthy or a healthy negative emotion. The main way to distinguish between a healthy and an unhealthy negative emotion is to look at their effects. According to REBT theory unhealthy negative emotions about negative As are unhealthy in the sense that they do not help people to change these negative As if indeed they can be changed, nor do they encourage them to make a constructive adjustment if these As cannot be changed. Healthy negative emotions do encourage productive attempts to change negative As and do facilitate constructive adjustment to As that cannot be changed. Also healthy negative emotions aid people in their pursuit of their basic goals and purposes, whilst unhealthy negative emotions impede people in this pursuit.

The third column gives the major inferences related to each healthy–unhealthy emotional pairing. To help you to understand inferences fully in the context of your client's emotional experiences, I need to introduce you to the concept of the 'personal domain'. This concept was first introduced in the mid-1970s by Aaron T. Beck (1976) and refers to the objects – both tangible and intangible – in which a person has an involvement. REBT theory distinguishes between ego and comfort-related aspects of the personal domain, although it does emphasize that these aspects frequently interact.

Inferences are personally significant hunches about reality that give meaning to it. Inferences go beyond the data at hand and need to be tested out by the person concerned. They may be accurate or inaccurate.

If you consider the 'inference' column in Figure 5.1, you will note that within each pairing, a healthy negative emotion and its unhealthy counterpart share the same inference. This makes the REBT position on emotions very clear, i.e. inferences contribute to, but do not determine emotions. Put slightly differently, whilst inferences are important in determining the flavor of a negative emotion, they do not determine the health of that emotion. For that we need to turn to the next column which outlines the type of belief associated with each pair of healthy–unhealthy negative emotions.

I have already reviewed these beliefs in chapter 1 and will say more about assessing them in Module 9, Unit 36. Here I just want to underscore the central part that beliefs play in determining emotions and to state once again that healthy negative emotions about negative As stem largely from rational beliefs and unhealthy negative emotions about these As stem largely from irrational beliefs.

The fifth column from the left in Figure 5.1 outlines what I have termed the cognitive consequences of experiencing different emotions. Whilst the inferences listed in column three give shape to the person's emotional experience (e.g. when the person faces a threat she will either experience anxiety or concern) the cognitive consequences listed in column five detail the kinds of thinking that the person engages in whilst experiencing different feelings. In other words, these different cognitions are the consequences of different emotions and their associated beliefs. As you will see if you inspect column five carefully, the type of thinking that people engage in as a result of experiencing healthy negative emotions is, in general, more functional than the type of thinking they engage as a result of experiencing unhealthy negative emotions.

The sixth column (i.e. the one on the far right) outlines the ways in which people TEND to act when they experience different emotions I term these 'action tendencies'. However, it is far from inevitable that a person will act in accordance with a particular action tendency. Let me give an example to illustrate these points. When a person is anxious, he will experience a strong tendency to withdraw from the situation in which he is anxious. However, he can go against his action tendency and remain in the situation until his feelings of anxiety dissipate and the behavioral principle of exposure (Marks, 1978) requires a person to do just this. Encouraging clients to act against their action tendencies is a core feature of REBT practice after you have helped your clients to dispute their irrational beliefs.

Unit 16: Five Approaches to Teaching Clients the Distinction Between Healthy and Unhealthy Negative Emotions

There are five approaches to helping yourself and your clients differentiate between healthy and unhealthy negative emotions. Before I list these, I do wish to stress that you can employ these approaches singly or together. As different approaches will be enlightening for different clients, I advise you to become familiar with all of them.

1. Using different terms

Because REBT theory distinguishes between unhealthy negative emotions and their healthy counterparts, in helping your clients to make this distinction in therapy it is important to use agreed terminology which reflects this important difference. There are two ways of doing this. First, you can use the REBT terminology as shown in [Figure 5.2]. This figure provides a brief reminder of these terms.

One problem with tacking this tack is that clients bring to therapy their own way of construing emotions and these constructions may be quite different to the REBT terms. It is quite common, for example, for clients to consider that shame and guilt are constructive emotions and as such they would resist the attempts of their therapists to construe them as unhealthy. In order to clarify the REBT position here, you would need to make use of one or more of the four other approaches described in this section.

Another problem with relying solely on REBT terminology is that clients may well consider that the healthy negative emotions are less intense than their unhealthy counterparts. For example, clients frequently consider healthy anger to be less intense than unhealthy anger. REBT's position on this issue is quite different. Thus healthy negative emotions can be very intense and still be constructive. Thus, one can be intensely healthily angry at someone's behavior without (a) demanding that he must not act in such a manner and (b) condemning him as a person for his behavior. REBT's theory of negative emotions posits qualitative rather than quantitative differences between healthy and unhealthy negative emotions, and thus one can be intensely healthily angry without being unhealthily angry. A quantitative approach to negative emotions would place anxiety on a single continuum with differing levels of intensity of this emotion placed on this one continuum. In contrast a qualitative approach would employ two continua: one for anxiety, the other for concern with increasing levels of intensity of each emotion represented on

Unhealthy Negative Emotions	*Healthy Negative Emotions*
Anxiety	Concern
Depression	Sadness
Guilt	Remorse
Hurt	Sorrow
Shame	Disappointment
Unhealthy anger	Healthy anger
Unhealthy jealousy	Healthy jealousy
Unhealthy envy	Healthy envy

Figure 5.2 Healthy and unhealthy negative emotions: REBT terminology.

each continuum. Thus, the quantitative approach does not keenly distinguish between anxiety and concern whilst the qualitative approach does. This crucial difference is shown in Figure 5.3.

In order to clarify these issues you will need to go beyond mere presentations of different terms and again use one or more of the four other approaches to distinguishing between healthy and unhealthy negative emotions to be described presently.

The second way of distinguishing between healthy and unhealthy negative emotions whilst solely relying on unelaborated emotional terms involves eliciting such distinctions from clients themselves. For example, one client may use the terms 'helpful anxiety' and 'unhelpful anxiety' seemingly to differentiate between what in REBT terminology is known as concern and anxiety. Another client may use the terms 'furious' and 'pissed off' instead of REBT's unhealthy anger and healthy anger. As in the first example, many clients use a different qualifier to distinguish between a healthy negative emotion and its unhealthy counterpart. In the first example then, 'helpful' and 'unhelpful' were the different qualifiers used by this client seemingly to denote a distinction between REBT's anxiety and concern. I say seemingly here because without exploring the matter further you will not know whether or not the client's terms match those

Qualitative Model

No anxiety	Intense anxiety

Increasing levels of anxiety (no distinction between anxiety and concern)

Qualitative Model

No anxiety	Intense anxiety

Increasing levels of anxiety (clear distinction between anxiety and concern)

No concern	Intense concern

Increasing levels of concern (clear distinction between anxiety and concern)

[Only the qualitative model reflects the REBT conceptualisation of negative emotions. According to REBT theory healthy negative emotions stem from rational beliefs and unhealthy negative emotions from irrational beliefs.]

Figure 5.3 Quantitative and qualitative models of negative emotions.

used by REBT. Thus, in the example we are considering, in the client's mind 'helpful' anxiety may be much less intense than 'unhelpful' anxiety. As explained above and shown in Figure 5.3 this represents a quantitative model of negative emotions rather than the qualitative model advocated by REBT theory.

The other problem with accepting clients' emotional terms without exploring the meaning behind them is that these terms may reflect a different perspective on emotions than that put forward by REBT therapists. If you do not find out what clients mean by their emotional terms then you have no way of discussing with them the problems that may be involved in their conceptualisations.

In conclusion, I hope you can see that relying solely on the 'using different terms' approach to helping clients distinguish between healthy and unhealthy negative emotions is fraught with problems. Consequently, you will need to employ one or more of the other four approaches to be discussed in this module to supplement this 'terms-based' approach.

2. Distinguishing between rational and irrational beliefs

As I have stated several times in this book, REBT theory holds that healthy negative emotions stem largely from rational beliefs and unhealthy negative emotions stem largely from irrational beliefs. It follows therefore that another approach to helping clients distinguish between healthy and unhealthy negative emotions involves referring to this part of theory.

For example, in helping a client distinguish between anxiety and concern you will want to point out that anxiety is based largely on irrational beliefs such as:

(a) This threat must not occur.
(b) It would be awful if this threat were to occur.
(c) I could not bear it if this threat were to occur and in ego anxiety:
(d) If this threat were to materialise, it would prove that I would be worthless.

You will also want to point out that concern is based largely on rational beliefs such as:

(a) I would prefer it if this threat did not occur, but there is no reason why it must not happen.
(b) It would be bad if this threat occurred, but it would not be terrible.
(c) If this threat occurred, it would be difficult to tolerate, but I could bear it. And in ego concern:
(d) I would be a fallible human being if this threat were to occur. It would not prove that I am worthless.

Having presented the two different sets of beliefs in the context of the client's specific problem, you can then ask your client to use these different beliefs to judge whether he was experiencing anxiety or concern. If you use this beliefs-based approach to helping your client to distinguish between healthy and unhealthy negative emotions, then you can refer back to the example you used to teach him the ABCs of REBT if you have already done so (see Module 4), or you can use this approach as a reminder when you do teach your client the ABCs.

3. Distinguishing between different cognitive consequences of unhealthy and healthy negative emotions

Another approach to helping your clients to distinguish between healthy and unhealthy negative emotions is to focus their attention on the different cognitive consequences that result from experiencing these different emotions. Here, then, the emphasis is on the utility of healthy and unhealthy negative emotions.

Continuing the example of teaching your client to distinguish between anxiety and concern, you will want to point out that anxiety has a number of cognitive consequences:

(a) Your client will tend to overestimate the negative features of the threat.
(b) He will tend to underestimate his ability to cope with the threat.
(c) When facing the threat, he will tend to create an even more negative threat in his mind.
(d) If he is carrying out a task while he is anxious, he will tend to have more task-irrelevant than task-relevant thoughts.

On the other hand, you will want to explain that concern has a different set of cognitive consequences:

(a) Your client will tend not to overestimate the negative features of the threat.
(b) He will tend to have a realistic view of his ability to cope with the threat.
(c) When facing the threat, he will not tend to create an even more negative threat in his mind.
(d) If he is carrying out a task while he is concerned, he will tend to have more task-relevant than task-irrelevant thoughts.

Having presented the two different sets of cognitive consequences in the context of the client's specific problem, you can then ask your client to use these different cognitive consequences to judge whether he was experiencing anxiety or concern.

4. Distinguishing between different action tendencies

As I explained in Module 1, Unit 3, when a person experiences an emotion she has a tendency to act in a number of ways. Because different emotions are associated with different sets of action tendencies, a fourth approach to teaching clients how to distinguish between healthy and unhealthy negative emotions is to focus their attention on these different sets of action tendencies.

Using the example of helping your client to distinguish between anxiety and concern, you will want to point out that when he is anxious, he will tend:

(a) to withdraw physically from the threat (i.e. by leaving the situa-tion);
(b) to withdraw mentally from the threat (e.g. by changing the subject if he finds a topic of conversation threatening);
(c) to ward off the threat (e.g. by using obsessive–compulsive or superstitious behavior);
(d) to tranquillise one's feelings (e.g. by the use of alcohol, legal and illegal drugs, food, cigarettes, etc.); and
(e) to seek reassurance so that the threat is neutralized, at least in his mind.

On the other hand, you will want to explain that concern is associated with a different set of action tendencies. When your client is feeling concern, he will tend:

(a) to face the threat; and
(b) to deal with the threat constructively.

Once you have reviewed the two different sets of action tendencies in the context of your client's specific problem, you can then ask him once again to use these different action tendencies as a yardstick to judge whether he was experiencing anxiety or concern.

5. Distinguishing between different symptoms

The final approach to helping your clients to distinguish between healthy and unhealthy negative emotions concerns focusing their attention on the difference in symptoms between the two different types of negative emotions. This is a somewhat problematic approach to use on its own as there is some overlap in symptoms associated with healthy and unhealthy negative emotions. For example, if you feel anxious you may well experience such symptoms as butterflies in your stomach, dry mouth and sweating. However, you may well experience these symptoms when you feel concerned and not anxious.

If you are going to use a 'symptoms-based' approach to differentiating between healthy and unhealthy negative emotions, the point to stress with your client is that when he has an unhealthy negative emotion (e.g. anxiety) he will experience more disabling symptoms and the degree of disability will be greater than when he has a healthy negative emotion (e.g. concern).

I have made the point earlier that it is advisable to use a combination of the five approaches when helping your clients to distinguish between their healthy and unhealthy negative emotions. I will demonstrate this in an illustrative therapist–client dialogue. But first, let me summarize the five approaches in Figure 5.4.

Approach 1: Distinguishing between emotional terms (Terms-based approach)

Approach 2: Distinguishing between rational and irrational beliefs (Beliefs-based approach)

Approach 3: Distinguishing between cognitive consequences (Cognitive consequences-based approach)

Approach 4: Distinguishing between action tendencies (Action tendencies-based approach)

Approach 5: Distinguishing between symptoms (Symptoms-based approach)

Figure 5.4 Five approaches to distinguishing between healthy and unhealthy negative emotions.

Unit 17: Teaching a Client to Distinguish Between an Unhealthy Negative Emotion (Unhealthy Anger) and a Healthy Negative Emotion (Healthy Anger): An Illustrative Dialogue

In this dialogue, I am counseling John who has been referred by his GP for 'anger management'. It is the second session and I am discussing a recent episode where he felt 'pissed off' at work. As will become clear, I am not clear at the outset whether by this he meant healthy or unhealthy anger. In the following part of the session I am attempting to clarify both for myself and for John whether his negative emotion was healthy or unhealthy. As you will discover, by 'pissed off' John meant unhealthily angry. As I will discuss later, it is important to help your client set goals which reflect healthy negative emotional responses to negative As and this is particularly important when the emotion is anger. However, I will not discuss this issue here with John.

Windy: So, If I understand you correctly you felt 'pissed off' when your boss did not put you on the Gwilliam account. Is that right?

John: Yes, that's right.

Windy: Now in the therapy that I practice, we make an important distinction between what we call healthy and unhealthy negative emotions. The former are constructive responses to negative life events, whilst the latter are not so constructive. I'm not sure whether 'pissed off' is a healthy or an unhealthy response to the 'Gwilliam' episode. Will you bear with me while I ask you a few questions to help us both become clearer on this issue?

John: OK.

Windy: More specifically I want to discover whether your anger was healthy or unhealthy. Does that distinction mean anything to you?

[This is an 'Approach 1' intervention]
John: Well, healthy anger seems much less intense than unhealthy anger.

Windy: A lot of people think that, John, but we consider that healthy anger can be an intense, but healthy emotion. Now if you were healthily angry in this situation, you would have a set of beliefs similar to the following:

(a) I really want my boss to put me on the 'Gwilliam' account, but he doesn't have to do so.
(b) It's really unfortunate that my boss hasn't put me on to this account, but it isn't terrible.
(c) I can stand being deprived in this way, although it is difficult to tolerate.
(d) My boss isn't a bastard for depriving me of this opportunity, just a fallible human being who has done what I consider the wrong thing.

However, if you were unhealthily angry rather than annoyed in this situation, you would believe something like the following:

(a) My boss absolutely should put me on the 'Gwilliam' account.
(b) It's terrible that he hasn't.
(c) I can't stand the deprivation.
(d) He is a bastard for depriving me of this opportunity.

Now which set of beliefs best accounted for your pissed off feeling at the time?

[This is an 'Approach 2' intervention]

John: Put like that I was unhealthily angry, because I believed that he was a bastard who shouldn't have treated me like that.

Windy: Right, but let's make doubly sure by looking at what you wanted to do in the situation.

Now, if you were unhealthily angry in the situation, you would have felt like attacking your boss physically or verbally; if not directly you would have felt drawn to getting back at him indirectly; or you would have felt like storming out. However, if you were healthily angry, your inclination would have been to assert yourself with him in an open and reasoned manner.

[This is an 'Approach 4' intervention]

John: Well, that clinches it then. I wanted to knock his block off.

Windy: So, it sounds as if you recognize that your anger was unhealthy rather than healthy. Do you generally refer to feeling 'pissed off' when you are unhealthily angry?

John: I've never thought about it before...No, I use it quite loosely.

Windy: So, because it is important to distinguish between a healthy negative emotion like healthy anger and an unhealthy negative emotion like unhealthy anger, we need to use terms to reflect this distinction. Does it make sense to you to use the terms unhealthy anger and healthy anger as I have described them or can you think of more apt terms?

John: Yes, that sounds reasonable.

Windy: So we'll use this distinction throughout our work together.

In this segment, I used a combination of three approaches to ascertain that John was unhealthily angry rather than healthily angry when he said he was 'pissed off'. First, I used the 'terms-based' approach (Approach 1). Here, I introduced the REBT terms, unhealthy anger and healthy anger, to see if John could see the difference between them. When he said that he could not, I used the 'beliefs-based' approach (Approach 2) and outlined the likely irrational belief that underpinned his 'pissed off' feeling if this was unhealthy anger and the likely rational beliefs that underpinned this feeling if it turned out to be healthy anger. When John said that he related most to the irrational beliefs, thus confirming that he was unhealthily angry, I used the 'action tendencies-based approach' (Approach 4) to double-check. Finally, I returned to the 'terms-based' approach to agree on a shared language when discussing anger-related issues with John during counseling.

How can you become more skilled at explaining the differences between healthy and unhealthy negative emotions to your clients? First, familiarise yourself with each of these different approaches. Second, pair up with a trainee colleague and, using a role-play format, practice explaining the differences between healthy and unhealthy negative emotions by employing arguments based on the five approaches. Tape-record the role-play and play it to you REBT trainer or supervisor for feedback. Becoming proficient at this skill will stand you in good stead when you come to assess your clients' problems using the ABC framework, a subject to which I now turn.

Module 6
Assessing Clients'
Problems: Introduction

I have already introduced most of what you need to know in order to carry out an accurate assessment of your clients' problems using the ABCs of REBT. I have explained that As are activating events which encompass both actual events and inferences and that As which trigger beliefs at B are called critical As. When carrying out an ABC assessment of your clients' problems, it is important to assess accurately these critical As. This is a complex skill and I will devote Module 8 to this issue.

As I explained in Modules 1 and 4, Bs are evaluative beliefs that are either rational or irrational in nature. The material in those modules contains the information you need to assess B. In Module 5, I considered at length the distinction between healthy and unhealthy negative emotions at C. This material provided the foundation for the task of assessing unhealthy negative emotions and for targeting these for change. Although C also encompasses dysfunctional behavioral consequences and cognitive consequences of holding irrational beliefs at B, in Module 7 I will concen-trate on assessing emotional Cs. Whilst I have covered the basic material for accurately assessing C in the previous chapter, there are a number of issues that still need to be covered. I will discuss these after I have emphasized the importance of specificity in the assessment process

Unit 18: Specificity in the Assessment Process

When clients discuss their problems at the outset of therapy they often do so in general terms. It is difficult to assess clients' problems when they are couched in general terms. REBT theory states that people make them-selves disturbed about specific events because they hold specific irrational beliefs about these events. Therefore, it is important for you to encourage your clients to provide specific examples of their emotional problems. Doing so will provide you both with the information you require to carry out an accurate assessment of these problems.

However, it is also important to give your client an opportunity to talk about his problems in his own way at least until he considers that you have listened to him and shown that you have understood him from his own frame of reference. As you do this you can begin to construct an overall picture of the problems he is experiencing in his life. On more advanced courses in REBT, I devote quite a bit of time to the development of a problem list on which your client lists the problems he wishes to deal with during therapy. As such, this topic is beyond the scope of this introductory book (see Blackburn and Davidson 1990).

After you have given your client an opportunity to talk about his problems in his own way, you will want to encourage him to discuss in greater depth the problem he wants to tackle first in therapy. This problem should be an emotional problem rather than a practical problem (Dryden, 1990b). Once you have agreed to tackle one of your client's emotional problems, you will be working on what is called, in REBT, a target problem. Explain to your client that you are going to assess this target problem and thus you will need to stay focused on it until you have adequately assessed it and helped your client to deal with it. Guard against switching from problem to problem. To help you do this and to gain the specific information you need in order to assess the problem thoroughly, you will want to encourage your client to provide a specific example of this target problem. This specific example might be:

(a) a recent example of the target problem;
(b) a typical example of the target problem; or
(c) a vivid example of the target problem.

What is important is that the problem is specific enough to provide you with a clear critical A and a definite unhealthy negative emotion at C. If you are successful in doing so, it makes assessing your client's irrational beliefs at B relatively straightforward.

Module 7
Assessing C

In this module, I will (a) encourage you to avoid A→C language in assessing C; (b) tell you how to respond when your client believes that a healthy negative emotion is unhealthy; (c) help you to deal with vague Cs; (d) advise you what to do when your client's C is really an A; and (e) suggest ways of intervening when your client gives you an extended statement when you ask for a specific C.

Unit 19: Avoid A→C Language in Assessing C

When asking questions about how your client feels in a specific situation, be careful not to use what we call in REBT, A→C language. When you use A→C language you reinforce the idea in your client's mind that A really does cause C. As this is the antithesis to the REBT position and runs counter to what you may have taught your client if you have already introduced the ABC model to him (see Module 4), by employing A→C language you will be giving your client conflicting and confusing messages. Here are some typical A→C questions that trainees ask at the beginning of their training in REBT:

* How did that make you feel?
* What feeling did that produce in you?
* Did that anger you?
* What feeling did that give you?
* What feeling did that provoke (or evoke) in you?
* What emotion did that give rise to?
* How did that lead you to feel?

I trust you can see that all these questions either explicitly state or strongly imply an 'A causes C' theory of human emotion. For example, the question, 'How did that make you feel?' makes explicit that the therapist thinks that 'that' (an unspecified event) can make the client feel something without recourse to any mediating variable (i.e. the client's beliefs). Therefore, A ('that') is deemed to cause C (the client's feelings).

How can you inquire about your client's feelings without explicitly stating or implying an A→C position? Let's examine two questions which avoid taking such a position.

* When that happened, how did you feel?

In this question, the therapist is putting forward a correlational relationship between A (the event) 'When that happened' and C (the client's feeling) 'how did you feel?' A causal relationship between A and C is neither made explicit nor implied.

*How did you feel about that?

In this question a correlational relationship between C ('How did you feel..') and A (..about that?) is again advanced. However, the word 'about' makes it clear that the client's feeling is closely related to the event. In the previous question the posited relationship between A and C is less close.

For the above reason, I recommend that you phrase your enquiries about A in such a way that you include the word 'about' in your question. If you do, you will find it difficult to posit an A→C model of emotions and you will make it clear that the client's C is closely related to the A in question.

Here are a number of things that you can do to guard against asking A→C questions.

1. Become aware of A→C phrases in people's language. Watch soap operas on TV, for example and write down phrases that explicitly state or strongly imply an 'A causes C' view of emotions.
2. Reformulate these A→C phrases into phrases that state a correlational view of human emotions.
3. Pair up with a trainee colleague and conduct a role-play of a counseling session. Have your colleague play the role of a client who makes numerous A→C statements. Correct the 'client' every time you identify an A→C statement. Tape record the session and in replay listen for any A→C client statements that you missed. Also listen closely to your reformulations of these statements and evaluate your responses. Improve your phrasing as needed.
4. Get used to using A–C correlational statements and questions in your everyday speech. Notice A→C phrases in the speech patterns of others with whom you converse. Reformulate them in your mind, but don't correct others on this point. Some trainees become overenthusiastic and correct A→C language whenever they hear it. In my view, this is an unwarranted intrusion into the social conventions of everyday conversation and I don't recommend that you do it.

5. Tape record your therapy sessions and listen to them carefully for instances of A→C thinking in your statements and questions. Correct these in your mind. Also listen to instances of A→C thinking in your clients' language. If you did not correct the most important of these determine which were the most important to correct and think about how you could have done so. It is important to be circumspect. It is legitimately irritating for clients to be corrected every time they utter an A→C statement. You need to correct the most salient of these statements; you don't need to correct each and every one of them!

6. Take to supervision or training your ongoing difficulties in dealing with A→C statements, either your own or your clients'.

Unit 20: When a Client Believes that a Healthy Negative Emotion is Unhealthy

In Module 5 I stressed the importance of helping your client to distinguish between a healthy negative emotion and an unhealthy negative emotion. This is very important to bear in mind while assessing C. If your client has a healthy negative emotion about a negative A, then this is not targeted for change in REBT as it is regarded to be a constructive response to an aversive situation.

Explaining the above to the client is useful because it helps to reveal one of two related situations. First, it brings to light the idea held by some clients that calmness or the absence of feeling is a desirable and healthy response to a negative A. At this point you can explain to your client that in order for him to be calm in the face of adversity, he would have to have an attitude of indifference about the adversity. Taking the example of John discussed in Module 5, Unit 17, he or she would have to believe: 'I don't care whether or not my boss puts me on the Gwilliam account' in order to feel calm about his boss's behavior. Put like this such clients generally understand the unrealistic nature of denying their healthy desires and no longer regard their healthy negative emotion as problematic.

Explaining the constructive nature of a healthy negative emotion may also reveal that a client may have a second-order problem. Here the client has an unhealthy negative emotion about what is in this case a healthy negative response. For example, Dina was intensely, but healthily angry about being refused permission to go on leave. She was, however, unhealthily angry with herself for getting so annoyed. Dina did not believe that she should not have any feelings about the refusal. Rather, she believed that she absolutely should not have such strong feelings about what had happened. She believed that only mild or moderate negative feelings were acceptable to her. Explaining to clients like Dina that healthy negative emotions can be strong is sometimes sufficient here. When it is not, then the real emotional problem is the client's meta-emotional problem which is then targeted for change (See module 10).

Unit 21: When a Client's C Is Vague

It will frequently happen that when you ask your clients for their feelings about negative As, they will give you vague feeling statements in reply. Here are some of the responses that clients will give you when you ask them how they felt about the negative As in their lives:

* I felt upset
* I felt miserable
* I felt bad
* I felt tense
* I felt bothered
* I felt hot and bothered
* I felt jittery
* I felt down
* I felt devastated
* I felt pissed off
* I felt blue
* I felt jumpy
* I felt gutted

There are two problems with the feeling statements listed above. First, it is unclear whether they refer to healthy negative emotions or their unhealthy counterparts. You may think that 'devastated' may refer to an unhealthy negative emotion, but without further exploration, you cannot be certain. Second, it is unclear in many cases to which pair of emotions the feeling statement refers. Take the word 'upset' as an example. Leaving aside the issue concerning whether this refers to a healthy or an unhealthy negative emotion and assuming for the sake of discussion that it is an unhealthy emotion; what kind of emotion is it? Is it an anxious upset, a depressed upset or a guilt upset? The answer is that we just don't know.

Whenever, a client's feeling statement is vague, it is very important that you try to clarify it. In Module 5, Unit 17, I showed how I clarified John's vague feeling of being pissed off. If you recall from that chapter I mentioned that in addition to the terms you and your clients may use to refer to emotional states, you can utilise the following information in clarifying whether a negative emotion is healthy or unhealthy:

(a) the type of beliefs your client holds (rational or irrational);
(b) the cognitive consequences of experiencing the emotion;
(c) her action tendencies; and
(d) her symptoms.

You can also use such information to clarify a vague negative emotion when you are unsure about its nature (e.g. whether it is anxiety/concern; depression/sadness; guilt/remorse etc). When you are unsure about the nature of a negative emotion, irrespective of its health, you can also refer to the person's inferences for clues. Thus, if the client is talking about a threat to his or her domain, he or she is likely to be anxious or concerned; if he or she is discussing hurting the feelings of a significant other, he or she is likely to feel guilt or remorse. Becoming very familiar with which pairs of negative emotions are associated with which inferences will be enormously useful in your quest to identify your client's specific unhealthy negative emotion. Having at your fin-gertips the knowledge outlined in Figure 5.1 is about the best preparation you can undertake for assessing your clients Cs.

Unit 22: When Your Client's C Is Really an A

It will also frequently happen that in response to your enquiries concerning their emotions about negative events, your clients will provide you with inferences. For example, your clients may say the following:

* I felt rejected
* I felt punished
* I felt betrayed
* I felt abandoned
* I felt used
* I felt criticized
* I felt frustrated

If you inspect these statements carefully you will note that none of them represents actual emotions. We do not have an emotion called 'rejection' or one called 'used', for example. Rather we have emotions about the inference that we have been rejected or used at A. Thus when you come across a client's C that is really an inferred A, you do need to deal with this situation. The following is a constructed therapist–client dialogue showing one way that this can be done.

Windy: How did you feel when Kevin said that to you?

Karen: I felt rejected.

Windy: Actually, Karen, rejection isn't a feeling. It is something that actually happened to you or something that you thought happened to you. Are you saying that you thought Kevin had rejected you?

Karen: Yes.

Windy: OK. Now, let's assume for the moment that Kevin did reject you, how did you feel about that rejection?

[Here it is important to note two things. First, I explained to Karen that rejection is not a C; rather, it is an actual or inferred A. Second, I said to Karen: '...let's assume for the moment that Kevin did reject you...' This is a typical REBT strategy. At this point, I did not challenge the validity of Karen's inference, i.e. that Kevin had rejected her. Rather, I encouraged her to assume temporarily that her inference was true so that in this case I could ascertain how she felt about this presumed rejection. REBT therapists tend to challenge the validity of their clients' inferences after they have identified, challenged and helped their clients to change the latter's irrational beliefs. REBT therapists argue that their clients are in a more objective (and therefore better) frame of mind to review the validity of their inferences once they are relatively free from the biasing effects of their irrational beliefs.]

Karen: When I thought that he had rejected me, I felt hurt.

Unit 23: When Your Client's C Is an Extended Statement

It is rare for people to have had any systematic psychological education. Consequently, people are quite unclear about the nature of emotions, how to discriminate among different emotions and what mainly determines their feelings. I have already commented that your clients are likely to give you vague feeling statements when you ask them how they feel about the negative As in their lives. Also I have noted that they may easily confuse their emotions with the inferences they make about A.

There is one other problem that you will encounter when you attempt to assess C that I wish to cover. This problem particularly occurs when you ask your clients questions about their emotions with the word 'feel' in it (e.g. 'How did you feel when that happened?'). Thus, when you ask such clients how they felt about given situations they provide you with an extended statement of what they thought about the events in question. This extended statement usually begins with the words 'I felt...' followed by the extended thought. It may also commence with the phrase 'I felt that....'. The one thing that your clients do not give you, however, is an accurate, clear account of their feelings.

Here are some examples of what I mean.

Example 1

Counselor: How did you feel when your mother interrupted you like that?

Client: I felt here she goes again, she never lets me finish a sentence.

Example 2

Counselor: How did you feel when your boss gave you that assignment to do?

Client: I felt that I would never be able to do it.

What can you do when your client gives an extended thought in reply to a question about her feelings? First, you can take the thought and find out what feeling was associated with it.

Counselor: How did you feel when your boss gave you that assignment to do?

Client: I felt that I would never be able to do it.

Counselor: And when you found yourself thinking that you would never be able to do it, what feeling did you experience in your gut?

Client: I felt very scared.

The points to note from this example are as follows.

(a) The counselor formed a bridge between the client's extended thought and her feeling. He labelled her initial response as a thought without explanation and asked for the feeling associated with the newly relabelled thought.

(b) The counselor added the words 'in your gut' to make it clearer that he was looking for a feeling not a thought.

The second thing you can do when your client gives you an extended thought instead of the feeling that you asked for is to explain what has happened. Tell your client that she has given you a thought rather than a feeling and then ask for the feeling again. When you do so, you might use the word 'emotion' rather than the word 'feeling', as for some people the word 'emotion' makes it clearer what you are looking for. For example:

Counselor: How did you feel when your mother interrupted you like that?

Client: I felt here she goes again, never lets me finish a sentence.

Counselor: Actually, 'here she goes again, never lets me finish a sentence' is a thought rather than a feeling. What emotion did you experience in your gut when she interrupted you?

Client: Oh, I see. I felt angry.

If your client still has trouble identifying an emotion, you might try giving him a list of emotions from which he is asked to select the closest one to his experience. It is also useful to limit your client to a one-word answer because this will curb his tendency to give you an extended statement.

Dealing with clients who have an ongoing difficulty in identifying their emotions is beyond the scope of this book and, as such, you will need to take such issues to supervision. An important part of assessing C is evaluating your client's motivation to change this unhealthy negative emotion and I will deal with this issue later. In the following module, I turn my attention to assessing A.

Module 8
Assessing A

In order for you to get the most from this chapter, I advise you to re-read the section on inferences in Module 1, Unit 1. I also suggest that you review Figure 5.1, particularly the part of the figure which links each pair of negative emotions with the relevant inference. For, once you have identified your client's unhealthy negative emotion, you will know what type of inference is associated with it.

Your major task at this point is to identify your client's critical A, which you will recall is that part of the A which triggers (in this case) your client's irrational belief which is at the core of her unhealthy negative emotion. This critical A can be an actual event, but more often than not it is an inference (which as you know may or may not be accurate). As I discuss the variety of ways of identifying a critical A, I want you to bear in mind one important point. Do not challenge your client's inferences. Assume that they are true until you have completed the assessment and disputing processes. There are, of course, one or two exceptions to this general rule but, at this point in your training, it is a sound rule to follow. This is such an important point that it bears repetition.

> While working to identify the client's critical A, assume temporarily that his inferences are correct. Do not challenge these infer-ences at this point.

How do you go about identifying your client's critical A? There are twelve methods of doing so. Don't expect to master them all at this stage of your training. It takes a good deal of practice and supervision before you become proficient at their use. What is important though is to have a working knowledge of most of them. To this end I will now discuss each in turn.

Unit 24: Inference Chaining

Have you ever played skimming stones at the seaside? You take a flat stone and skim it over the water and it 'bounces' several times until it sinks. Imagine that every 'bounce' represents an inference and you have inference chaining. Now you may think that the last time the stone hits the water and disappears it represents the critical A; after all it is the last link in the chain. However, the last link in the inferential chain is not necessarily the critical A. I'll explain why in a minute. Let me first give you an example of inference chaining. In this example,it has been ascertained that the client's C is anxiety which arose in the broad context of giving a brief speech at prize day at her old school.

Windy: So when did you become anxious?

Sue: Well, I was all right until I got up on the platform.

Windy: What were you anxious about at that point?

Sue: All those faces looking up at me.

[Here the client has narrowed her attentional focus and identifies what is probably an actual A.]

Windy: And what were you anxious about when you saw all those faces looking up at you?

[This is a typical question used in inference chaining. What you do is take the target emotion – in this case anxiety – and link it with the question 'What were you...about?'. You then insert the A that the client has just given you. The phrasing of the question: 'What were you anxious about' is important here in that it avoids A→C thinking. If I had asked, for example: 'What made you anxious about seeing all those faces looking up at you?', I would have implied that something about the faces looking at her MADE her anxious, which is of course an A→C view of the situation.]

Sue: That they seemed to expect a lot from me.

[This statement is clearly an inference as Sue cannot know what the members of her audience are thinking.]

Windy: Let's assume that. What's anxiety-provoking in your mind about them expecting a lot from you?

[This is another typical question used in inference chaining. The formula here is as follows. 'What's x-provoking in your mind about y?' where x = the target emotion and y = the inference that the client has just provided. One problem with this question is that it may convey that an inference can provoke an emotion directly. Thus, take care when asking such questions.]

Sue: I might not give a good talk.

[Another inference]

Windy: And what would be scary about not giving a good talk?

Sue: They would laugh at me.

[Another inference]

Windy: And if they did laugh at you, what would be scary about that in your mind?

Sue: I'd just want to rush off the stage.

[This is probably a behavioral reaction associated with being laughed at. It is probably not an inference.]

Windy: Why?

[Because the previous client response is probably a behavioral response, the question 'why?' is asked to get the client back on the trail of the critical A. You can ask 'why' questions whenever clients provide emotional and behavioral consequences (Cs) in reply to your enquiries about their inferences. Sometimes, though, these Cs are, in fact, inferences and should be treated as such. This is an advanced point which is beyond the scope of this book.]

Sue: Because I couldn't bear to be laughed at.

[Here, the client has revealed an irrational belief. This may be a sign that I have found the critical A. To test this I will review the chain with the client, as follows.]

Windy: Let's back up a bit. I'm going to go over what you've told me. As I do so, think carefully about which of the scenarios you were most anxious about.
    You mentioned the following: (1) seeing the faces looking up at you; (2) the audience expecting a lot from you; (3) you might not give a good talk; and (4) the audience laughing at you. Which of these were you most anxious about when you were up on the platform?

[If you don't want on rely on your memory, you might wish to write down the different inferences in the inference chain as your client provides them. You can do this privately for yourself or publicly on a large white board, for example. Clients often find it helpful to see their inferences written down.]

Sue: Definitely the last.

[Because the client has said that she was most anxious about the prospect of being laughed at, this is her critical A in the ABC under assessment. If she had chosen one of the other inferences, then that would become the critical A, unless you, as therapist, have reason to think otherwise. If this is the case then you need to explain your reasons.]

Focus on meaning

Another way of doing inference chaining is to focus your questions on the concept of meaning. Here is how the inference chain with Sue would have gone if I had used this form of questioning.

Windy: So when did you become anxious?

Sue: Well, I was all right until I got up on the platform.

Windy: What were you anxious about at that point?

Sue: All those faces looking up at me.

Windy: And if they looked up at you what would that mean to you?

Sue: That they expected a lot from me.

Windy: And if they expected a lot from you that would mean...?

Sue: That I might not live up to their expectations.

Windy: By failing to do what?

Sue: By not giving a good talk.

Windy: And if you did not give a good talk, what would that mean?

Sue: That they would laugh at me.

Windy: And if they did laugh at you, that would mean...?

Sue: Ugh. I couldn't bear to be laughed at!

Theoretical inferences

There are times when your client may provide you with what I call 'theoretical' inferences. These are inferences which point to possible occurrences, but in truth these are not real preoccupations for the client. The client provides them because you have continued to ask for more inferences. Here's an example with Sue.

Windy: And if they did laugh at you, what would be scary about that in your mind?

Sue: ...(long pause)... Er. They'd tell everybody about me?

Windy: And if they told everybody about you, what would be scary about that?

Sue: ...(long pause)...Nobody would talk to me again?

Windy: And if nobody talked to you again?

Sue: ... (very long pause)... I'd be a recluse?

Windy: And if you became a recluse...?

In this example, the client revealed the following typical signs that we had started to deal with theoretical inferences:

1. The emotional intensity went out of her voice.
2. She looked confused by my questions.
3. The latency of her response time increased.
4. Her answers were phrased in the form of questions.

If you suspect that your client is providing you with theoretical, but clinically unimportant inferences you need to check this out with her. Here is an example of how to do this.

Windy: And if they did laugh at you, what would be scary about that in your mind?

Windy: Because if they did laugh at you what would be scary about that?

Sue: ...(long pause)... Er. They'd tell everybody about me?

Windy: You sound very doubtful about that.

Sue: I am.

Windy: Is that because you think I expect you to come up with something else?

Sue: That's right.

Windy: So I'm hearing that your bottom line anxiety is about being laughed at.

Sue: Yes, it is.

So far I have discussed inference chains where the C is constant. In the dialogue with Sue, for example, the emotion that 'drove' the chain, so to speak, was anxiety. Thus I kept asking questions like, 'What was anxiety-provoking in your mind about...?' and 'What was scary about...?'. In other chains, the emotion will change when the content of the inference changes. When you consider that this may have occurred in the chain you are developing with your client, check this out by asking a question directed to your client's feelings. An example will make this clearer.

Windy: So you are saying that you are very reluctant to get close to a woman, but on the other hand you yearn for intimacy. How do you feel about the prospect of getting close to a woman?

Thierry: Scared.

Windy: What's scary about getting close to a woman?

Thierry: Well, I might tell her something about myself that she doesn't like.

Windy: And if you do tell her something about yourself that she doesn't like, what's scary about that?

Thierry: She might tell other people about this.

[Note that up to this point, Thierry's inferences have been mainly threat-related. Thus the questions I have been asking have all reflected anxiety (i.e. What's scary about...). This will change with Thierry's next statement.]

Windy: And if she does, that would mean...?

Thierry: That she would have betrayed my trust.

[Note that the content of this statement has changed from threat to betrayal of trust. REBT theory hypothesises that the two negative emotions associated with betrayal of trust are hurt (unhealthy) and disappointment (healthy) – see Figure 5.1. Given that Thierry's emotion is likely to change at this point from anxiety to hurt (if his negative emotion is unhealthy), I ask him about his feelings about the inferred betrayal of trust.]

Windy: And if she betrays your trust, how would you feel about that?

Thierry: Very hurt.

Windy: What would be hurtful for you about her betraying your trust?

[At this point I continue using inference chaining, but with hurt as the driving emotion instead of anxiety.]

A thorough understanding of the inferential themes associated with each negative emotion pairing (as shown in Figure 5.1) will help you to know when to ask feeling-directed questions in inference chaining.

As the above material demonstrates, inference chaining is a difficult skill and you need to practice it a lot if you are to become proficient at it. You can best do this with your trainee colleagues on their actual emotional problems. Tape record your efforts and get feedback from your trainer on your efforts. If you want to learn more about inference chaining, Moore (1988) has an excellent article on the subject.

Unit 25: The "Going for Broke" Method

If inference chaining can be likened to the game of skimming stones, the 'going for broke' method can be likened to the other games kids play on the beach. This involves throwing a stone as far as one possibly can without, of course, skimming it. In REBT, where the stone drops is the critical A. I call this method 'going for broke' because you are trying to identify the critical A at the first attempt. As such it is something of a risky procedure. Let me use the example of Sue to demonstrate the 'going for broke' method.

Windy: So when did you become anxious?

Sue: Well, I was all right until I got up on the platform.

Windy: Now think carefully, Sue. What do you think you were most anxious about?

Sue: ...pause...I was scared that the audience would laugh at me if I did not give a good talk.

In this scenario, Sue in fact did provide the critical A; however, I do not know this at this point. So I use inference chaining to check.

Windy: And what would be anxiety-provoking in your mind about being laughed at?

Sue: Oh! I couldn't bear to be laughed at.

As Sue provides an irrational belief in response to my request for a further inference, I make the assumption that 'being laughed at' is her critical A.

However, what if Sue does not provide a critical A in response to my 'going for broke' question? Because I do not whether or not her response is a critical A, I again use inference chaining to check as follows.

Windy: So when did you become anxious?

Sue: Well, I was all right until I got up on the platform.

Windy: Now think carefully, Sue. What do you think you were most anxious about?

Sue: That the audience would be expecting a lot from me.

Windy: And if they expected a lot from you, what would be scary about that?

Sue: That I might not give a good talk.

Windy: And that would mean...?

Sue: That they would laugh at me.

Windy: And if they laughed at you, what would be scary about that?

Sue: Oh! I couldn't stand that.

In conclusion, even though you may ask a 'going for broke' question, it is still important to use inference chaining to check whether or not the client's inference is her critical A. In my experience, clients do sometimes provide you with their critical A in response to a 'going for broke' question. But, more frequently, they provide an inference located in the middle of the inference chain. So, don't assume that your client has provided you with a critical A just because you have asked for it. As a general rule use inference chaining after your 'going for broke' question as a check.

Unit 26: The Listing Approach

The third approach to finding the critical A is called the listing approach. Here, you ask your client to list all the possible As that she may have been disturbed about in the example being assessed. As your client lists the possible As, write these down on a sheet of paper or on a white board. Then, ask your client to imagine that she is actually in the situation and ask her what she thinks she was most disturbed about. Next, take this A and use inference chaining as a check. Here is how I might have used the listing approach with Sue.

Windy: So when did you become anxious?

Sue: Well, I was all right until I got up on the platform.

Windy: Now see if you can list all the things you may have been anxious about. Don't worry about getting them in any kind of order, just list them.

Sue: Let me see. I was anxious about giving a poor talk...the audience seemed to expect a lot from me, I remember being anxious about that...I was scared about them laughing at me if I screwed up...and I first got anxious when I looked down and saw their faces looking up at me.

Windy: Right. Now I'm going to recap on your list. As I do so, think carefully which of the items you were most anxious about at the time. OK?

Sue: OK.

Windy: (1) Giving a poor talk; (2) the audience expecting a lot from you; (3) the audience laughing at you; (4) seeing the faces looking up at you. Which of those were you most anxious about?

Sue: Definitely, the audience laughing at me.

Windy: Can you think of any other issue that you were more anxious about than the audience laughing at you?

[This is an additional approach to checking whether the client has provided you with the critical A. Alternatively, I could have initiated inference chaining as another way of initiating this check.]

Sue: No.

Unit 27: The Subtraction Method

The fourth way of determining whether or not a particular A is critical is the subtraction method. To use this method you first need to employ inference chaining or the listing method to develop a number of As that your client is anxious about. You then ask your client to rank the listed As according to how anxious she would be if she actually faced them; the highest ranked item is at the top of the list and the lowest at the bottom. In many cases inference chaining provides you with a list of As that has already been rank ordered. However, as this is not invariably the case, I advise you to ask your client to rank order the list of As derived from inference chaining.

You then take the first, top-ranked item and ask the client whether she would still be anxious, for example, if she could cope productively with it if it happened. If the client says that she would not be anxious under these circumstances or that she would be significantly less anxious, then you have probably identified a critical A. However, if your client states that she would still be significantly anxious then that A is probably not critical and you proceed to the next item, subtract that A from the list and assess the effect of that subtraction. Here is how I would have used the subtraction with Sue.

Windy: So when did you become anxious?

Sue: Well, I was all right until I got up on the platform.

Windy: Now see if you can list all the things you may have been anxious about. Don't worry about getting them in any kind of order, at this point. Just list them.

Sue: Let me see. I was anxious about giving a poor talk...the audience seemed to expect a lot from me, I remember being anxious about that...I was scared about them laughing at me if I screwed up...and I first got anxious when I looked down and saw their faces looking up at me.

Windy: Right. Now I'm going to recap on your list and then I am going to ask you to rank order them in terms of how anxiety-provoking they were for you in your mind at that time. OK?

Sue: OK.

Windy: (1) Giving a poor talk; (2) the audience expecting a lot from you; (3) the audience laughing at you; (4) seeing the faces looking up at you. Now I am going to ask you to rank order them. Which of those were you most anxious about?

Sue: The audience laughing at me.

Windy: And then?

Sue: Giving a poor talk.

Windy: And then?

Sue: The audience expecting a lot from me.

Windy: And finally, their faces looking up at you?

Sue: Yes.

Windy: Now I want you to imagine that the audience laughing at you was not an issue for you. You could handle it successfully if it happened Can you imagine that?

Sue: Yes.

Windy: Good. How anxious, if at all, would you feel about not giving a good talk then

Sue: Well, I still wouldn't like it, but I wouldn't be nearly so anxious.

[This response makes it clear that Sue's critical A was the audience laughing at her. However, it would not have been the critical A, if she replied as follows.]

Sue: I would still be very anxious.

Windy: Now I want you to imagine that giving a poor talk was not an issue for you. If you did not give a good talk, you could handle that quite well. How anxious, if at all, would you feel about the audience's high expectations of you?

Sue: If I could handle not giving a good talk, then I would not be that anxious about their expectations of me.

[This response makes it clear that in this scenario Sue's critical A was not giving a good talk.]

Unit 28: The "2 x 2" Method

When you are working to identify your client's critical A in the ABC you are assessing, you may well find that there are two main ele-ments in the A that the client is disturbed about. Whilst you could choose to make both elements the critical A, this may lead to other problems because the client may have different beliefs about each element. How can you tell which element may be more critical? By using what I call the '2 x 2' method. Those of you who are familiar with statistics may also think of it as the 'chi-square' method. Let me give an example of this method which will make clear what it is and how to use it.

Ian is seemingly anxious about both gaining people's approval and the uncertainty that he experiences whenever he is unsure about others' opinion of him. I am not clear whether the prospect of disapproval or the uncertainty is his critical A. So I decided to use the '2 x 2' method to clarify this.

Windy: So, Ian, you are anxious about being disapproved of and about not knowing how people think of you. I want to find out whether you are most anxious about disapproval or uncertainty. Are you clear about this?

Ian: No, I'm not.

Windy: Let me draw a diagram which will help us both determine the answer to this question.

[NB The diagram that appears in Figure 8.1 is best drawn on a large whiteboard. The numbers that appear on Figure 8.1 represent a rank ordering of the scenarios thus depicted and are entered as the client answers the therapist's questions.]

As you see there are four possible scenarios. Let me outline them one by one and as I do so I want you to consider which scenario you would be most anxious about, which the next etc.
OK?

Ian: OK.

Windy: Now in the first scenario you know that people approve of you; in the second scenario you know that people disapprove of you: in the

	Approval	Disapproval
Certainty	4	3
Uncertainty	2	1

Figure 8.1 The '2 x 2' method of uncertainty/certainty and approval/disapproval as the two variables.

third scenario, you suspect that people like you, but you are unsure; whilst in the final scenario, you suspect that people disapprove of you, but again you are unsure about this. Now which of these scenarios would you be most anxious about?

Ian: Well clearly, I would be most anxious about thinking that people disapprove of me, but not being sure (Square 1). Also, obviously, I would not be anxious at all if I knew that people approved of me (Square 4).

Windy: Right. Now we have two scenarios left. Would you be more anxious if you knew for sure that people disapproved of you or if you suspected that they approved of you, but you were basically uncertain about this?

Ian: I know it sounds strange, but I would be more anxious in the uncertainty scenario (Square 2).

[This response shows that Ian's critical A involves uncertainty. If he had chosen the scenario where he knew for certain that others disapproved of him then his critical A would involve disapproval.]

Unit 29: The Hypothesis-Advancing Method

In the hypothesis-advancing method, the therapist puts forward a hypothesis about the client's critical A based (a) on the information that the client has already provided about the ABC episode in question and about himself in general and (b) on the therapist's knowledge about REBT theory as it pertains to the relationship between unhealthy negative emotions and inferences. Generally, the therapist advances a hypothesis in this way when the client has provided limited information about the A despite the fact that the therapist has employed some of the other methods designed to elicit a critical A discussed in this module.

In general then, this method is used after such methods as inference chaining and 'going for broke' have been employed. It is used particularly when the client has provided the therapist with some information about the A, but where this information is sketchy. When this happens the therapist uses this sketchy information, considers what the unhealthy negative emotion in the episode under consideration is and refers back to previous ABCs the client has discussed. The therapist takes all this information and advances a hypothesis concerning the possible nature of the critical A. In doing so, the therapist needs to make clear to the client that his hypothesis is just that and if he is wrong the client should indicate so. The task of the therapist is to put this in such a way that the client is able to say 'no'. Here is how I might have used this method with Sue, if the information she had provided me with was sketchy.

Windy: So, Sue, we know that you were anxious while you stood on the platform and you think that your anxiety had something to do with the audience. Is that right?

Sue: Yes. That's right.

Windy: OK. Now I have a hunch what you might have been anxious about and I'm going to put this to you in a moment. But let me make it clear that it is only a hunch and I may well be wrong. If I am wrong or off beam please tell me and we can take it from there. OK?

Sue: OK.

Windy: Based on what you've told me about this incident and from what you've told me about other incidents, my guess is that you were most anxious about the audience laughing at you if you didn't perform well. What do you make of that?

Sue: Yes! That's it. That's what I was anxious about.

[The definite quality of Sue's response is, I would argue, an indication that my hypothesis can be confirmed. The following is an example where my hypothesis can be rejected.]

Windy: OK. Now I have a hunch what you might have been anxious about and I'm going to put this to you in a moment. But let me make it clear that it is only a hunch and I may well be wrong. If I am wrong or off beam please tell me and we can take it from there. OK?

Sue: OK.

Windy: Based on what you've told me about this incident and from what you've told me about other incidents, my guess is that you were most anxious about not giving a good talk. What do you make of that.

Sue: ...(pause)...Well...I suppose it could be.

Windy: It sounds to me as if my hunch doesn't really ring a bell for you.

[The tentative nature of Sue's response is, I would contend, sufficient evidence to reject the hypothesis that I have put to her, and in my following response I say as much. Sometimes, however, an incorrect therapist hypothesis can be a stimulus for the client to identify the critical A for herself. This happens in the following interchange.]

Windy: Based on what you've told me about this incident and from what you've told me about other incidents, my guess is that you were most anxious about not giving a good talk. What do you makeof that?

Sue: ...(pause)...Well...No, I don't think it's that. It's more how they will respond to me. Yes, that's it. I'm scared that they will laugh at me.

Unit 30: The Theory-Derived Method

In the theory-derived method, the client has provided the therapist with an unhealthy negative emotion (e.g. anxiety), but cannot give any clue to what she may have been anxious about other than the broad situation she was in. In this case, the therapist uses his general knowledge about the kind of things people who find themselves in the same broad situation as the client are anxious about. The therapist then provides a verbal list of these possibilities and asks the client to indicate which item the client thinks may apply to her. The therapist then uses imagery to create an A featuring the chosen item and encourages the client to report on her response. This is how I would have used the theory-derived method with Sue.

Windy: OK, Sue. So you know that you became anxious while you were standing on the platform, but you don't know what you were anxious about? Have I understood you correctly?

Sue: Yes, you have.

Windy: As I need to know more precisely what you were anxious about, do you think it might help if I list the kind of things that people become anxious about when in the same situation that you were in; namely, standing on a platform about to give a talk?

Sue: Yes, I think it might help.

Windy: OK. I'll mention them one by one and, as I do so, I'd like you to think which, if any, of the items on my list you may have been anxious about. Don't make a decision until you have heard the entire list. OK?

Sue: OK.

Windy:
(1) Some people become anxious about the prospect of giving a poor talk. Here they have some standard of performance that they believe they must live up to and they get anxious in case they don't live up to this standard. They are anxious about disappointing themselves rather than disappointing their audience.
(2) Other people are more anxious about how the audience will respond to them. They are anxious in case the members of the audience display their boredom, show overt hostility, ridicule or laugh at them, walk out or throw things.
(3) Yet other people are frightened of making a fool of themselves. Here, they are scared of saying or doing something which in their minds reveal how shameful they are. This group of people are more focused on the prospect of their own foolish behavior than they are on the reactions of the audience.
(4) The final group of people are anxious about features of their own

anxiety. They are scared of the symptoms of their anxiety and thereby increase the likelihood in their minds of losing control of themselves. For example, such people are scared of such things as their mind going blank, fainting and being unable to speak.

Now do you think you may have been anxious about any of the items that I listed?

Sue: Well, when you mentioned the audience laughing that seemed to provoke a reaction in me.

Windy: Well, let's test that out. Close your eyes for a moment and imagine that you are standing on the platform ready to begin your talk. Can you picture that?

Sue: Yes, I can.

Windy: Now keep imagining that you are on the platform. As you do so start to think that you may say something that the audience finds funny that you do not intend to be humorous. They are laughing at you, not with you. How do you feel?

Sue: Well, as soon as you said that the audience were laughing AT me, I could tell that this is what I've been scared about all along.

[Sue's response indicates that I have managed to identify her critical A.]

Unit 31: Identifying the Critical A by Assessing B

I have found that sometimes I have been able to identify a client's critical A while assessing her irrational beliefs. As such, I occasionally make deliberate use of this method with the intention of identifying a critical A. Let me demonstrate how to use this method by showing how I would have employed it with Sue.

Windy: So when did you become anxious?

Sue: Well, I was all right until I got up on the platform.

Windy: What do you think you were anxious about?

Sue: I'm not sure.

Windy: Well, do you remember what mainly determines the way we feel?

Sue: Yes, our beliefs.

Windy: Right, so what do you think you were telling yourself about standing on the platform that led to your anxiety?

[Note here that having failed to find any kind of specific A above, I switch my attention to the client's beliefs. I thus work with a broad A, but as you will soon see I identify more specific As by focusing on B, not A.]

Sue: That the audience were expecting a lot from me.

[Note that in response to my deliberately vague question about her beliefs, i.e. what do you think you were telling yourself about...?, Sue provided me with an inference. Because I am primarily interested in identifying her critical A and not her irrational beliefs, I do not correct her here. I would do so if my purpose was actually to discover her irrational beliefs.]

Windy: And what were you telling yourself about the audience expecting a lot from you that led to your anxiety?

Sue: That I might not give a good speech?

[Note again that Sue provides me with another inferred A rather than an irrational belief.]

Windy: And what were you telling yourself about not giving a good speech that led to your anxiety?

Sue: That the audience will laugh at me.

[Yet another inference]

Windy: And again what were you telling yourself about the audience laughing at you that led to your anxiety?

Sue: Oh! I couldn't bear that.

[Finally, Sue has provided me with an irrational belief about an A (the audience laughing at her). This is a probable sign that this A is critical. This still needs to be checked out and I refer you to the section on inference chaining for how to carry out such a check.]

You will note the similarity between this method and inference chaining. However, there is a crucial difference. In inference chaining you are using the C (e.g. anxiety) to discover a critical A. Thus you will ask questions like: 'What was anxiety-provoking in your mind about A...?' to go deeper into the person's chain of inferences until the critical A is discovered. However, in the present method you are using a general B-directed question to identify the critical A, e.g. 'What were you telling yourself about this broad A to make yourself feel...?' The information that you obtain is the same, but the focus of the questions is different. Some clients respond very well to inference chaining, whilst others will provide you with inferences only when you ask about their beliefs or thoughts. As mentioned earlier, the more methods of identifying critical As you can become proficient in, the better, so that if you draw a blank with inference chaining you can switch to another method such as the current one of identifying the critical A by assessing B.

Unit 32: Identifying the Critical A by Questioning Musts

It is also possible to identify a client's critical A while questioning one of his musturbatory beliefs. Here, you have tried to identify your client's critical A by using one of the other methods already described in this chapter. However, you have only succeeded in identifying an A that is probably not critical. What you do then is identify a musturbatory belief about that A and question it. It is important to realize that your main purpose here is not to dispute your client's must. Rather, it is to question this must to promote identification of the critical A. In response to your questions you hope that your client will take you deeper into his chain of inferences until you identify his critical A. Here is how I would have used this method with Sue.

Windy: So when did you become anxious?

Sue: Well, I was all right until I got up on the platform.

Windy: What was scary about standing up on the platform?

Sue: I could see people's faces looking up at me?

Windy: What was scary about them looking up at you?

Sue: ...(pause)...I don't know....

[After several different attempts to identify the client's critical A, I switch the focus of my questioning to identify the client's irrational demanding belief.]

Windy: Well what were you demanding about the audience looking up at you that led you to feel anxious?

Sue: I was demanding that the people in the audience must not look up at me like that.

Windy: Why must the audience not look up at you?

Sue: Because if they do they will expect a lot from me.

[Here Sue provides an inferred A in response to my question. Since my purpose is to identify a critical A rather than helping her to dispute her irrational beliefs, I take this new A and ask another question of her implied must.]

Windy: And why must they not expect a lot from you?

Sue: Because I may not give a good talk.

[This is another inferred A and serves as the trigger for the next question.]

Windy: Why must you give a good talk?

Sue: Because the audience will laugh at me if I don't.

Windy: And why must the audience refrain from laughing at you?

Sue: Because it would be terrible if they did laugh at me.

[The evaluative irrational belief 'it would be terrible...' provides a clue that the client may have referred to a critical A. Reviewing the chain would be a useful check here (see p. 97).]

You will again note that I am developing an inference chain, not by using inference chaining but by seeming to dispute must statements. As noted above I am not actually disputing such beliefs, I am questioning them in order to elicit inferences that I have failed to elicit using more traditional methods.

Unit 33: The "Relive It Now" Method

In the 'relive it now' method of identifying a critical A, you attempt to have the client relive the experience that you are assessing as if it were happening to her now. While you do so, encourage your client to verbalise any thoughts that go through her mind. Keep your own interventions to a minimum, but verbally encourage the client to go on with her account if she gets stuck (e.g. by asking 'what is happening now?' or by saying 'go on'). Many clients find this task easier if (a) they close their eyes and (b) they have had an opportunity to describe the environment in which the event took place. However, this is not true for all clients and if your client, for instance, wants to relive his experience with his eyes open by all means encourage him to do so. Before you ask your clients to undertake this reliving experience, it is important that you explain why you are asking him to do it. If he agrees encourage him to describe the experience as if he is going through this now. Have him slow down the 'action' if his thoughts come too quickly for him to report. This method can well elicit strong affect in the session and it is best to inform your client of this. Indeed, the sudden shift of affect from weak to strong is one indicator that your client is encountering a critical A.

There are two ways in which your client can use this method. First, he can do it as if he is directly going through the experience. Second, he can do it as if he is experiencing it indirectly by seeing himself go through the experience on video, for example. Here is an example of how I would have used the 'relive it now' method with Sue.

Windy: So when did you become anxious?

Sue: Well, I was all right until I got up on the platform.

Windy: What was scary about standing up on the platform?

Sue...(pause)... I really don't know.

Windy: Well, it's important that we find out because knowing what you were most anxious about will enable us to help you deal with it effectively. Can you see that?

Sue: Yes, I can.

Windy: One way that we can find out what you were anxious about would be for you to relive the experience in imagination as it were and give me an ongoing account of what is going through your mind. What do you think?

Sue: I'm not sure I can do it, but I'll give it a try.

[At this point I give Sue some 'warm-up' imagery exercises so that she doesn't begin the method 'cold'. Then I proceeded as follows, with Sue electing to keep her eyes closed.]

Windy: Now you may experience strong emotion as you do this, but that is a good thing because it may well mean that we have discovered what you are anxious about. Is that OK?

Sue: Yes.

Windy: Let me start by asking you to describe the hall where you are giving the talk.

[Sue provides the description.]

You are now being introduced to the school by the headmistress. Take it from there.

[It is useful to have the client begin the 'relive it now' exercise at a time before they began to experience the target unhealthy negative emotion. This 'lead in' time helps to orient the client to the broad A.]

Sue: I have begun to stand up...

Windy: I am beginning to stand up. Describe it as if it is happening now and use the present tense.

[At the beginning you will need to interrupt the client a few times so that he reports on his current experience.]

Sue: I am beginning to stand up. The room is quiet and I am looking down. I can see all those eager faces looking up at me. I am thinking: 'they expect a lot of me'. I am looking down at my notes. I've got to give a good talk. My anxiety is beginning to build. I suddenly picture them laughing at me and my anxiety soars....I am beginning my talk. I somehow find myself talking but I'm so anxious.

[At this point I can use a number of methods already described to review the As Sue came up with and select her critical A. I think it is already apparent from her account what this is.]

The 'relive it now' method is a good example of what I call 'Vivid REBT'. For more vivid ways of identifying the critical A see Dryden (1986).

In addition to using the 'relive it now' method in the consulting room, you can also employ it with your client outside in a relevant aspect of his environment. You can accompany the client and encourage him to report his inferences in an ongoing manner. Sacco (1981) develops this method in an interesting way and his chapter is worth reading.

Unit 34: The Opposite of The Client's Most Cherished Desire

Another way of determining the client's critical A, but one that is perhaps less vivid than the 'relive it now' method involves you first identifying the client's most cherished desire relevant to the situation in which her problem appears. Second, you ask the client what the opposite of this desire would be and how this would be manifest in the situation. The client's response may well represent the client's critical A. Let's see how I would have used this method with Sue.

Windy: So when did you become anxious?

Sue: Well, I was all right until I got up on the platform.

Windy: What were you anxious about at that point?

Sue: I'm not too sure.

Windy: Let me put this another way. What did you really want to happen in that situation – your most cherished desire, so to speak?

Sue: I would have wanted to be admired for giving a great talk.

Windy: And what would be the anxiety-provoking opposite of this for you?

[Note that I say 'anxiety-provoking' here because anxiety is the client's target emotion.]

Sue: To be ridiculed.

Windy: And how may the audience have shown that?

[Here I ask for the specific manifestation of the client's general fear that is relevant to the example that we are assessing.]

Sue: By laughing at me if I didn't give a good talk.

Windy: And if they did laugh at you, what would be scary about that in your mind?

[Note here that I ask an 'inference chaining' question to determine whether or not being laughed at is the critical A in this emotional episode.]

Sue: I'd just want to rush off the stage.

Windy: Why?

Sue: Because I couldn't bear to be laughed at.

[Here it is reasonable to conclude that being laughed at is Sue's critical A. First, it is the embodied opposite of the client's most cherished desire in the situation and the use of inference chaining does not reveal a more critical inference.]

Unit 35: The "Take a Wild Guess" Method

If you have drawn a blank after using the above methods, you may still be able to identify your client's critical A by asking him to 'take a wild guess'. I have listened to many of Albert Ellis's therapy sessions and I have been struck by the positive response he has had to this method. You might use this technique in its own right or as part of another method (e.g. 'going for broke' or inference chaining). However, you should use it sparingly and only when your client is stuck.

I have covered the twelve methods of identifying critical As in some detail because these As trigger clients' irrational beliefs. Having done so, in the following chapter I will now consider the assessment of irrational beliefs.

Module 9
Assessing Irrational
Beliefs

You have now identified your client's major unhealthy negative emotion and have discovered his critical A. You are now in a position to assess his irrational beliefs. If you have taught your client the ABCs of REBT (as discussed in Module 4) you will have taught him the role that musts play in emotional problems. In some of the teaching examples shown in that chapter (i.e. the money and lateness examples) you will also have alluded to the role that awfulizing plays in such problems.

If you have not previously gone over the ABCs with your client, now would be a good time to do so and I refer you back to Module 4 for how to do this. If you have already gone over this material, you will still need to review it at this point. You will also need to expand your teaching to cover awfulizing in more detail and to introduce the concepts of low frustration tolerance and self/other downing. (It is worth reviewing Module 1, Unit 2 before proceeding). The best way to do this is also to teach the rational alternatives at the same time. Let me demonstrate how to do this with Sue (from the example discussed above).

Unit 36: Assessing Irrational Beliefs: A Teaching Transcript

Windy: So to sum up, Sue, you were anxious about the prospect of the audience laughing at you.

Sue: Right.

Windy: Now your anxiety is what we call C, your emotional consequence. So let me write this up on this whiteboard under C. Next, the prospect of the audience laughing at you is that part of the activating event that you were particularly anxious about. This is what I call the critical A, so I'll write this up on the whiteboard under A.

A = Prospect of audience laughing at me
B = ?
C = Anxiety

Now, do you remember when I taught you the ABCs of REBT what B stands for?

Sue: My beliefs about a situation.

Windy: Correct. As you see from the whiteboard we don't yet know what your beliefs are about the audience laughing at you that led to your anxiety. This is what we need to do now. OK?

Sue: OK.

Windy: Now do you recall from the money example what type of belief underpins people's emotional problems?

Sue: Their absolute musts.

Windy: That's right. And what were the healthy alternatives to musts?

Sue: Preferences.

Windy: Let me write these down under two main headings. Preferences are the main type of rational beliefs; so I'll write that down under the heading 'rational beliefs' and musts are the main type of irrational beliefs. Now 'rational' basically means beliefs that will help you to achieve your basic goals and purposes, whereas 'irrational' means beliefs that will stop you from achieving these goals. I'll come back to the terms 'rational' and 'irrational' later.

Rational Beliefs   *Irrational Beliefs*

Preferences   Musts

Any questions so far?

Sue: No that's quite clear. You've just summed up what you showed me earlier.

Windy: Right. What I want to do now is to show you the three other rational beliefs that stem from your preferences and the three other irrational beliefs that stem from your musts. Then we can apply this to determine which set of beliefs you were holding when you became anxious about being laughed at. OK?

Sue: Fine.

Windy: Now if you hold a non-dogmatic belief about something you believe that you want it, but you don't insist that you must have it. If you believe that, then if you don't get what you want are you likely to believe (a) 'it's bad that I haven't got what I want, but it's not terrible' or (b) 'it's awful that I don't have it'?

Sue: I'd believe that it's unfortunate.

Windy: Right, now if you believe that you absolutely have to have the object in question, which of those two beliefs that I have outlined will you hold?

Sue: I'd believe that it would be awful.

Windy: Right. Let me put that up on the board.

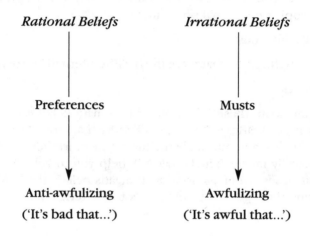

Rational Beliefs	*Irrational Beliefs*
Preferences	Musts
Anti-awfulizing	Awfulizing
('It's bad that...')	('It's awful that...')

[I have drawn a line from preferences and musts to anti-awfulizing/ awfulizing to emphasize for the client that the latter are derived from the former. Not all REBT therapists hold that musts and preferences are primary and that awfulizing/anti-awfulizing and the other irrational and rational beliefs that I will describe presently are derived from these primary beliefs. These REBT therapists would therefore omit the connecting lines.]

Windy: Any questions on awfulizing?

Sue: Well, is that different from when I say 'It's awful weather'.

Windy: It is. When you are disturbed, 'awful' means that it is worse than 100% bad and it must not be as bad as it is. Whereas when you say that it is awful weather you really mean that it is bad weather and you aren't usually emotionally disturbed about it. Does that answer your question?

Sue: Yes, that's clear.

Windy: Now on to the next set of beliefs. When you hold a non-dogmatic preference and you don't get what you want, then will you tend to conclude that the resulting situation is tolerable, albeit difficult to bear or will you believe that you can't stand it when you don't get what you want?

Sue: I'd believe that it is tolerable.

Windy: Right, now if you believe that you absolutely must have the object in question, which of those two beliefs that I have outlined will you hold?

Sue: I'd believe that it would be intolerable.

Windy: That's right. Let me add that to the board.

Rational Beliefs	*Irrational Beliefs*
Preferences	Musts
↓	↓
Anti-awfulizing	Awfulizing
('It's bad that...')	('It's awful that...')
High Frustration Tolerance	Low Frustration Tolerance
('I can stand it')	('I can't stand it')

Any questions, Sue?

Sue: No. That's perfectly clear.

Windy: And do you go along with it or not?

Sue: No. It makes very good sense and I can already see how it applies to me.

Windy: I'm pleased about that; but I've got one other concept to go over before we see how it all applies to you. OK?

Sue: OK.

Windy: Now let's suppose that you believe that it would be preferable for you to do well in a forthcoming test, but that you don't have to do well. You believe that it is desirable for you to do well, but it's not necessary. Now let's suppose that you fail the test. Would you believe (a) that you are a fallible human being for having failed or (b) that you are a thoroughgoing failure for having failed?

Sue: I'd believe that I was fallible.

Windy: But what if you believe that you absolutely have to do well in the test, which of those two attitudes towards yourself would you tend to hold?

Sue: I see what you're getting at. I'd believe that I was a failure.

Windy: This concept also applies to how you view other people, but we will get to that when it becomes relevant. Any questions or comments or should I put this concept up on the board?

Sue: Put it up on the board.

Windy: OK.

Rational Beliefs	*Irrational Beliefs*
Preferences	*Musts*
↓	↓
Anti-awfulizing	*Awfulizing*
('It's bad that...')	*('It's awful that...')*
High Frustration Tolerance	*Low Frustration Tolerance*
('I can stand it')	*('I can't stand it')*
Self/Other-Acceptance	*Self/Other Downing*

Now, let me give you a handout which is basically the same as I have on the board which you can use for future reference.

Now, Sue, I've gone over the heart of the model that I use to help people to understand their emotional problems. Before we apply it to the problem that we have been focusing on, do you have any final questions or observations to make?

Sue: No. It seems to be a good model.

Windy: Any doubts or reservations?

Sue: Only about applying it.

Windy: Well, we'll come to that in due course. Now let's apply the model and see if we can determine the irrational beliefs that underpinned your anxiety about being laughed at by the audience.

[At this point I am going to use the four irrational beliefs that I have discussed with Sue as a guide to the assessment questions I am about to ask. My questions will therefore be theory-driven.]

Windy: Now, what demands, if any, were you making about being laughed at?

Sue: The audience must not laugh at me.

Windy: Did you have any awfulizing beliefs about being laughed at?

Sue: It would be terrible if they laughed at me.

Windy: Any LFT beliefs? LFT stands for low frustration tolerance.

Sue: (looking up at the whiteboard)...That's the 'I can't stand it belief', isn't it?

Windy: Yes.

Sue: I wouldn't be able to stand it if they laughed at me.

Windy: Finally, were you putting yourself down, the audience down, both or neither?

Sue: I was putting myself down.

Windy: What did it sound like?

Sue: If they laugh at me it would prove that I was incompetent.

Windy: As a speaker or as a person?

Sue: Both.

Windy: So, let's complete the ABC on this problem that we started earlier...(writing on the board)

A = Prospect of audience laughing at me
B = (i) The audience must not laugh at me
    (ii) It would be terrible if the audience laughed at me
    (iii) I wouldn't be able to stand it if the audience laughed at me
    (iv) If the audience laughed at me it would prove that I am an incompetent person
C = Anxiety

Now, Sue, is this an accurate assessment of your anxiety about being laughed at?

Sue: Very accurate.

The above is a theory-driven way of assessing your client's irrational beliefs. It involves two basic steps: first you teach the client the irrational beliefs that underpin emotional disturbance in general, dealing with any doubts, reservations and misunderstandings he may have along the way and second, you apply this viewpoint to the client's target problem. For a different, less theory-driven way of assessing clients' irrational beliefs see Dryden (1990b). I prefer the theory-driven method of assessing irrational beliefs because it has an educational as well as a therapeutic purpose. Here you actively teach your clients which irrational beliefs to look for in both the target problem and in the other emotional problems they wish to cover during therapy. As such, it tends to save therapeutic time and encourages them to take responsibility for assessing their own problems.

Unit 37: Assessing the Effect of Irrational Beliefs on Inferences

In Module 8, I focused on the importance of assessing inferences that trigger irrational beliefs; these I have called critical As. The importance of assessing a critical A accurately is that doing so enables you to identify the irrational beliefs that your client held in the situation in which the critical A prevailed.

In Module 1, Unit 4, I mentioned the principle of psychological interactionism. This refers to the fact that different psychological processes interact with one another, often in complex ways. Part of the broad picture of psychologica linteractionism is what I call cognitive interactionism. This refers to the fact that different types of cognition interact with one another, again often in complex ways. What I am concerned with at this point is the fact that irrational beliefs can also produce inferences as well as be triggered by them. Indeed, I have done research which shows that people who hold irrational beliefs about a situation will subsequently go on to make more distorted inferences about elements of that situation than people who hold rational beliefs about the same situation (e.g. Dryden, Ferguson and Clark, 1989).

The relevance of the influence of irrational beliefs on inferences to the assessment process becomes clear when deciding what to do with very distorted negative As. So far, I have only dealt with the situation where very distorted negative As are deemed to trigger irrational beliefs. In this scenario you are encouraged to assume temporarily that the particular A is true so that you can identify the irrational beliefs that the inference triggered. However, as irrational beliefs also produce inferences, an alternative strategy here is to help the client understand how his irrational beliefs produced his very distorted negative As and that if he will dispute these beliefs then this will either decrease the likelihood that he will make such distorted inferences or encourage the production of more realistic inferences.

This latter strategy is best employed when you have a strong sense that it is very unlikely that you can help your client to think rationally about such a distorted negative A. Here is an example of how to use the 'irrational beliefs producing inferences' concept in the assessment process. In this example, Gerry experiences panic attacks and I have asked him to give me an example of his panic.

Gerry: Well, the last one I had was yesterday. Will that do?

Windy: Yes.

Gerry: I was walking up the road to get some pipe tobacco and a wave of panic came over me.

Windy: What were you panicking about?

[Gerry has provided me with his unhealthy negative emotion, panic. I then ask him the standard REBT question to try and determine his critical A.]

Gerry: What I usually panic about, that I am having a heart attack.

[Theoretically, I could use inference chaining here; that is I could encourage Gerry to assume temporarily that he was having a heart attack and then ask him what was anxiety-provoking in his mind about having a heart attack. However, he would probably look at me as if I were mad, because for him and other clients who experience panic attacks having a heart attack is a sufficient reason to panic. I have experimented with using inference chaining with clients who have panic attacks and it is not useful for this reason.

Theoretically, I could also treat the inference 'I am having a heart attack' as Gerry's critical A, encourage him to assume temporarily that this inference was correct and show him that it was his irrational beliefs about having a heart attack that led to his panic rather than the inference itself. I have briefly experimented with using this strategy, but again I have found it unhelpful.

What is helpful in such conditions where the client's inference is obviously distorted in a negative direction is to teach the client the process that leads to the production of such an inference. This is the line I chose to take with Gerry.]

Windy: So you have thought that you were having a heart attack before?

Gerry: Many times. I've even been taken to casualty and had my heart checked.

Windy: And what did they find?

Gerry: What you might expect, that there was nothing wrong with me.

Windy: Yet you find yourself still thinking that you are having a heart attack. Do you know why?

Gerry: No.

Windy: Well, let me give you one explanation and see if it makes sense. To do this properly I'll have to ask you a number of questions about your experiences leading up to the panic attack. Is that OK?

Gerry: Yes, that's fine.

Windy: Also I'll ask you to imagine things in slow motion. This is important if we are to understand the process of your panic attack fully. It may seem strange to do this, but it is important. Again is that OK?

Gerry: Yes.

[Slowing the panic experience down is an important part of the assessment process here. As I will show you, your task here is to identify the sequence of As and irrational beliefs that occur in your client's mind. Each A triggers an irrational belief and each irrational belief an increasingly distorted negative A.]

Windy: Now I want you to take yesterday's example and tell me about what was happening before you started to panic.

Gerry: Well as I said, I decided to go down the road to buy some pipe tobacco.

Windy: How did you feel as you left the house?

Gerry: I felt fine. It was a nice sunny day and I was in good spirits.

Windy: Now before what you call the wave of panic came over you and slowing the experience right down, what do you think was the first sign that you were becoming anxious?

[I am attempting to identify the first A in the client's A-irrational belief chain.]

Gerry: ...(pause)...Let me think. I was aware of my breathing.

Windy: In what way?

Gerry: It was a little irregular.

Windy: So that's what I call your first A in the chain. Now, let's look at what your beliefs were about this. Before we do so, I want to stress that your beliefs were very much below the surface of your awareness and we will have to reconstruct them. Do you think that you were thinking rationally or irrationally about your irregular breathing?

[It is useful to have taught your client the distinction between the four rational beliefs and the four irrational beliefs as shown above before attempting to assess the A-irrational belief chain.]

Gerry: You're right, I wasn't aware of any of my beliefs, but according to your model I must have been thinking irrationally.

Windy: And what demand do you think you were making about your breathing?

Gerry: I must make it regular.

Windy: I think you're right. Now, this next step is the key to the whole process. Did that belief get rid of your anxiety or serve to increase it?

Gerry: It served to increase it.

Windy: Again slowing down the process, how did you experience that increased anxiety.

Gerry: ...(pause)... I began to get a little breathless.

[The second A in the chain]

Windy: And what do you think your belief was about your breathlessness?

Gerry: I must control my breathing. I'm beginning to catch on to what you're getting at.

Windy: Good, but let's not jump ahead. What effect do you think that belief had on your anxiety?

Gerry: ...(pause)... I began to feel tight in my chest.

[The third A in the chain]

Windy: And what did you believe about that?

Gerry: That it's terrible to feel that way.

Windy: Which led to?

Gerry: The thought that I was having a heart attack.

[The final A in the chain]

Windy: Let me put this chain on the whiteboard.

$$A1 = \text{Irregular breathing}$$
$$\downarrow$$
$$B1 = \text{I must make my breathing regular}$$
$$\downarrow$$
$$A2 = \text{Breathlessness}$$
$$\downarrow$$
$$B2 = \text{I must control my breathing}$$
$$\downarrow$$
$$A3 = \text{Tightness in the chest}$$
$$\downarrow$$
$$B3 = \text{It's terrible to feel this way}$$
$$\downarrow$$
$$A4 = \text{I'm going to have a heart attack}$$

Now my view is this. If I can help you to identify the initial A in this chain which is irregular breathing (A1) and encourage you to think rationally about this then you will be less likely to experience breathlessness at A2. If I then help you to think rationally about your breathlessness at A2 then you are less likely to get a pain in your chest at A3 and so on. My hypothesis is is that working in this way you will be far less likely to think you are having a heart attack than if you think irrationally about each A in the chain. What do you think of this viewpoint?

Gerry: It certainly makes sense and it's worth trying.

Let me recap on the steps you need to take when your client's negative A is very distorted and you consider it very unlikely that you can help him to think rationally about it.

Step 1: Identify the client's C.
Step 2: Help the client to select a time in the episode prior to the development of the C.
Step 3: While encouraging the client to run the experience in slow motion, help him to identify the first A that he was aware of. This is A1.
Step 4: Identify the client's major irrational belief about A1.
Step 5: Identify the next A in the chain (A2).
Step 6: Identify the client's major irrational belief about A2.
Step 7: Repeat steps 5 and 6 until you reach the distorted A that the client mentioned in the first place.
Step 8: Teach the impact of irrational beliefs on the client's inferences.
Step 9: Target an early A-irrational belief pairing for change.

As with other REBT skills I suggest that you pair up with a trainee colleague and practice this skill in peer counseling where you both present real problems.

In the following module I will deal with the final assessment issue – assessing your client's emotional problems about their emotional problems or what I call their meta-emotional problems.

Module 10
Assessing Meta-Emotional Problems

Your clients will frequently make themselves emotionally disturbed about their emotional problems, thus unwittingly giving themselves a 'double dose' or 'two problems for the price of one'. I now call these secondary emotional problems 'meta-emotional problems', a term which literally means emotional problems about emotional problems (Dryden, 1994b). Like primary emotional problems, meta-emotional problems are characterised by unhealthy negative emotions.

There are two major issues that arise in REBT which pertain to meta-emotional problems. The first concerns assessment and the second relates to which emotional problem you target for change first: the client's primary emotional problem or her meta-emotional problem. I will deal with both these issues in this module.

Before showing you how to assess your clients' meta-emotional problems, let me deal with a training issue. Some REBT therapists routinely determine whether or not their clients have meta-emotional problems, whereas others will inquire about their existence only when their clinical intuition leads them to suspect that meta-emotional problems may be present. At this stage of your career as an REBT therapist, you probably lack such intuition, so it might be advantageous for you to ask your clients routinely how they feel about their primary emotional problems. The drawback to doing this is that you may become confused. Many trainees find the REBT assessment process difficult enough when dealing with their clients' primary emotional problems. Introducing meta-emotional problems into the picture at a time when they are struggling with primary problems would prove too much for these trainees at this juncture. Whilst I will show you how to assess meta-emotional problems, I urge you to consider carefully your own skill and confidence level as an REBT practitioner when deciding whether or not you are going to deal with your clients' meta-emotional problems. Discuss this issue with your REBT trainer or supervisor.

There is no definite point in the assessment process to determine best whether or not your client has an emotional problem. You can do so (i) as soon as your client has mentioned that he has a primary emotional problem; (ii) after you have assessed his primary problem; or (iii) after you have disputed the irrational beliefs that underpin his primary problem and he has started to effect some change on the problem. Another way of determining that your client has a meta-emotional problem is by investigating reasons why he is not making expected progress on his primary problem. One reason for this may be that he has a meta-emotional problem which is getting in the way of the work that he otherwise would be doing on the primary problem.

Unit 38: The ABCs of Meta-Emotional Problems

You carry out an assessment of your client's meta-emotional problem in the same way as you do his primary emotional problem. Here are some illustrative examples.

Larry is anxious about giving presentations at work. I assessed the ABC of his primary problem as follows:

A = Won't get promotion (if I don't give an excellent presentation)

B = (i) I must not be denied promotion when I deserve to achieve it
       (ii) Poor me!

C = Anxiety

I then explored the possible presence of a meta-emotional problem as follows:

Windy: Now, Larry, some people have what I call secondary emotional problems about their primary problems...

[I usually refrain from using the term meta-emotional problems with clients as it can come over as psychological jargon.]

... What I mean by this is that if someone is unhealthily angry, for example, then she may feel guilty about experiencing such angry feelings. The unhealthy anger is her primary problem and the guilt she feels about her anger is her secondary problem. Am I putting that clearly?

Larry: Yes, she has two problems; unhealthy anger and the guilt she feels about her anger.

Windy: Right. Now let's see if you have a secondary problem about your primary anxiety. OK?

Larry: Yes.

Windy: Now when you are anxious about the prospect of not getting promotion, how do you feel about being anxious?

Larry: I'm anxious about it.

Windy: What's anxiety-provoking in your mind about being anxious in that situation...?

[I am now using inference chaining on Larry's meta-emotional problem.]

Larry: I get the feeling of being out of control.

Windy: And what's scary about feeling out of control?

Larry: I might lose control.

Windy: In what way?

[Here I'm trying to clarify a vague A.]

Larry: I might faint.

Windy: And if you faint, what would be scary about that?

Larry: Oh, God. I'd make a complete fool of myself.

Windy: Now if fainting or losing control in any noticeable way was not a possibility, would you still be anxious about that sense that you were out of control?

Larry: Yes. I can't stand not feeling in control.

[By using the subtraction method I determined that Larry's critical A in his meta-emotional problem was 'feeling out of control'. The other A that he subsequently mentioned, i.e. fainting, was produced by his irrational belief about his out of control feeling.]

Windy: So, if you are most anxious about feeling out of control, using the sheet of irrational beliefs I've given you, let's see if we can figure out what your beliefs were about feeling out of control that led to your secondary anxiety...

The ABC of Larry's meta-emotional problem turned out thus:

A = Feeling out of control

B = (i) I must always feel in control
     (ii) It is terrible to feel out of control

C = Anxiety

It is often helpful to your client to put both his primary emotional problem and his meta-emotional problem on the whiteboard so that he can see them clearly in diagrammatic form. Otherwise, your client might get lost in a welter of words. Figure 10.1 shows a diagrammatic form of Larry's two problems.

A1 = Won't get promotion (if I don't give an excellent presentation)

B1 = (i) I must not be denied promotion when I deserve to achieve it
       (ii) Poor me!

C1 = Anxiety

$\downarrow$

A2 = Feeling out of control

B2 = (i) I must always feel in control
       (ii) It is terrible to feel out of control
C2 = Anxiety

Figure 10.1 A diagrammatic representation of Larry's primary and meta-emotional problems.

Notes: (i) The notation A1, B1, C1 represents Larry's primary emotional
       problems and A2, B2, C2 represents his meta-emotional problem.
       (ii) Larry's anxiety at C1 becomes his critical A at A2. This means
       that feeling out of control is for Larry the most anxiety-provoking
       aspect of his primary anxiety.

Unit 39: C1→A2 Transformations

You will note from the material above that when I focused on Larry's
primary anxiety (C1) and treated it as an interim A, inference chaining
with Larry's secondary anxiety (C2) as the driving emotion yielded the
critical A: 'feeling out of control' (A2). In other words what Larry found
most anxiety provoking about his primary anxiety was the sense that he
was losing control. I call the situation where the most anxiety-provoking aspect of feeling anxious (C1) was feeling out of control (A2) a
C1→A2 transformation. Here are some commonly encountered C1→A2
transformations:

1. Unhealthy anger → Hurting significant others

C1 = Unhealthy anger

$\downarrow$

A2 = Hurting significant others

B2 = I must not hurt people who are significant to me

C2 = Guilt

Here the person feels guilty about her unhealthy anger because she has inferred that the expression of her anger has 'caused' hurt to significant others and she believes that she must not hurt those who are significant to her.

2. Unhealthy jealousy → Immaturity

C1 =Unhealthy jealousy

A2 = Immaturity

B2 = I must not be immature

C2 = Shame

Here the person feels ashamed of his unhealthy jealousy because he has inferred that jealousy is a sign of immaturity and he believes that he must not be immature in this respect.

3. Unhealthy Envy → Unacceptable Trait

C1 = Unhealthy Envy

A2 = Very undesirable trait

B2 = I must not have such a trait

C2 = Unhealthy anger at self

Here the person is most angry about her unhealthy envy because she sees it as a very undesirable trait in herself which she believes she must not have.

Unit 40: Focusing on the Meta-Emotional Problem as the Target Problem

When you have ascertained that your client has a meta-emotional problem, you are faced with a choice: (a) do you start to work on her primary emotional problem (or continue to work on this target problem if you have already started to work on it) or (b) do you start to work on her meta-emotional problem (or switch to this target problem if you have started work on her primary problem)? First, let me reiterate what I said earlier. If you are unsure of your REBT skills and consider that working in therapy at both the level of your client's primary emotional problem and her meta-emotional problem is too daunting or confusing for you at this stage of your career as an REBT therapist, then just work at the level of your client's primary emotional problem.

If you want to develop your skills at working with your clients' primary and meta-emotional problems then practice doing so in peer counseling. Pair up with a trainee colleague with another trainee as observer and have your 'client' choose a primary personal problem about which he has a meta-emotional problem. Assess both problems and choose which problem to start with; this then becomes the target problem. Tape record the interview and stop the tape when you become confused or lose your way. Review the tape at the place where you began to have difficulties and with the help of the observer and your 'client' get back on track. Do this whenever you become stuck until you can deal with primary and meta-emotional problems with confidence. This process should help you to develop competence at working productively at the level of primary and meta-emotional problems with your real clients.

Having made these points, here are four criteria for dealing with the client's meta-emotional problem before his primary emotional problem

1. When the presence of the meta-emotional problem interferes with the work that you are trying to do on your client's primary emotional problem in the session.

For example, I was working with Don on his unhealthy anger problem, but he seemed quite distracted. When I asked him what he was focusing on, Don replied that he was racked with guilt over the harm that he had caused his partner with his temper. It was only when I had helped him feel remorseful about such harm (rather than guilty about it) that he could give his full attention to working on his unhealthy anger.

2. When the presence of the meta-emotional problem interferes with the work that the client is trying to do on her primary emotional problem outside the session.

For example, Sally was attempting to identify and challenge the irrational beliefs that underpinned her anxiety about disapproval whenever she felt anxious in social situations. However, she failed to do so and was puzzled as to the reason why. In the next therapy session it became clear that Sally felt ashamed about her anxiety, which she regarded as a personal weakness which she believed she absolutely should not have. Sally was able to carry out the work she needed to do on her anxiety once she overcame her emotional shame problem.

3. When the meta-emotional problem is clinically more important than the primary emotional problem.

There are certain client problems where the meta-emotional problem is clinically more important than the primary emotional problem. You will get to know these as you become more clinically more experienced. However, two common client problems where the meta-emotional problem is more crucial are (a) generalised anxiety where the client's anxiety about anxiety is more of a feature than the primary anx-iety and (b) certain mild obsessive thought problems where the secondary intolerance of the original disturbing thought is the most salient feature of the problem. The final criterion for beginning with the meta-emotional problem is:

4. When the client sees the sense of addressing his meta-emotional problem before his primary emotional problem.

Even though the above three criteria for addressing your client's meta-emotional problem before his primary problem are sound, if your client does not see the sense in doing so, then proceeding with his meta-emotional problem will threaten the therapeutic alliance that you have developed with your client. Thus, it is useful to present your client with a plausible rationale for starting with his meta-emotional problem. Only begin this work when he sees the sense of so doing.

On this point, a good training exercise is for you to practice presenting such rationales in peer counseling to your fellow trainee 'client'. Tape record your rationales under each of the three conditions listed below:

(i)   When your 'client' is distracted by his meta-emotional problem when you are attempting to work on his primary emotional problem in the session.

(ii) When your 'client' is distracted by his meta-emotional problem when attempting to work on his primary problem outside the session.

(iii) When the meta-emotional problem is more significant than his primary emotional problem.

Play your tapes to your REBT trainer or supervisor and get feedback on your performance.

In the next module, I will outline the steps that you need to take when teaching clients the REBT view of therapeutic change.

Module 11
Teaching The Rebt View Of Therapeutic Change

I have found it useful in my clinical work to explain to clients how therapeutic change occurs, at least as viewed from an REBT perspective. It is possible to do this in many ways and which method you choose will depend on many factors including your client's interest in this subject. Before I outline the steps, let me make a few general comments about this educational issue.

Unit 41: General Issues

First, you will probably introduce these steps at different points in the therapeutic process. I have found it most useful to educate the client about each step before he and I do any therapeutic work in the step itself. If you do this, you will help your client to understand what is coming next and you will decrease the chances that your client will be resistant to the work that you plan to do at that point in therapy. It will also help him to engage in the tasks that the therapeutic step calls upon him to carry out.

Another way of explaining what your client needs to do in each step is to do so if the work that you and your client are doing in that step is not going well. One reason for this may be that your client does not understand what is expected of him in that step. If you provide the relevant explanation, then this may help dissolve the impasse. For me, this is a less successful approach than the first approach because the former seeks to prevent the development of problems in therapy, whilst the latter seeks to deal with problems once they have arisen. In a phrase, an ounce of prevention is better than a dollar of cure.

Finally, it is possible to teach your client about the entire process of change before you start work on the first step. I prefer not to do this because (i) you will be presenting your client with a lot of information at a time when he may wish to start discussing his problems and (ii) he may not understand what is expected of him and may become unduly confused. However, I have used this approach with several clients who like to see the big picture before they will commit themselves to therapy.

The second point that I want to stress is that educating clients about the REBT change process is a different order of intervention from the specific work that you and your client will be doing in each step. To use an analogy here: when you teach someone the rules of tennis you are engaged in education, whereas when you teach that person the various skills he will need to win the game you are engaged in therapy.

Let me now spell out the steps that clients need to take if they are to effect therapeutic change and show you how to get the salient points over to your client. In this context, note the liberal use I make of analogies. I wish to stress, however, that the analogies I use are illustrative and as you gain experience as an REBT therapist, you will want to develop your own. The following analysis assumes that your client acknowledges that she has a problem which, on balance, she wishes to change and has some idea of how she would like things to be different (see Module 12). Dealing with reluctant clients is outside the scope of this volume.

In discussing the seven steps, I will focus my discussion on what has been called philosophic change. Such change involves a substantial shift in your client's belief system toward greater rationality. There are, as I have shown earlier, other forms of change (inferential, environmental and behavioral), but they all involve making various compromises with your preferred REBT strategy of targeting and helping your client to change her irrational beliefs (see Dryden, 1987, for a fuller discussion of compromises in REBT).

Unit 42: Step 1. Acknowledging the General Principle of Emotional Responsibility

The first step that your client needs to take in order to embark upon therapeutic change is to acknowledge that she is largely (but not exclusively) responsible for creating her own emotions and her psychological disturbance. Unless your client acknowledges this, then it is unlikely that she will derive much lasting benefit from REBT or any other approach to psychotherapy come to that. Why? Because she will blame other people and/or life conditions for her problems and will implicitly believe that she can only change if the other people in her life and the conditions that she finds herself in change first. If she holds these views she will have what psychologists call an exclusively external attributional style. Unless you help such a client acknowledge that she is largely (but not exclusively) responsible for her emotions in general and her problems in particular, then either therapy will not get off the ground or you will both be working at cross-purposes.

How, then, do you help such clients begin to accept the general principle of emotional responsibility and to realize that she largely (but not exclusively) creates her psychological problems and is therefore largely responsible for her own therapeutic change process? One way is to use the 'hundred people technique'. Let me illustrate this technique.

The hundred people technique

Windy: So, Mary. You're saying that your boss makes you unhealthily angry and that's the end of it. Is that right?

Mary: Exactly.

Windy: Well, let's see. Imagine that a hundred women, your age, background and intelligence level all worked for your boss — separately of course — but they all worked for your boss at one time or another. Imagine too that he behaves equally obnoxiously to them as he does towards you. Now would all one hundred women feel the same way about him as you do?

Mary: Well, most would.

Windy: Maybe, but would they ALL?

Mary: I guess not.

Windy: That's right. Many, as you say, would be unhealthily angry, some would be healthily angry, some would feel guilty...

Mary: Guilty? You mean some women would actually feel guilty about that son of a bitch?

Windy: Oh yes. What would they have to think to feel guilty?

Mary: Beats me.

Windy: Well wouldn't they have to think something like: 'It's my fault he's so nasty. I've done something very wrong which proves that I'm a bad person?'

Mary: I suppose they would. I've never thought about it like that.

Windy: And by the same token, wouldn't some of these women be healthily angry, but not furious about his lousy behavior?

Mary: I guess they would.

Windy: What do you think they would have to think in order to be healthily angry, but not furious about the way he behaves?

Mary: Something like, 'I don't like it but that's the way he is. Tough!'

Windy: That's probably very true. Now strange as it may seem one or two of these women will even feel pleased about the way he treats them. Do you know why?

Mary: No, why?

Windy: Well, what would they have to think about his bad behavior to feel pleased about it?

Mary: It's good that he is treating me badly?

Windy: Right.

Mary: But, come now. Who in her right mind will be pleased about such bad behavior?

Windy: Well, the person may not be in her right mind. But I can think of at least one non-crazy reason why a woman may feel pleased about being treated so badly.

Mary:....(long pause)...well I can't think of any. Put me out of my misery. I'm dying to know.

Windy: Well what if she thought something like: 'I hope he continues because if he does I'm going to report him to his superior. That'll get him into trouble.'

Mary: You're right!

Windy: Now note, Mary, that by saying this I'm not condoning his bad behavior. If you're right and from the evidence you've given me, I've got no reason to doubt it, his behavior does stink and is bound to have some influence on how you will feel, but from what we've just discussed do you think that he makes you feel unhealthily angry?

Mary: No. I can see what you mean. I'm glad that you said that his behavior does have some bearing, otherwise I would have thought you were saying that my feelings had nothing to do with him and I certainly wouldn't have bought that...

[This is a common client misconception that you need to keep your eyes and ears open for. Namely: 'If you say that my boss doesn't make me angry then you are saying that he has nothing to do with it; it's all me.' To counteract this tendency it is important to stress, as I did with Mary, that the behavior of others and/or environmental conditions do CONTRIBUTE to your client's disturbed feelings, but they do not CAUSE these feelings. Rather, it is the client's way of thinking about the event that is often the most important factor to consider.]

...but as you've acknowledged that he has something to do with it, I can see that the different ways people think about the same event have quite an influence on the way they feel about it.

Now, of course, the client's last statement is not quite true. You will recall earlier that a person disturbs herself at C about the most relevant (for her) part of the A. As I discussed in that book, this is called the critical A and is often inferential. Thus, strictly speaking, the hundred women in the above example are not all evaluating the same event. They are evaluating their critical As. It is for this reason that the 'hundred people' technique is NOT a good way of teaching the ABCs of REBT. However, please remember that you are NOT teaching the specific role that rational and irrational beliefs have on people's negative emotions at this point. I call this the SPECIFIC principle of emotional responsibility which is step 3 of the REBT therapeutic change framework. Here, you are making the general point that people need to take responsibility for the way they think about events. I call this the GENERAL principle of emotional responsibility.

In other words you are concerned here with emphasising the general point: 'You feel the way you think' and not the specific REBT point: 'You disturb yourself largely by your irrational beliefs'. That point comes later. However, I should stress that there are a number of REBT therapists who would rather teach the specific REBT point first and would thus dispense with the more general point, i.e.: 'You feel the way you think'. These REBT therapists argue that because the specific point: 'You disturb yourself largely by your irrational beliefs' is the core of the REBT model AND that by using it first you can also teach your client the principle of emotional responsibility, then teaching the general principle of emotional responsibility is a redundant exercise. I tend to be in this latter camp myself. However, as you will need to teach some of your clients the general principle of emotional responsibility, you will need to learn some of the methods outlined in this section. Having made this point, let me outline another way of teaching this general principle.

Using diagrams

A good way of teaching your client the general principle of emotional responsibility is by using diagrams. In Figure 11.1 I outline what might be called the general principle of emotional irresponsibility in that the client is claiming that A (a situation) can directly cause her feelings at C.

The diagram in Figure 11.2, on the other hand, represents the general principle of emotional responsibility that I am suggesting that you teach your clients. It shows that it is the person's beliefs about the existing negative event that are largely responsible for the person's disturbed feelings.

As a training exercise, pair up with a trainee colleague and have him/her play the role of a client who believes that 'A causes C'. Using the diagrams outlined in Figures 11.1 and 11.2, help your 'client' understand that a more accurate representation is that shown in Figure 11.2. Tape record the dialogue and play the tape to your REBT trainer or supervisor for feedback.

A (Negative Event) ——————————————— C (Disturbed Feeling)

No A (No Negative Event) ————————— No C (No Disturbed Feeling)

Therefore:

A (Negative Event) ————————————————➤ C (Disturbed Feeling)

Caused

Figure 11.1. Argument used to justify 'A causes C' model.

A (Negative Event) ——————————————— C (Disturbed Feeling)

No A (No Negative Event) ————————— No C (No Disturbed Feeling)

A (Negative Event) x B (Belief) ——————————➤ C (Disturbed Feeling)

Figure 11.2. A × B→C explanation.

Two common client objections to the general principle of emotional responsibility

As you will soon discover, some clients find it difficult to accept the general principle of emotional responsibility. Your clients will come up with several objections, but here I will concentrate on the two most common: (a) 'But I would not have felt that way if the event didn't happen' and (b) 'If I accept the general principle of emotional responsibility, then I will blame myself.'

(a) 'But I would not have felt that way if the event didn't happen'

Here is an example of how to deal with this argument. Let's suppose that Susan has made this objection in the course of a therapy session. This is how I would have responded.

Susan: Well, that's all well and good, but if my mother didn't interfere in my life, I wouldn't get angry. Therefore, she makes me feel angry.

[When Susan and I refer to anger here we both mean unhealthy anger and when we refer to annoyance we both mean healthy anger.]

Windy: Can I put your argument on the white board and show you an alternative view?

[You will recall earlier that I advocate asking your client for permission before proceeding with an explanation.]

Susan: OK.

Windy: Correct me if I've got you wrong, but your argument seems to be as follows....(writes diagram on the whiteboard; see Figure 11.3). You recognize that you are angry when your mother interferes in your life. Right?

Susan: Correct.

Windy: Then you recognize that when your mother does not interfere in your life you have no need to be angry. Is that right?

Susan: Right.

Windy: As a result you conclude that your mother's interference makes you angry. Have I understood your argument?

Susan: Yes, that's it.

Windy: Now can I offer you an alternative view? [Again I ask for permission to proceed.]

Susan: OK.

Windy: This view recognizes that you are angry when your mother interferes in your life. It also notes that when she doesn't interfere in your life you have no need to be angry. So far this model is the same as yours. Can you see that?

Susan: Yes I can.

Windy: Now. I want you to imagine a number of scenarios. Some will sound a bit strange, but there is an important point to be made, so please bear with me. OK?

[Note that I have prepared the client in advance for the 'strangeness' of some of the scenarios, thus making it less likely that she will find them strange than if I had not so prepared her. Again, I stressed this point in earlier in this volume.]

Susan: OK.

Windy: Now how would you feel about your mother's interference if

A (Mother's interference) ———————————————— C (Anger)

No A (No interference from mother) ———————— C (No Anger)

Therefore:

A (Mother's interference) ——————————————→ C (Anger)

Caused

Figure 11.3. Susan's argument used to justify 'Mother made me angry'.

you had sad thoughts about her behavior?

Susan...(pause)...I guess I'd feel sad.

Windy: Let me write that up on the whiteboard. Now, how would you feel if you had guilty thoughts about her interference?

Susan: Guilty.

Windy: (writes the client's last response on the board). Now I know this is going to sound strange, but how would you feel if you had happy thoughts about her behavior?

Susan: (laughs) I'd feel happy.

Windy: (writes that on the board). Now, how would you feel if you had angry thoughts about you mother's interfering behavior?

Susan: Angry.

Windy: (writes that on the board). Now. here's the $64 000 dollar question. Does your mother's interference make you angry directly, or does your anger stem from your angry thoughts about her behavior?

Susan: I see what you mean. Put like that, my anger stems from my angry thoughts about her interfering behavior.
Windy: That's right. Her interfering behavior contributes to your anger by triggering your angry thoughts; but your angry feelings largely stem from your angry thoughts. (This is shown in Figure 11.4).

(b) 'If I accept the general principle of emotional responsibility, then I will blame myself.'

Some clients will resist accepting the point that they are largely responsible for disturbing themselves because they would blame themselves. For such clients responsibility is equivalent to blame. This is how I generally deal with this issue.

A (Mother's interference) ———————————————— C (Anger)

No A (No interference from mother) ——————— C (No anger)

A (Mother's interference) x Sad thoughts (B) = C (Sadness)

A (Mother's interference) x Guilty thoughts (B) = C (Guilt)

A (Mother's interference) x Happy thoughts (B) = C (Happiness)

Therefore:

A (Mother's interference) x Angry thoughts (B) = C (Anger)

Figure 11.4. Argument used to explain that Susan's anger (C) stems from B (her angry thoughts).

Susan: You say that I am largely responsible for my anger about my mother's interference. But if I accept that then that means that I'm to blame for my anger, doesn't it?

Windy: No. There is an important distinction to be made between responsibility and blame. Responsibility here means that you largely make yourself angry about your mother because you have angry thoughts about the way she interferes in your life. These thoughts are your thoughts and no one else's. Given that you have ownership of these thoughts you can be said to be responsible for them. However, I employ the term responsibility (as distinct from blame) to include the following beliefs: (i) I wish that I didn't have angry thoughts about my mother, but there's no universal law that states that I must not have them. I have them and unfortunately all the conditions are in place for me to have them and (ii) I am a fallible human being and not a bad person for having angry thoughts about my mother. Blame involves ownership of your angry thoughts plus a very different set of beliefs, namely: (i) I (in the case of self-blame) absolutely should not have angry thoughts about my mother and (ii) I am a bad person for having such thoughts towards her. Have I made myself clear?

Susan : I think so.

Windy: Can you put it into your own words so I can see if I have explained the difference clearly?.

Susan: Well, you seem to be saying that responsibility is something which is down to you, but which you don't blame yourself for and blame is the same thing down to you which you do blame yourself for.

Windy: That's exactly the point. Let me put that on the board to reinforce the difference (see Figure 11.5). Now, often people are reluctant to take responsibility for what is down to them because they would blame themselves if they did so. They confuse responsibility and blame.

Susan: I did at the start, but you've helped me to see the difference.

Figure 11.6 presents the general difference between responsibility and blame more formally.

Responsibility = What's down to you (angry thoughts) + preferences and self-acceptance

Blame = What's down to you (angry thoughts) + musts and self-downing

Figure 11.5. The difference between responsibility and blame in Susan's case.

Responsibility = Acknowledged ownership of what is in one's control + preferences and self-acceptance

Blame = Acknowledged ownership of what is in one's control +
   musts and self-downing

Figure 11.6. The difference between responsibility and blame.

Having considered how to teach clients the general principle of emotional responsibility we can now go on to the second step of therapeutic
change.

Unit 43: Step 2. Recognizing That One Can Effect Change in One's Psychological Problems

Unless your client acknowledges that she is able to effect change in the
problem that she has taken responsibility for in step 1, then it is unlikely
that she will proceed much further in therapy. In the above section I
mentioned two common blocks to clients taking responsibility for their
problems: (i) believing that an event causes one's problems because one
does not feel disturbed in the absence of that event and (ii) blaming oneself for having the problem for which one is responsible. Other clients
will resist accepting the point that they are largely responsible for disturbing themselves because they think that they cannot change. As such
this obstacle touches at the heart of step 2: encouraging your client to
see that she can change and that she is not a hopeless case. Here are
some examples of how I generally deal with clients who believe that
they cannot change and that therefore they are a hopeless case. I will
again present examples where the client is reluctant to accept responsibility for her problem because this is where the belief that one cannot
change becomes particularly manifest.

Example 1: Change is possible — the general argument

In the first example, I employ a general instance where change occurs. It is
useful to select an issue where change is particularly difficult, but still possible to achieve. If you choose an issue which the client perceives is easier
to overcome than she does her particular problem, then she may say something like: 'Yes, but that is an easy problem to deal with compared with
mine.' The implication here is that change is possible on easy issues, but
not on difficult issues like hers. It is for this reason that you should select
an issue that the client is likely to see as more difficult to overcome than
her own. In effect, your aim is to help your client conclude: 'If they can

overcome this difficult problem, then perhaps I can overcome my (less difficult) problem.'

Susan: You say that I am largely responsible for my anger about my mother's interference. But if I accept that then that means that I can't change.

Windy: Why not?

Susan: Well, I've always gotten angry with her when she's interfered in my life; therefore, I always will.

Windy: So you believe that because you have always made yourself angry with your mother, you're doomed to continue to do so. In other words, you have no choice in the matter. Is that right?

Susan: Well, yes.

Windy: Do you know any instances where people have changed longstanding patterns?

Susan: No.

Windy: Do people ever get over alcoholism or overcome longstanding addictions to drugs?

Susan: I guess so.

Windy: Do you think it is easier to break an addiction to drugs or to get over your anger about your mother's interference?

Susan: (laughing) ... I see your point.

Windy: What's my point?

Susan: That I may think that I can't change, but that doesn't mean that I can't.

Windy: Good. Indeed, the more you think you can't change the more you will make that statement come true, because you won't do anything to effect a change.

Example 2: Change is possible — the specific inspirational argument

Here, you choose a specific example where a given individual, preferably well known, has effected change in his or her life. Again it is important to choose an example where the person has overcome a more difficult problem than your client's problem, otherwise the client may dismiss the example as trivial and of no relevance to his or her 'very difficult' problem. For some clients, it helps if the example you choose is inspirational in nature in the sense that it encourages the client to conclude, 'If she or he can do it, so can I.' However, other clients are put off by so-called inspirational examples and are more responsive to non-inspirational examples.

Susan: You say that I am largely responsible for my anger about my mother's interference. But if I accept that then it means that I can't change.

Windy: Why not?

Susan: Well, I've always gotten angry with her when she's interfered in my life; therefore, I always will.

Windy: So you believe that because you have always made yourself angry with your mother, you're doomed to continue to do so. In other words, you have no choice in the matter. Is that right?

Susan: Well, yes.

Windy: Have you ever heard of Jimmy Boyle?

Susan: The name's familiar, but I can't place it.

Windy: Well, he grew up in Glasgow where he had a very deprived childhood and led a life of violent crime for many years until he decided to reform himself whilst in prison for murder. And with the help of a number of people he did just that. He was eventually released from prison and now is well respected as a writer and social commentator. Now do you think that changing your angry feelings will be more difficult for you than the changes Jimmy Boyle brought about in himself?

Susan: I get your point.

Windy: What's my point?

Susan: That I may think that I can't change, but that doesn't mean that I can't.

Windy: Good. Indeed, the more you think you can't change the more you will make that statement come true, because you won't do anything to effect a change.

Example 3: Change is possible — using self-disclosure

Another way to show clients that change is possible is to relate a personal example where you effected change on one of your personal problems. The field is divided over the value of therapist self-disclosure (see Dryden, 1991 and Segal, 1993 for both sides of the argument). However, I and other REBT therapists advocate using self-disclosure with clients unless there are good reasons not to do so. As you will see from the example below, it is important to get your client's permission to provide a personal example before you begin to self-disclose.

Susan: You say that I am largely responsible for my anger about my mother's interference. But if I accept that then that means that I can't change.

Windy: Why not?

Susan: Well, I've always gotten angry with her when she's interfered in my life; therefore, I always will.

Windy: So you believe that because you have always made yourself angry with your mother, you're doomed to continue to do so. In other words, you have no choice in the matter. Is that right?

Susan: Well, yes.

Windy: Would it be helpful if I told you a personal anecdote which is relevant to this issue? It may help you to re-think your position on this issue.

[Again it is important to ask permission here. If you launch into self-disclosure, it may be unproductive in that your client may not value therapist self-disclosure. Also listen carefully to the tone of your client's agreement. Is she definite in her response? If not, explore any doubts first.]

Susan: (firmly) OK.

Windy: You've probably noticed that I have a stammer.

Susan: I have, but it's only a slight one.

Windy: Well it used to be a lot worse. I would avoid talking to people and used to get very anxious about speaking in public. I now go on the radio which I never dreamed I would be able to do. Now I realized I made myself anxious, but do you think I concluded that this meant I would always stammer badly and always be anxious about speaking in public?

Susan: Obviously, not.

Windy: What do you think would have happened if I had concluded that?

Susan: Presumably you wouldn't have even tried to overcome your problem. I get your point.

Windy: What's my point?

Susan: That I may think that I can't change, but that doesn't mean that I can't.

Windy: Good. Indeed, the more you think you can't change the more you will make that statement come true, because you won't do anything to effect a change.

Here are some other reasons that clients give for not being able to change:

* I'm too old to change.
* I'm too weak to change.
* I'm too disturbed to change.
* My family won't allow me to change.
* I don't have the energy to change.
* I've thought this way for too long to change now.

It is important that you are able to challenge these arguments when your client uses them. One good way of doing this is for you to pair up with one of your trainee colleagues and have him/her take the role of a client who holds to each of these positions. Use as many arguments as you can think of to challenge your 'client's' views. Tape record the role plays and play them to your REBT trainer or supervisor for feedback.

Unit 44: Step 3. Acknowledging the Specific Principle of Emotional Responsibility

You will recall that I have distinguished between the general and specific principles of emotional responsibility. The general principle states that clients create, to a large (but not exclusive) degree their own psychological disturbances. When you teach this principle (as shown in Unit 42) you keep your explanation of how your client does this fairly vague. Thus you may choose to follow the lead of Epictetus who said that 'People are disturbed not by events, but by their views of events' or you may show your client that his feelings are largely determined by the way he thinks. However, when you teach your client the specific principle of emotional responsibility, which is equivalent to the REBT model of human emotions, it is important that you show him that emotional and behavioral disturbances stem largely from irrational, absolutistic beliefs.

Earloer in this book (in Module 4), I outlined three examples of how to teach your client the central role that irrational beliefs play in his psychological problems and I suggest you re-read these at this point. However, as it is useful to have a number of such methods in your therapeutic armamentarium, let me give you two more. The first is called the Rubber Hammer method, whereas the second example is one that I originated myself, called Dryden's Invitation Technique.

The Rubber Hammer method

The following is an example of how to use the Rubber Hammer method when teaching the specific principle of emotional responsibility.

Windy: So what you're saying, Susan, is that your mother makes you angry.

Susan: That's right. Every time she interferes with my plans she makes me so wild.

Windy: May I offer you an alternative perspective on this point and one which I think will help you to achieve your goal of anger control?

[It is again important to ask your client for permission to present an alternative view. If she grants permission she is also more likely to listen openly to what you have to say than if you proceed without gaining her agreement on this matter.]

Susan: OK.

Windy: This way of explaining it may seem strange, but bear with me if you will. OK?

[Note that I have again sought the client's permission here. Also I have acknowledged myself that the method may seem strange to the client. Doing this, I have found, has the paradoxical effect of making the method seem less bizarre in the client's eyes.]

Susan: OK (laughing warily).

Windy: Now this is a rubber hammer. I'd like you to take it (I pass it to the client who takes it). Now again I'd like you to bear with me. I want you to imagine that my passing you the hammer represents your mother's interference, whereas the hammer represents the belief: 'My mother absolutely must not interfere in my life.' Now hit yourself over the head with it. It won't hurt, I promise.

Susan: (hits herself over the head with the hammer which makes a squeaky noise. The client laughs and says...) That's a relief.

Windy: Now, how will you feel if you believe that your mother absolutely must not interfere in your life?

Susan: Angry.

Windy: That's right. Now let me have the hammer back...(Susan passes me the hammer)...Now once again my passing you the hammer represents your mother's interference in your life, but this time the hammer represents a different belief, namely: 'I'd prefer it if my mother did not interfere in my life, but there's no reason why she must not.' Now, hit yourself over the head again...(the client does so)...How would you feel if you believed that it would be preferable if your mother did not interfere in your life, but that there is no law of the universe which states that she must not do so?

Susan: Well I still wouldn't like it, but I guess I wouldn't be nearly as angry.

Windy: Right, you wouldn't like it. You'd even strongly dislike it, but you wouldn't be angry. You'd be annoyed or even strongly annoyed. Now, note that your mother's interference is the same in both situations. What's different?

Susan: My beliefs.

Windy: Your mother's behavior contributes to your feelings, but your anger largely stems from your demanding belief, whilst your annoyance stems from your healthy non-demanding preference. Now, I'm not sure I've made myself clear. Can you put into your own words the main point about what I've said?

[Once again it is important to determine whether or not the client has grasped the main point.]

Susan: That my mother doesn't make me angry. I do that, with my demanding belief about her behavior.

Windy: Correct.

Dryden's Invitation Technique

The 'Invitation Technique' is best used to illustrate the specific principle of emotional responsibility when the client applies to himself the actual or inferred put-down from another person or group of people. Here's how I used it with a client, Bill.

Windy: So, Bill. You felt depressed when your friends laughed at you because you thought they considered you worthless. Have I understood you correctly?

Bill: That's right.

Windy: So who made you depressed?

Bill: They did by considering me to be worthless.

Windy: Can I explain something to you which might help you to see that in a different perspective and help you over your depression?

[Note that I ask for permission to put the alternative view.]

Bill: OK.

Windy: Bear with me for a few minutes if I seem to be going off track and if I seem to be asking a lot of irrelevant questions. I'm not and I think you will understand why in a few moments. OK?

[Here I explain that there is a reason behind my apparent deviation.]

Bill: OK.

Windy: Have you ever been invited to a wedding?

Bill: Yes, I have.

Windy: What did the invitation say?

Bill: It announced the wedding of the couple and invited me to attend.

Windy: Was there a reply card?

Bill: Yes, I think there was.

Windy: What did it say?

Bill: Something like: 'Thank you for inviting me to the wedding. I accept or I decline.

Windy: That's right. You are given a choice. Now, let's put your friends' view of you in the same format. I'm assuming for the moment that they actually considered you to be worthless.

[As I showed you in in Module 8, assuming temporarily that the client is correct is a typical REBT strategy.]

It would go something like this: 'We consider Bill to be worthless and invite him to consider himself worthless. RSVP.'

Now, here's what's on the reply card:

'Thank you for your invitation for me to consider myself worthless. I accept or I decline.'

Now Bill, put like that what did you reply in your own head?

Bill: I accept.

Windy: And how did you feel as a result of believing that you were worthless, for that is what the statement 'I'm worthless' is, a belief?

Bill: Depressed.

Windy: How would you have felt if you replied in your head: 'I decline to consider myself worthless' which is a more healthy belief?

Bill: Well. I still wouldn't have liked them laughing at me, but I wouldn't have felt depressed. I would have felt sad or displeased.

Windy: So who made you depressed – : your friends with their laughter and their invitation for you to consider yourself worthless or your acceptance of that invitation, your belief – : 'Yes, they're right. I am worthless?'

Bill: Put like that, it was my belief, my own acceptance of their put-down in my own head. I'm beginning to see what you mean. I'm mainly responsible for my depression.

Windy: That's right. They contribute to your depression by putting you down, let's assume. But you really depressed yourself by your own self-downing belief.

[Let me stress one point here. On realising that the specific principle of emotional responsibility applies to them and therefore they are largely responsible for making themselves disturbed, a minority of clients will disturb themselves about this. As such it is worthwhile adding a statement like the following.]

Windy: Yes, and you don't have to condemn yourself for doing this because we all do it when we are depressed and anxious, to give but two examples. In a sense, the fact that you mainly depress yourself is good news. Because if you have the power to depress yourself, you also have the power to undepress yourself. Now, let's see if we can figure out together how you can use this latter power to help you undepress yourself about your friends laughing at you.

Unit 45: Step 4. Detecting Irrational Beliefs and Distinguishing Them From Rational Beliefs

According to REBT, irrational beliefs are the core of psychological disturbance and rational beliefs are the core of psychological health. After acknowledging that psychological disturbance is largely determined by irrational beliefs in step 3 of the change process, it is important that your client learns to detect his or her irrational beliefs and to be able to distinguish them from rational beliefs at step 4. I will deal with these two different but related tasks in turn. First, let me show you three ways of helping your client to detect his irrational beliefs.

Detecting irrational beliefs

1. Give your client the following basic instruction. 'Whenever you have a disturbed feeling like anxiety, depression, unhealthy anger, hurt, guilt, shame, unhealthy jealousy or unhealthy envy, do the following:

(a)   Write down the letters ABC like this:

A

B

C

(b)   Make a note of your disturbed emotion at C.
(c)   Ask yourself: 'What am I most disturbed about?' and write down your answer at A.
(d) Finally, look for one or more of the following irrational beliefs: must, awful, I can't stand it and I/he or she/they are no good and write these beliefs under B.

2. A shorter version of this instruction is as follows:

Whenever you feel disturbed look for and write down one or more of the following irrational beliefs: must, awful, I can't stand it and I/he or she/they are no good and say what you were most disturbed about.

In asking your client to do this you hope that he or she will be able to identify a relevant A in reporting his irrational belief. For example, one of my clients recently used this instruction and came up with the belief: 'My sister must ask me how I am when I talk to her on the telephone.' If your client does not report an A, then you can train him or her to do so, by giving him some examples of what you are looking for.

3. Ellis's basic instruction:

If you listen to as many of Albert Ellis's therapy tapes as I have, you will soon become familiar with the following basic instruction that he gives to his clients very early on in therapy to help them to detect their irrational beliefs:

'Whenever you disturb yourself, *cherchez le should, cherchez le must*; look for the should, look for the must.' Sometimes he adds: 'If you find it difficult to find your must, just make a note of what you disturbed yourself about, bring this in and I will help you find it.'

Note that with this instruction, Ellis is deliberately guiding his clients towards detecting their musts. He does not even mention the three other irrational beliefs, namely: awfulizing, low frustration tolerance beliefs and self/other downing. This is consistent with Ellis's view, discussed in earlier that musts are primary irrational beliefs and that the others are secondary irrational beliefs in that they are derived from the musts.

Distinguishing irrational beliefs from rational beliefs

One major purpose of encouraging your client to detect his irrational beliefs and to be able to distinguish them from his rational beliefs is so that he can dispute them effectively. It is therefore particularly important that your client is able to discriminate carefully between rational and irrational beliefs. Otherwise he may dispute his healthy rational beliefs or other non-disturbing cognitions. Here are some ways whereby you can help him to sharpen his discriminatory powers on this issue.

(a) Teach your client the difference between absolute and non-absolute shoulds. In the mid-1980s, I wrote a paper on language and meaning in REBT where I made the point that it is important to distinguish between words and meanings (see Dryden, 1991). Take the word 'should'. In REBT, we argue that only absolute shoulds are the core of much psychological disturbance. Thus, it is important to help your client to distinguish between absolute shoulds and other forms of the word 'should'. In particular, your client needs to distinguish between absolute shoulds and preferable shoulds. One way of doing this is to encourage him to use the relevant qualifier. Thus, when your client's should is rational, encouraging him to use the phrase 'I preferably should...', for example, and when it is irrational, the phrase 'I absolutely should...' makes the meaning clear. To help your client to understand the non-absolute nature of these shoulds have her say, 'I preferably should be approved by my boss, but he doesn't have to do so.'

However, there are other meanings of the word 'should' which are non-absolute and which your client needs to understand so that he doesn't mistake them for absolute shoulds. In addition to preferable shoulds the following is a list of non-absolute shoulds:

(i) *Recommendatory shoulds*. These shoulds point to what your client recommends to herself or to others e.g. 'You really should go and see the new play at the local theatre.' If your client uses the phrase 'I recommend that you...', then he or she will see the recommendatory meaning of this particular should. To help your client understand the non-absolute nature of these shoulds encourage him or her to say, 'You really should go and see the new play at the local theatre, but there is no reason why you have to do so.'

(ii) *Predictive shoulds*. These shoulds represent your client's predictions about the future, e.g. 'I should pass my driving test tomorrow.' Using the phrase, 'I predict that...', instead of 'I should...' should (I predict!) make the meaning of this 'should' clear. To help your client to understand the non-absolute nature of these shoulds, encourage her to say, 'I should pass my driving test, but there is no law of the universe that states that I must do so.'

(iii) *Ideal shoulds*. These shoulds point to the existence of ideal conditions, e.g. 'People should be nice to one another.' Substituting the phrase, 'In an ideal world, people would...' will probably reveal the ideal nature of such shoulds. To help your client to understand the non-absolute nature of these shoulds, encourage her to say, 'People should be nice to one another, but they obviously don't have to do so.'

(iv) *Empirical shoulds*. These shoulds point to the existence of reality, e.g. 'My mother should interfere in my life.' What this really means is this: 'Because all the conditions exist for my mother to interfere in my life therefore she should do so.' Not surprisingly, your client will not use the empirical should very frequently and needs to be encouraged to do so.

(b) Teach your client the difference between unconditional and conditional musts. Your client will often use the word 'must' in its conditional sense which you and she might mistake for an unconditional must. An unconditional must is, as you know, the one that is the core of much emotional disturbance. If your client, for example, states 'I must pass my exams', how do you both know whether or not this is a disturbance-creating must? There are two major ways of finding out.

   (i) *Ask for the consequences of the A (in this case, 'passing my exams') not occurring*. If a must is unconditional, it is likely that your client will give one of the irrational belief derivatives as a reply to your question. For example:

Windy: So you say that you must pass your exam. Is that right?

Peter: That's right.

Windy: And if you don't pass your exams?

Peter: That would be unthinkable.

Windy: Why?

Peter: Because it would prove that I would be a failure.

However, if a must is conditional then the client will give you a negative A in reply. Thus:

Windy: So you say that you must pass your exam. Is that right?

Simon: That's right.

Windy: And if you don't pass your exams?

Simon: Then, I won't get into the law.

[Note that this client's must is really specifying the conditions that have to be met in order for him to achieve the object of his desire. In other words, his true desire is getting into the law and the condition that have to be met for this to happen is 'Passing my exams'.

   Also note one very interesting thing about my short interchange with Simon. As his must is conditional and he gives me the negative A ('I won't get into the law') that will result if the conditions ('passing my exams') aren't met, this constitutes the beginning of an inference chain (see Unit 24). Given this, I would then say: 'And if you don't get into the law, then what...?']

   (ii) *Ask for the meaning about the consequence*. You may find that by just asking for the consequence of the client's violated must you will get a negative A in response even though the must is unconditional and disturbance-creating. This is because 'pure consequence' questions tend to pull negative A responses from clients.

One way round this problem is to ask for the meaning of the consequence. I will first demonstrate this approach with a client whose must is unconditional.

Windy: So you say that you must pass your exam. Is that right?

Peter: That's right.

Windy: And if you don't pass your exams, WHAT WOULD THAT MEAN?

[Note that I am asking for the consequence: 'And if you don't pass your exams...' AND for the meaning of the consequence: 'WHAT WOULD THAT MEAN?']

Peter: It would mean that I was a failure.

Now let me demonstrate this with a client whose must is conditional.

Windy: So you say that you must pass your exam. Is that right?

Simon: That's right.

Windy: And if you don't pass your exams, WHAT WOULD THAT MEAN?

Simon: It would mean that I won't get into the law.

Windy: And if you don't get into the law, what would that mean...?

[Again note that I am now doing inference chaining by asking for the client's meaning of the negative inferred As in his mind (see unit 24) for more information on this critical A assessment technique.]

(c) Teach your client the difference between awful and very bad. You will have already noted that REBT therapists use particular words in precise ways. You will have also grasped the point that it is important for you to make clear to your client the meaning of these terms (see Dryden, 1988, for a fuller discussion of this important issue).

Continuing this theme, it is important to help your client understand the difference between the terms 'awful' and 'very bad'. If you recall (see Dryden, 1995), awful (and its synonym 'terrible') means, in REBT theory, more than 100% bad and worse than it absolutely should be. On the other hand, very bad means just that, very bad. This evaluation of badness can be located on a scale ranging from 0% to 99.99% badness. Note, then, that it is not possible to achieve 100% bad; to quote again from Smokey Robinson's mother 'From the time you are born till you ride in the hearse, there's nothing so bad that it couldn't be worse.' Awful, however, exists on a magical scale from 101% badness to infinity.

The difficulty in explaining this distinction lies in the fact that clients often use the term awful to mean bad or very bad. How, then, do you clarify this difference? Here is one example.

Windy: So you are saying that you feel hurt because you believe it is awful that you were rejected by your boyfriend. Is that right?

Rosemary: Yes.

Windy: Now can I clarify something. By awful do you mean that it is the end of the world or very bad but not the end of the world?

Rosemary: Well it feels as if it is the end of the world. I know it's not, but that's the way it feels.

Windy: And when it feels that way, what do you believe?

Rosemary: That it is the end of the world.

[Note that at this point the client is referring to her feelings. As you are encouraging her to identify her belief then this is a very good way of getting her to do so. Later when you move on to the disputing stage of the change process you will want to show your client that her feelings are not a good guide for judging the rationality of a belief.]

(i) *Pain in the neck hassle vs end of the world horror*. Another good way of helping your client to distinguish between awful and very bad was originated by the late Howard Young who worked with lower-class clients from West Virginia, USA (Dryden, 1989). His approach was to put two categories on a board: 'Pain in the Neck Hassle' and 'End of the World Horror' and have clients assign the event being discussed to one or other category. Whilst this method is valuable, in my experience it is not a good technique to use when the client has experienced a personal tragedy because the client will have a negative reaction to his tragedy being seen as a 'pain in the neck hassle', however great that hassle is. In such situations a different approach is called for.

(ii) *Tragedies aren't awful*. If your client has experienced a personal tragedy such as losing a child or learning that she has an inoperable tumour, then it is important that you go out of your way to empathise with her situation and emphasize that this A is a personal tragedy. For reasons discussed above, do not label it as 'a pain in the neck hassle' or 'something unfortunate'. Call it what it is — a tragedy. However, the rational position is that tragedies are tragic, but not awful. This is so because unfortunately such events do happen and no one is immune from them. Because a tragedy is tragic (but not awful), encourage your client to express strong healthy distress about it and help her to see that when she believes such things as 'this absolutely should not have happened to me', a demand which leads to awfulizing, then she is adding emotional disturbance to personal tragedy.

(d) Teach your client the difference between unconditional and conditional self-acceptance. I noted earlier that unconditional self-acceptance is a rational, healthy perspective on the self. REBT views the self as an intrinsically fallible, complex, ongoing ever-changing process which defies the ascription of a single global rating. Sometimes, however, when clients believe that they accept themselves, they do so only conditionally. Thus, your client may say that even though she has made a series of errors, she can accept herself as a fallible human being for so doing. However, on further examination, it transpires that your client is only accepting herself because her mistakes were minor and that she would condemn herself if these errors were more serious. Thus, what seems to be a rational belief turns out, on further exploration, to be an irrational belief. In this case, your client is still adhering to the principle of conditional self-acceptance. Unconditional self-acceptance, on the other hand, means accepting oneself as a fallible, complex, ongoing process no matter how serious one's errors.

(e) Help your client to specify his full rational belief. One reason why your client may not be able to differentiate his irrational beliefs from his rational beliefs is that he fails to specify the full version of his rational beliefs. As I mentioned earlier, the full version of a rational belief has two components: the assertion of a rational component and the negation of an irrational component. The main reason that I strongly suggest that you help your client to specify the full form of his rational beliefs is that otherwise he may easily change the partial form of his rational to an irrational belief. He will especially tend to do this when his rational belief is strong. Let me now illustrate some of these points; in doing so I will put the full version of the rational belief first. Then I will give the partial version of the rational belief and show how your client may impli-citly change this partial rational belief into an irrational belief. I want to stress at the outset that the only reliable way of helping your client to distinguish between irrational beliefs and rational beliefs is by contrasting an irrational belief with the full form of the rational belief. The following examples will help you to see why. If they do not, discuss the examples with your trainee colleagues and/or ask for guidance from your REBT trainer or supervisor.

(i) Distinguishing preferences from absolute musts.

Full preference: 'I would like to do well in my new job, BUT I DON'T HAVE TO DO SO.'

Partial preference: 'I would like to do well in my new job.'

Partial preference changed implicitly into a must: 'I would like to do well in my new job (and therefore I must do so).'

Must: I must do well in my new job.

(ii) Distinguishing anti-awfulizing from awfulizing beliefs.

Full anti-awfulizing belief: 'It would be bad if I did not do well in my new job, BUT IT WOULDN'T BE AWFUL.'

Partial anti-awfulizing belief: 'It would be bad if I did not do well in my new job.'

Partial anti-awfulizing belief changed implicitly into an awfulizing belief: 'It would be bad if I did not do well in my new job (indeed it would not only be bad it would be awful).'

Awfulizing belief: 'It would be awful if I did not do well in my new job.'

(iii) Distinguishing high frustration tolerance (HFT) from low frustration tolerance (LFT) beliefs.

Full HFT belief: 'With difficulty I could tolerate not doing well in my new job; HOWEVER, THERE'S NO REASON WHY I COULDN'T STAND IT.'

Partial HFT belief: 'With difficulty I could tolerate not doing well in my new job.'

Partial HFT belief changed implicitly into an LFT belief: 'With difficulty I could tolerate not doing well in my new job (but really this would be too much to stand).'

LFT belief: 'I couldn't stand not doing well in my new job.'

(iv) Distinguishing self-acceptance from self-downing beliefs.

Full self-acceptance belief: 'If I do not do well in my new job, I can accept myself as a fallible human being. MY WORTH TO MYSELF DOES NOT CHANGE, NO MATTER HOW WELL OR POORLY I DO AT WORK.'

Partial self-acceptance belief: 'If I do not do well in my new job, I can accept myself as a fallible human being.'

Partial self-acceptance belief changed implicitly into a self-downing belief: 'If I do not do well in my new job, I can accept myself as a fallible human being (however, I would be more worthy if I did well at work than if I did poorly).'

Self-downing belief: 'If I do not do well in my new job, I am less worthy.'

Having now covered step 4 in some detail, we are ready to move on to the next step.

Unit 46: Step 5. Recognizing That One Needs To Dispute One's Irrational Beliefs to Change Them

Disputing irrational beliefs is such a central part of the practice of REBT that a number of researchers have unfortunately equated the entire therapeutic approach with disputing. As I will show you later, REBT is much more than its disputing elements. However, as these elements are so core, it is important that you help your client to understand this step in the process of therapeutic change. Later in this book I will devote a lot of space to disputing as a skill. Here, however, I will consider it as part of your overall task of teaching your client the REBT change process.

(a) Disputing involves asking questions and giving explanations

As you will see later in this book, disputing basically involves the application of two main skills: asking questions and giving explanations. Whilst you could explain this to your client at this point, it is better if you can help him to see this for himself. One way of doing this is to ask your client how he would respond to you if you held a belief that he considered harmful to you. Let me illustrate.

Windy: So you can now see the role that your irrational beliefs play in 'creating' and maintaining your psychological problems and the importance of distinguishing these beliefs from their rational counterparts.

[These are, of course steps 3 and 4 in the REBT change process as described above.]

Now what do you think you need to do with these beliefs?

Jack: Change them.

Windy: How do you think you could do this?

Jack: I don't know. I'm hoping you can tell me.

Windy: Well, let's see if you can answer that question for yourself. This is going to sound strange...

[Note how I prepare the client for what may well seem strange to him.]

...but bear with me, because I think you'll be able to get the answer to your question in a way that will be more memorable than if I told you direct. Will you bear with me?

[Note that I ask permission before proceeding.]

Jack: OK.

Windy: Imagine that our roles were reversed — I was the client and you were my therapist. It transpires that I have a belief about myself that I am worthless because my girlfriend left me. Is that a healthy idea for me to hold?

Jack: No, of course not.

Windy: Is it important for me to change it?

Jack: Undoubtedly.

Windy: So let's start the role play and let's record it so you can hear later which methods you used to help me to change. Remember you're the therapist and I'm your client. I'll start off.

Windy (as client): I'm so depressed. My girlfriend left me and that proves I'm worthless.

Jack (as therapist): Is everyone whose girlfriend leaves them worthless or just you?

Windy: But I don't care about everyone. I'm the one who is depressed and I'm the one who is worthless.

Jack: But just because she left you, how does that prove you are worthless?

Windy: Because I feel in my gut that I am.

Jack: But that feeling proves nothing apart from that you have an emotional pain in the gut. What you are doing is taking a painful event like losing your girlfriend and proving to yourself that this means that you are worthless. But it means nothing of the kind. It means that you are the same person as you were before she left you, but you are now without her.

Windy (as therapist): That was very good, Jack. Now let's play back the tape and review what you did to try and help me re-evaluate my unhelpful belief.

[We then review the tape and I encourage Jack to categorise his responses.]

Windy: So, Jack, how did you try to help me to change my belief?

Jack (as client): Well, I started off by asking you questions and then when it looked as if I wasn't going to get anywhere with my questions, I explained to you why you weren't worthless.

Windy: Now, that's exactly what I plan to do with you. I plan to ask you questions about your irrational beliefs so that you can re-evaluate them. If we get stuck then I'll give you short explanations on important points.

(b) Disputing involves using empirical, logical and pragmatic arguments

As I will show you later in this book (see Module 15), REBT therapists use empirical, logical and pragmatic arguments to help their clients re-evaluate their irrational beliefs. In that module, I will demonstrate how to employ such arguments in the context of your disputing work. My objective here, however, is different. It is to help you to educate your client to understand these arguments before you use them. I will now show you how I use one such method which is based on the idea of embodying these arguments in the person of three different professionals.

Windy: So, Jack, you now know that I will be using a combination of questions and explanations in helping you to re-evaluate your irrational beliefs. In doing so, I will be using three major arguments with you. Do you know what these arguments might be?

Jack: I have no idea at all.

Windy: Most people don't, but it is important that you understand what these arguments are before we start. Now these arguments are based on the approach of three different types of professionals. Each of these categories has a different way of understanding their subject. The three professionals are scientists, philosophers and personal finance consultants. Let's start with scientists. How do scientists go about understanding the world?

Jack: Well, they look for evidence.

Windy: That's right. First, they set up hypotheses based on an underlying theory and then they look for evidence in the world that either strengthens or disconfirms their hypotheses. In REBT we call arguments based on the scientific method empirical arguments and in using them we are basically interested in helping you judge whether or not your irrational beliefs are consistent with reality.

Now let's consider philosophers and here I have in mind philosophers who are particularly concerned with logic. What do they do?

Jack: Well, they're concerned with looking at those funny looking formulas and judging what's logical or not.

Windy: That's right. In REBT we employ logical arguments and in using them we are basically interested in helping you judge whether or not your irrational beliefs are logical.

Finally, let's consider personal finance consultants. What do they do?

Jack: They line their own pockets, selling you bad investments.

Windy: (laughs) So you've met some! OK, what are they supposed to do?

Jack: Those on your side give you advice concerning which investments will be best for you.

Windy: Right, and if you want to invest in something that won't give a good return they use arguments showing you that it isn't in your best interest to make such an investment. In REBT we call these pragmatic arguments and in using them we are basically interested in helping you judge whether or not your irrational beliefs lead to good or bad emotional and behavioral results. So when I dispute your irrational beliefs sometimes I will be acting like a scientist, sometimes like a philosopher interested in logic and sometimes like a personal finance consultant who has your interests at heart. Do you have any questions?

Jack: Is this something that I can do for myself?

Windy: Thanks for reminding me. That's a very important point. Yes indeed, this is something that you can do for yourself. After a while, as we get into the disputing process, you'll find that you will be able to use the empirical, logical and pragmatic arguments with yourself when you are able to identify the irrational beliefs that underpin your disturbed emotions.

(c) Disputing involves weakening irrational beliefs and strengthening rational beliefs.

The goals of disputing are twofold: first, to help clients to weaken their conviction in their irrational beliefs and, second, to help them to strengthen their conviction in their rational beliefs. How can you help your client to understand this? I often use the following analogy.

Windy: Do you know what you can realistically expect from disputing?

Jack: No.

Windy: May I use an analogy to explain?

[Note once again that I seek permission before proceeding.]

Jack: OK.

Windy: Imagine that you have grown up believing that the number 13 is bad luck. Being a rational individual you want to overcome this superstition. How would you go about doing that?

Jack: Well I would show myself all the reasons why the superstition is probably false and ...(pause)...

Windy: Well there are really two ideas. The first idea is that 13 is unlucky.

You really believe it is true, although you can see it is probably false and you want to change it. The other idea is that 13 is neither unlucky nor lucky. You want to believe this, but at present you don't. Now as you said you can review all the reasons why the idea '13 is unlucky' is probably false...

Jack: Oh, I see. I would also review the reasons why the idea '13 is neither lucky nor unlucky' is probably true.

Windy: Exactly. You can do this using logic and evidence as discussed above. You can do the former just by using your mind, but the latter involves coming into frequent contact with the number 13 and seeing what happens. Now, let's suppose that you do this. What will happen to your degree of conviction in the two ideas?

Jack: Well, I'd gradually stop believing in the idea '13 is unlucky' and gradually start believing in the idea '13 is neither lucky nor unlucky'.

Windy: That is exactly right and this is what happens when you dispute your irrational beliefs. You weaken your conviction in your irrational beliefs and...

Jack: Strengthen my conviction in my rational beliefs. That makes sense. I wouldn't have expected to change my irrational beliefs just like that. (Clicks his fingers to indicate a magical change.)

You have now educated your client in three respects concerning disputing. First you showed that you will be asking questions and giving explanations. Second, you explained the nature of the three main arguments you will be using as part of the disputing process. Finally, you helped him to understand that disputing involves weakening irrational beliefs and strengthening rational beliefs. I will discuss the more technical and strategic aspects of disputing in Modules 15–18. Having prepared your client to understand step 5 of the change process, you are now ready to proceed to step 6.

Unit 47: Step 6. Recognizing That One Needs To Work Towards the Internalization of New Rational Beliefs by Employing Cognitive, Behavioral and Emotive Methods of Change

Clients often come to therapy with a number of implicit ideas about the process. Some believe, for example, that all they have to do is to attend therapy sessions and that something magical or mystical will happen as a result. Others realize that they have to be active in the therapeutic process, but believe that all change occurs within therapy sessions. REBT's response is a tough one for such clients to digest. It argues that there is nothing magical about the process of therapy, that change involves active participation of the client both within and particularly outside counseling sessions and that, generally speaking, the more change you desire the harder you need to work on yourself outside therapy. How do I know that most clients want an easy ride from therapy? Because of their response to the following technique. Try it for yourself and see.

Windy: Now, Jill, let me ask you a few questions concerning your view of therapy. First, would you like to make progress very quickly, moderately quickly or slowly.

Jill: Very quickly.

Windy: Now would you like therapy to be very uncomfortable, moderately uncomfortable or comfortable?

Jill: Comfortable.

Windy: So you want therapy to be a comfortable experience where you make progress very quickly?

Jill: The way you've put it, it sounds unrealistic.

Windy: Why?

Jill: Because things don't work that way.

Windy: How do they work?

Jill: The quicker you want to change the more uncomfortable it will be.

Let me now show you how to deal with a number of issues that are relevant to the process of internalising rational beliefs.

(a) Helping your client to distinguish between intellectual insight and emotional insight

During the process of disputing your client's irrational beliefs, it is likely that she will say something like: 'What you say makes perfect sense to me, but I don't believe it' or ' I see what you're saying in my head, but I don't feel it in my gut.' When your client makes such a statement, she is in effect saying that she has intellectual insight into the rational point you have been making, but she does not have emotional insight into the concept. In a brief but important paper published over thirty years ago, Albert Ellis (1963) considered intellectual insight to be a light, occasionally held conviction in a rational belief which does not have an impact on the person's feelings and behavior, whereas emotional insight is a strong, frequently held conviction in a rational belief which does make a difference to the way the person feels and acts. How can you get this point over to your client? The following are two examples that I use frequently.

(i) The 'Weed–Flower' Analogy I

Windy: So what you are saying is that whilst you see what I'm saying about not needing your mother-in-law's approval you don't believe it.

Jill: Exactly.

Windy: This is an important point. Will you bear with me while I use another analogy to help you understand the point?

[Once again I ask for my client's permission here, for reasons that you should (hopefully!) recall.]

Jill: OK.

Windy: Do you have a garden?

Jill: I do.

Windy: Are you a keen gardener?

Jill: I wouldn't say I was a keen gardener, but I do a bit.

Windy: Does your garden have any weeds in it?

Jill: Weeds? They're the bane of my life.

Windy: Mine too. How do you control them?

Jill: By digging them out at the roots and putting down weedkiller.

Windy: Right. Do you have flowers in your garden?

Jill: Some.

Windy: After you plant them, do they require any attention?

Jill: Yes, I have to water them and make sure the birds don't get at them.

Windy: Why do you do that?

Jill: Because I want them to grow to their full capacity.

Windy: And if you didn't look after them, what would happen?

Jill: They would have stunted growth or if I neglected them totally they would die.

Windy: That's right. What relevance do you think this has for your rational and irrational beliefs?

Jill: That if I don't dig up or dispute my irrational beliefs, I won't change them and if I don't look after or prove the rationality of my rational beliefs, they won't grow.

Windy: Excellent. Now let me extend this analogy to help you distinguish between intellectual and emotional insight. Let's take the garden situation first. Suppose you know what to do in order to have a nice garden, but you don't do it. What effect would your knowledge alone have on your garden?

Jill: None at all.

Windy: Why's that?

Jill: Because knowledge without action isn't going to water the flowers or uproot the weeds.

Windy: Exactly. That kind of knowledge or what we call intellectual insight in REBT has no impact on action and as you say without action the garden will deteriorate. Now if we apply this point to rational and irrational beliefs, what conclusion do we come to?

Jill: That knowing why a belief is irrational and why another belief is rational won't make a difference unless one acts on that knowledge.

Windy: Good point. Unless you think and act against your irrational beliefs and in ways that are consistent with your rational beliefs, your insight into rational principles will be intellectual; you won't really believe them and thus your knowledge will have little if any impact on your feelings and behaviors. However, what is more likely to happen if you do act on your knowledge that you need to think and act against your irrational beliefs in a way that is consistent with your rational beliefs?

Jill: I am likely to really believe it.

Windy: That's right. Your insight into your rational belief, for example, will be emotional in the sense that you really believe it and that strong conviction will make a real difference to how you feel and act.

(ii) The Tennis Player Analogy I

This analogy makes a similar point to the Weed–Flower Analogy I. In addition, it is particularly useful when you wish to make the point that changing an ingrained habit like irrational thinking involves putting up with and working through an uncomfortable phase of unnaturalness.

Windy: Now, how often do you think you will have to question and change your irrational beliefs before you begin to believe the alternative rational beliefs?

Ian: Quite frequently.

Windy: Why?

Ian: Because I've held my irrational beliefs for a long time.

Windy: That's right. Now let me use an analogy to help you to understand a few important points about change. Is that OK?

Ian: Fine.

Windy: Imagine when you were much younger you wanted to play tennis and had saved up your pocket money for some lessons from a tennis coach. On your way to your first lesson you met your favourite uncle who asked you where you were going and you explained about the tennis lessons. He told you that he could play tennis very well and offered to teach you for nothing. The thought of the free lessons and the idea of all the other things you could do with your pocket money was very enticing to you so you agreed. Over the next six months, your uncle gave you weekly tennis lessons, but unfortunately he taught you incorrectly, but as you were very enthusiastic, you diligently practiced the wrong strokes not knowing at that time that you were developing some very bad habits. However, the more you played against other young tennis players, the more defeats you suffered. Later you realized what had happened, so you went to have some tennis lessons from a professional tennis coach. She was able to diagnose your faults and taught and demonstrated how to play the various tennis strokes properly. Now would knowing how to play the correct strokes help to improve your game?

Ian: No, of course not.

Windy: Why not?

Ian: Because I would not have done any practice.

Windy: Right. Now let's suppose that you started to practice the new strokes. Would you be comfortable playing the new strokes?

Ian: Not at all.

Windy: Why not?

Ian: Because I would be accustomed to playing the old, incorrect strokes.

Windy: So it would feel natural to play the old stokes and unnatural to play the new ones.

Ian: Yes.

Windy: But would that unnatural feeling stop you from correcting the stroke when you started to play in the old, incorrect but natural manner?

Ian: No, it wouldn't.

Windy: Now it's the same with changing your irrational beliefs. The next time you fail to master something new the first time you will undoubtedly think that you are a failure. Why do I say undoubtedly here?

Ian: Because that is what I've believed in the past and it's natural for me to think that way.

Windy: That's right. However, if you go against that natural feeling you can detect, dispute and change your belief to a rational belief and keep doing so until...?

Ian: Until the rational belief becomes more natural to me.

Windy: Also the more you act against the old irrational belief and according to the newer rational belief, the more you will be convinced by the new rational belief and the less you will believe the old belief. This is what some people call going from 'head thinking' to 'gut thinking'. What do you understand by these terms?

Ian: 'Head thinking' sounds like it means understanding something in your head, but not truly believing it, whereas 'gut thinking' sounds like it means believing it in your guts.

Windy: That's exactly it. Which type of thinking is likely to change your feelings and actions when you fail to master something the first time?

Ian: 'Gut thinking' obviously.

Windy: Does believing something new in your gut take a lot of practice or does it happen without too much practice?

Ian: No, it sounds like it will take a lot of practice.

Windy: Are you willing to do that practice if it increases your chances of getting over your anxiety about trying new things?

Ian: Yes, I am.

(b) Helping your client to understand the importance of between-session as well as in-session work

Whilst the above methods which help your client distinguish between intellectual and emotional insight imply that she needs to work to effect change between sessions as well as within sessions, it is still important to make this point explicit. I often use an extension of the Tennis Player Analogy to underscore the central role that between-session work has in the REBT change process.

(i) The Tennis Player Analogy II

Windy: Now, let me go back to the tennis analogy for the moment, if I may, to stress another point about the change process. Is that OK?

Ian: Fine.

Windy: Remember that you have decided to go for tennis lessons to correct the bad habits you developed when your uncle taught you all the wrong strokes and you practiced them diligently.

Ian: Fine.

Windy: Imagine this scenario. You attend tennis lessons once a week and each lesson lasts for one hour. In the first part of the lesson your coach watches your game, points out your errors and models the correct strokes, whilst in the second half you practice what you have learned with the occasional prompt from your mentor. Now let's suppose that you do no practice in between sessions. What will happen to your tennis game?

Ian: Well, I won't improve.

Windy: Why not?

Ian: That's obvious. I won't improve because I'm not practicing what I am learning.

Windy: Yes you are, you're getting in the practice in the second half of the lesson.

Ian: But that's not enough.

Windy: Why not?

Ian: For two reasons. First, in order to become proficient at the skill I need to practice it much more frequently than once a week, particularly when I have first learned that skill.

Windy: And the second reason?

Ian: Well, I need to work extra hard to practice that new skill because my old poor habits are still well ingrained. And once a week practice won't really do anything to change things around.

Windy: What do you need to do then?

Ian: If I can find the time, I'd need to practice once a day rather than once week.

Windy: Now let's apply this to the therapy situation and the practice you need to do to change your irrational beliefs. What do you think the implication of this is for therapy?

Ian: Well, the implication seems to be that if I only practice thinking rationally in this room, then I won't get much benefit from therapy.

Windy: What do you need to do to benefit from therapy, which in this case means making the new rational beliefs your own?

Ian: I need to practice disputing my irrational beliefs and strengthening my rational beliefs fairly frequently.

Windy: Like once a day?

Ian: Like once a day.

After your client has understood that he needs to work fairly frequently if he is to begin to internalize his rational beliefs, you can begin to raise the issue of how much work your client is prepared to do. Note that I did this in a general way at the end of the Tennis Player Analogy II. In the following approach, I seek to encourage my client to commit himself to a specified number of hours of DELIBERATE psychological work. I have stressed the word 'deliberate' here because I do not wish to preclude the client from doing such work at other unplanned times.

(ii) The 168 hour week

Windy: So, Ian, you can see the importance of doing therapy work between sessions otherwise it is unlikely that you will derive much benefit from therapy. Is that right?

Ian: Yes, I can see that.

Windy: Now, let's talk about how much time you are prepared to commit yourself to doing that work on yourself in a planned fashion. Now there are 168 hours in a week minus this therapy hour leaving us 167 hours. How many of these hours are you prepared to commit to helping yourself over your emotional problems?

Ian: Let me see. I guess fourteen hours.

[It is important to note that, when you ask the above question in the way that I have done, you will invariably get an unrealistic answer from your client. Very few clients will be prepared to commit as many as ten hours per week to therapy work. Note how I deal with this issue. However, I maintain that helping clients to negotiate downwards on the number of hours they are prepared to work on themselves per week is more effective than helping them to negotiate upwards. This hypothesis awaits empirical enquiry.]

Windy: Are you sure you want to commit yourself to two hours' self-therapy every day given your busy lifestyle?

Ian: No, I guess that is a bit unrealistic.

Windy: What would be more realistic?

Ian: I guess half an hour a day would be possible.

Windy: When in the day would you do this?

Ian: In the morning before work would be possible.

Windy: But don't you jog every morning before going to work?

Ian: That's a point. I'd forgotten about that.

Windy: Given that fact, when would be the best time?

Ian: Well in the week, I think between 7pm and 7.30 pm would be a good time and on weekends between 4 pm and 4.30 pm would be possible.

Windy: Only possible?

Ian: No, definite.

Windy: So. let me recap. You agree to do 30 minutes planned work on yourself a day. In the week that will take place between 7 pm and 7.30 pm and on Saturdays and Sundays between 4 pm and 4.30 pm. Agreed?

Ian: Agreed.

Windy: Let's shake on it.

[As I will discuss further in Module 11, Unit 50, it is important to encourage clients to think carefully about when they are to carry out between-session (or homework) assignments and to commit themselves to do them. Note how I intervened to help Ian make an informed decision and commitment on the issue of planned self-therapy.]

Now can you see that this doesn't stop you from using what you learn here at other times when relevant issues crop up?

Ian: Yes, I can.

(c) Helping your client to see the importance of using cognitive, emotive and behavioral methods of change

Whilst REBT is properly considered to be one of the cognitive-behavioral therapies, it does not neglect emotion in the process of personal change. However, because there is an emphasis on promoting philosophic change in REBT, much time in therapy sessions is spent on its cognitive restructuring aspects. This could lead clients to think that any between-session work that they will be invited to do will be exclusively cognitive in nature. This is far from the case, for REBT argues that clients need to use cognitive (including imaginal) methods, behavioral and emotive methods if they are to internalize a rational philosophy. How might you get this point over to your client? By using the following arguments.

(i) The importance of behavioral methods used in conjunction with cognitive methods

Windy: So, Brian, you can now see that believing that you must not be rejected by a woman that you ask out for a date is irrational and it would be far better for you to believe that it would be undesirable if you were rejected, but there is no law that says that you must not be turned down. Is that right?

Brian: Yes it is.

Windy: You also understand that in order to weaken your irrational belief and strengthen your rational belief you need to do what?

Brian: A lot of work between therapy sessions.

Windy: Right. But the question is what kind of work. Let me outline a number of ways in which you could do this work. I'll outline them all and then you can tell me which way would be most effective. OK?

Brian: OK.

Windy: The first way would be for you to sit at home every night imagining that you are asking women out, picturing them rejecting you and practicing your new rational belief to the image of rejection. The second way would be for you to ask women out in reality until you are rejected a number of times. However, while you do so you do not deliberately try to change your irrational beliefs, hoping that the exposure alone will lead to belief change. The third and final way involves the same exposure as I discussed in the second approach, but this time you deliberately show yourself the rational belief. Thus before, during and after any rejection, you show yourself that it is undesirable to be rejected, but there's no reason why you must not be rejected.

Now which of these three methods are likely to be most effective in helping you internalize your new rational philosophy?

Brian: The last.

Windy: Why?

Brian: Because it involves both action and rethinking.

Windy: That's very well put. Now what about the remaining two approaches?

Brian: Well, they have their strengths and weaknesses. The imagery one is good because it gets me to practice the new way of thinking. But it doesn't involve me doing anything. It lacks that immediate punch of being rejected which would be present if it actually happened.

[Brian's point that imagery doesn't provide him with the necessary 'punch' is true for many but certainly not all clients. Clients vary widely according to their ability to imagine critical As in a vivid fashion.]

Brian (cont.): This approach might be a good preparation for the acting-rethinking approach.

Windy: And that's how it is frequently used. Now, what about the behavioral approach without the rethinking?

Brian: Well, that's good because it gets me actually to go out and ask women out, but if I don't consciously remind myself of the new belief as you said a minute ago, before, during and after the event, I may well go back to my old way of thinking.

Windy: Right, so what do you conclude from all this?

Brian: That the best way to really sink in the new belief is by actually doing what I am afraid of doing while practicing the new belief at the same time.

Windy: Right. You can't do this for every problem, but where you can it really is the best approach.

(ii) The importance of emotive force in the change process

Windy: So far, Brian, we've seen that using behavioral and rethinking methods hand in hand is a powerful way to 'sink in' the new belief as you called it. Now there's another important point about the change process that is important in this respect. It's relevant in a number of areas, but I'll just mention one if I may?

Brian: Fine. Go ahead.

Windy: Let me first take the scenario where you actually go out and ask a woman for a date and she rejects you. Is it better to say to yourself in a quiet, weak manner: 'This is undesirable, but there's no reason why she must accept my invitation' or to say to yourself in a very forceful, emotive manner something like: 'THIS IS UNDESIRABLE, BUT THERE'S NO DAMNED REASON WHY SHE HAS TO GO OUT WITH ME!'?

Brian: Definitely the latter.

Windy: Why?

Brian: Because it is powerful and I am more likely to listen to myself. If I'm too meek in what I say to myself, I may not even hear myself and I may go back to my irrational belief.

Windy: That's right. Indeed, it is for this reason that I recommend that people use strong, good old Anglo-Saxon swear words in their head. In the past when you have been anxious about asking women out, did you express your irrational thoughts to yourself in quiet, polite language?

Brian: Not at all. My language would have made a sailor blush!

Windy: That's why I recommend that you use profanity, to get through to yourself and to fight fire with fire. Does that make sense?

Brian: Definitely.

[A number of therapists consider this suggestion controversial. But it is best seen as helping the client to use his or her own language. If your client claims not to use profane language to herself, it is often best to refrain from suggesting that she begins to do so.]

Windy: The point I want to stress here, Brian, is that the more you can engage your emotions in the change process, the better. Going over your new beliefs in a strong and forceful manner is one very good way of doing this.

[I should point out that it is important that your client does, in fact, have intellectual insight into the rational belief before using this approach. If she does not, the use of emotive force won't help her to acquire it.]

(iii) Emotional change often lingers behind behavioral and cognitive change

There is one clinically observed fact about the change process that your client needs to understand fully if she is to persist at working to internalize her new rational beliefs. It is that your client's emotions will change after she has changed the way she acts and after she has begun to change her irrational beliefs. If your client does not appreciate this she may well give up changing her behavior and beliefs with the predictable result that she will relapse. The reasons why emotions are the last to change are complex, but need to be explained, in simplified form, if your client is to persist at carrying out forceful, cognitive-behavioral assignments without experiencing immediate or even intermediate affective benefit. Here is how I convey this to clients. Note that I normally do so after I have shown them the importance of carrying out such assignments.

Windy: OK, Brian. So far you have seen the importance of carrying out behavioral and rethinking methods at the same time and, if you can, to do this with emotive force. Right?

Brian: Right.

Windy: Now, there's an important point that I want to make in this context. My experience as a therapist has led me to the following conclusion: you will need to keep changing your behavior and your way of thinking for quite a time before you notice any significant change in your emotions. I wish things were otherwise, but this is what most of my clients report.

Brian: Why should that be the case?

Windy: Well, I'm not entirely sure, but my hunch is as follows. It is fairly easy to change behavior. I know that you find it difficult asking women out, but you'd do so to save the life of a loved one. Wouldn't you?

Brian: Certainly.

Windy: Now it is also relatively easy to change your self-statements at least at one level. Thus, you can fairly easily tell yourself something like, 'It is undesirable to be rejected, but there's no reason why I must not be rejected.' You won't believe it at first, of course, and you will need to do a lot of rethinking and behavioral change to begin to believe it deeply. Now it is at this stage when your emotions begin to change in a significant way. But you need to do a lot of forceful cognitive and behavioral work first before this happens. Thus, when you begin to get discouraged when your feelings haven't changed even though you are working hard at the cognitive and behavioral levels, what do you need to say to yourself?

Brian: That it's worth persisting because my feelings take longer to change than my behaviors and my thoughts.

Windy: Think of it like this. Imagine that you are going to have a bet on a greyhound race. It is a three-dog race, one dog is called 'Behavior', one called 'Thinking' and the third is called 'Emotion'. Having read about all three dogs, you decide to put your money on 'Emotion' even though it is a very slow starter indeed. Now, the race gets under way and, true to form, 'Emotion' stays in the trap while 'Behavior' and 'Thinking' are out there racing around the track. Would you tear up your betting slip and quit?

Brian: No, I wouldn't.

Windy: Why not?

Brian: Because I know that my dog is a notoriously slow starter, so I would hang in there and wait until it decides to get started. I know that it will catch up in the end.

Windy: Excellent reasons. Now that is exactly what I want you to do with your cognitive and behavioral assignments. Keep doing them because your feelings are like the dog called 'Emotion' — slow to get started but, after a while, quick to catch up.

Brian: I'll remember that.

(iv) Therapeutic progress is uneven

Even when your client consistently works hard to challenge irrational beliefs and acts on his rational beliefs, his progress will be uneven. It is important to forewarn your client of this ubiquitous therapeutic phenomenon, otherwise he may well become discouraged and give up working to change himself. How can you get the 'uneven progress' idea over to your client? Here is one way.

The Golf Analogy

Windy: Once your emotions do start to change and you can see that you are making progress, do you think that your rate of progress will be smooth or even?

Brian: I'm not sure.

Windy: Well, let's suppose that you have been learning to play golf and that you have started to feel comfortable playing all the correct shots. Now do you think that the more you continue to practice, the more you will improve?

Brian: Yes, as long as I don't practice morning, noon and night.

Windy: That's a good point, you can spoil your game by too much practice. But within sensible limits...

Brian: Within reasonable limits, the more you practice the more you will improve.

Windy: But do you think that even though the overall curve will be upwards, you will experience downturns along the way?

Brian: Yes, I see what you mean, I would go backwards at times.

Windy: Even professional golfers go through bad patches.

Brian: That's right. I remember reading that this happened to Seve Balles-teros a while back.

Windy: Now do you think that the same will happen in therapy?

Brian: Yes, I suppose that it would.

Windy: So when you practice the skills that you are learning here regularly and steadily outside, your overall curve will be upwards, but...?

Brian: Within that, my progress will be uneven. A matter of two steps forward and one step back.

Windy: And sometimes even one step forward and two back. Now we'll be closely monitoring your progress together and sometimes it will be apparent why you are not going forward. But at other times, there won't be any reason other than 'progress is uneven'.

Brian: That it is a natural part of change.

Windy: You've put that more clearly than I have. Exactly. So when you notice that you are not going forwards or even that you are going backwards despite working steadily on yourself, what could you say to yourself?

Brian: That this is part of the territory of therapy. There may be a specific reason for it in which case we can find it and do something about it. On the other hand, it might be just one of those things which happens from time to time and if I persist, I'll come out of it.

Windy: Now do you find that discouraging or hopeful?

Brian: On the hopeful side, although I can't say I'm jumping up and down with joy about it.

Windy: I'd be very concerned if you did!

(v) Dealing with lapses and relapses

The final point that I want to make with respect to the 'internalization' process concerns dealing with lapses and relapses. I define a lapse (or a set-back) as a small or moderate return to previous unhealthy functioning, whereas a relapse is a significant return to unhealthy functioning. As I have shown above, small or moderate set-backs are a frequently occurring (and almost inevitable) part of the change process. To the extent that your client is able to deal constructively with lapses, she will help herself significantly to avoid a more significant relapse, as relapses tend to occur when lapses are not dealt with in a healthy manner. The best way to help your client to avoid relapse is to engage in relapse prevention with her. How might you introduce this concept? Here is one example.

Windy: Well, Rachel, you've made quite a lot of progress on overcoming your bulimia and it seems to me that you have made significant inroads into changing your irrational beliefs.

Rachel: I think so too.

Windy: Now there's one issue that I want to raise with you to help you to maintain and extend your progress. OK?

Rachel: OK.

Windy: I want to do two things here. First, I want to help you to develop a list of activating events both external and internal that you would have difficulty dealing with, that if you don't handle well might lead you to binge. Then I want to help you to develop some solid coping strategies underpinned by healthy rational beliefs that you could use in the face of these As.

Rachel: That sounds like a really good idea.

Windy: After we have done that how would you feel about seeking out some of these situations in graded fashion so that you can practice dealing with them in constructive ways?

Rachel: I don't like the sound of that.

Windy: I didn't think you would. However, it's a bit like having an injection against diphtheria.

Rachel: What do you mean?

Windy: When you are inoculated against a disease like diphtheria, the injection contains a small dose of the disease. Why do you think that is?

Rachel: To mobilise the body's defences to fight against the disease if I encounter it.

Windy: Right. So why do you think that I am asking you to seek out small doses of situations that you are vulnerable to?

Rachel: To mobilise my ability to cope with situations if I encounter them later in full force.

Windy: Now what do you think of the idea?

Rachel: I still don't like it, but it makes sense.

Windy: Will you commit yourself to doing it?

Rachel: Yes.

Windy: Now the second point I want to raise is this. Let's suppose you have a lapse and have a binge–purge episode. How can you turn this into a full-blown relapse?

Rachel: I'm not sure I understand you.

Windy: Well, if you have a lapse as I've described, you can either view that as an unfortunate event which you can learn from or as something that absolutely must not happen in which case you will disturb yourself about it. Which attitude will more likely lead to a relapse?

Rachel: The latter.

Windy: So if you want to stop a lapse turning into a relapse, what do you have to do?

Rachel: Develop a healthy attitude towards it.

Windy: And I'll help you do that.

Unit 48: Step 7. Recognizing That One Needs To Continue the Process of Challenging Irrational Beliefs and Using Multimodal Methods of Change for the Rest of One's Life

It would be nice if we could help our clients to eradicate their irrational beliefs entirely but, as Ellis (1976) notes, this is inconsistent with the human condition which is to create demands out of preferences, particularly when these desires are strong. Given this, how can you educate your client concerning the fact that he needs to work at the process of self-therapy for the rest of his life if he is to maintain and enhance his gains? The following is one such way.

The 'Weed–Flower' Analogy II

Windy: Do you know what you can realistically expect from therapy?

Jack: To eliminate my irrational beliefs?

Windy: Well that would be nice, wouldn't it. But that isn't possible. Do you know why?

Jack: No. Tell me.

Windy: Do you remember the 'Weed–Flower' Analogy?

Jack: I do.

Windy: You will remember, then, that in order to control the weeds in the garden you will have to do what?

Jack: Dig them out and put down weedkiller.

Windy: Which is like showing yourself why your irrational beliefs are irrational. What do you have to do to ensure that your flowers thrive?

Jack: Water them and give them the right protection.

Windy: Which is like showing yourself why your rational beliefs are rational. Now will there ever be a time when you can stop weeding your garden and stop tending the flowers?

Jack: No, you will always have to tend your garden.

Windy: Because if you don't?

Jack: Then the flowers won't grow and the weeds will get out of control.

Windy: Right. Now it's the same thing with your beliefs. There will never be a time when your irrational beliefs will be totally eradicated and your rational beliefs will grow without attention.

Jack: So that means that I will always have to do some work on myself.

Windy: That's right.

Jack: I don't care for that.

Windy: Do you clean your teeth, eat and wash every day?

Jack: Of course.

Windy: Why?

Jack: To maintain physical well-being.

Windy: Do you object to doing that?

Jack: No.

Windy: So why object to doing regular work to maintain your mental well-being?

Jack: I see what you mean. That makes really good sense.

Windy: A well-kept garden is easier to keep than a neglected one, but it will always need attention. And a rational mind is easier to keep healthy than an unhealthy one...

Jack: But it will always need attention.

All the analogies I have used in this module have their limitations. As a training exercise, work with a trainee colleague to identify the limitations of any of the analogies that I have used here and practice ways of dealing with these limitations. Have your colleague play a client who criticises your analogy and see if you can develop good counter-arguments. Take any 'client' criticisms that you cannot counter to your REBT trainer or supervisor. Notwithstanding the limitations of ana-logies, I consider that they nicely show what your client can realistically expect from REBT and they also make clear what he or she has to do to achieve these realistic goals.

Having presented the series of seven therapeutic steps, I will now focus on an important initial stage of facilitating client change: goal-setting and eliciting a commitment to change.

In the following two modules, I will consider two important therapeutic issues. The first concerns effective goal-setting and the second involves you eliciting from your clients a commitment to change. Dealing effectively with these two issues will mean that you will get the REBT change process off on the right foot. Failing to deal with these issues successfully will mean that you will struggle with your clients from the outset.

Module 12
Goal-Setting

It is easy sometimes to lose sight of the fact that the purpose of therapy is to help clients achieve their goals. However, it should also not be forgotten that therapists have goals in therapy. Thus, in a seminal book entitled *The Goals of Psychotherapy* (Mahrer, 1967), the book's editor, concluded from his review of the contributions to the book that therapists have two major types of goals: (a) those concerned with the reduction of psychological disturbance and (b) those concerned with the promotion of psychological health. As a therapist, the more you can encourage your client to be explicit about his or her goals and the more you can be explicit about your goals, the better. Doing so will enable the two of you to work cooperatively toward agreed goals. Such cooperative striving towards the achievement of agreed goals is, as Bordin (1979) has argued, an important hallmark of effective therapy.

As I have already argued, REBT is an approach to psychotherapy that stresses the importance of explicit, open communication between therapist and client. It also recommends that you set goals with your clients. Thus, this therapeutic system encourages you to engage in the very activities that will help promote effective therapeutic change.

In this module, I will deal with goals at three levels. First, I will consider goals in relation to dealing with specific examples of your clients' problems. Then, I will consider goals in relation to your clients' problems as these are broadly conceptualised. Third, I will consider the issue of goals as they relate to the distinction between reducing disturbance and promoting growth.

Unit 49: Setting a Goal With a Specific Example of Your Client's Problem

Let me outline the steps for effective goal-setting in REBT as these relate to specific examples of your client's target problem. As you will see, this is not the simple process it may appear at first sight.

Steps for effective goal-setting

In this section I will outline the steps that you need to take in order to set therapeutic goals with your client with respect to specific examples of his or her target problems. Whilst your client may well have more than one problem, I will deal with the situation where you are working with a given client problem. I want to stress one point at the outset. Whilst I will outline the steps you need to take to elicit your client's goals for change in the sequence that I suggest you carry them out, it is important for you to note that you will do so at more than one point in the therapeutic process. For example, I make an important distinction between the client's DEFINED PROBLEM and his ASSESSED PROBLEM. The defined problem is the way the client sees or defines his or her focal concern, whereas the assessed problem is the same problem put into an ABC format. I argue below that it is important to elicit goals for both the defined problem and the assessed problem but, and this is the point that I want to underscore here, this will be done at different times in the REBT therapeutic process. The work you are likely to do on your client's goal as this relates to the assessed problem will occur later, and sometimes much later than the work you will do eliciting his goal as this relates to the defined problem. Remember this as I deal with the following steps.

Step 1: Ask for a specific example of your client's target problem

The first step in the goal-setting process is to encourage your client to give you a specific example of his or her more general problem. As discussed in Unit 18, you can best assess your client's target problem if he or she provides you with a specific example of it because this will help you to identify a specific critical A, a specific unhealthy negative emotion and specific irrational beliefs.

Step 2. Communicate your understanding of the problem from the client's point of view and come to an agreement with him or her on this defined problem

The second step is for you to understand how he or she sees the problem and to communicate this understanding to the client. This is important for two reasons. First, it helps your client to 'feel' understood. Second, knowing how your client sees the problem will help you to assess it using the ABC framework. It is at this point that your basic counseling skills come into play. As you need to convey understanding, the skills of clarification and reflection are particularly useful. In addition, you will need to phrase your attempts at understanding as just that — attempts. As such, there needs to be a tentative quality to your interventions which need to be put as hunches to be confirmed or denied rather than as incontrovertible facts.

For example, it is best to say: 'So, you seem to find it difficult getting down to studying when you know that your friends are out having a good time. Have I understood you correctly', rather than 'You find it difficult getting down to studying when you know that your friends are out having a good time.'

In the former statement, the therapist has phrased the statement in a tentative fashion and has put understanding as a hunch which he or she is testing. This enables the client to correct the therapist if the therapist is off track. In the latter statement, however, the therapist has phrased the statement more definitely and has not checked out his or her understanding of what the client has said, assuming that he or she has got it right. This makes it more difficult for the client to correct the therapist if he or she is off beam.

The purpose of being tentative and testing out one's hunches is that you want to come to an agreed understanding with your client on the problem as he or she sees it. I call this 'coming to an agreement with the client on the DEFINED PROBLEM'. Later in the goal-setting process, you will need to arrive at an agreement with the client on the ASSESSED PROBLEM.

Step 3. Elicit the client's goal with respect to the defined problem

It is useful to elicit the client's goal in relation to the defined problem. Whilst this goal may change once you have assessed the problem, nevertheless it is helpful to learn in which direction your client is thinking with respect to what he or she considers a satisfactory outcome of the problem. Indeed, it is here that you will frequently discover that your client has unrealistic or unobtainable goals for change. If so, you will need to confront this issue. Whether you do so at the point when your client has revealed his unrealistic or unobtainable goal or whether you choose to do so later, you do have to deal with the issue; otherwise, your client will think that you agree with the problematic (i.e. from your perspective) goal when, in fact, you don't. I will discuss how to deal with unrealistic and unobtainable goals in a moment, but first let me show you how you might usefully elicit your client's goal with respect to the defined problem.

Let me use the example that I introduced above. As a reminder the client (whose name is Clare) defined her problem as follows: 'I find it difficult getting down to studying when I know that my friends are out having a good time.'

Here is how I would work with Clare to identify her goal as it relates to this defined problem.

Windy: So you find it difficult getting down to studying when you know your friends are out having a good time. What would you like to achieve from counseling on this issue?

[Alternative questions might include:

(i) What would you like to be able to do instead?
(i) How would you like to change?
(iii) What would be in your best interests to do?]

Clare: To be able to study even when I know my friends are out enjoying themselves.

If Clare replied that she didn't know, I would have employed other techniques such as:

* Imagery: This involves having your client imagine a preferred solution to her problem (e.g. 'Close your eyes and imagine a scene where you are doing what is productive for you even when your friends are out enjoying themselves. What would you be doing in that image?'). Having elicited this preferred scenario, ask the client to give reasons for her choice.

* Time projection: This involves your client projecting herself into the future and stating how she would like to have acted at the time in question (e.g. 'Imagine that we are a year in the future. Looking back, would you rather have studied at the time we are discussing or not?'). Then, ask the client to explain her answer.

* A best friend's suggestion: This involves asking your client to imagine how her best friend would suggest she handle the problem. (e.g. 'Would your best friend suggest that you study even though you know that she and others might be out enjoying themselves? If so, why do you think she would say that?'). If you use this technique you need to ensure that your client's best friend does, in fact, have her interests at heart.

* A worst enemy's suggestion: This is the opposite of the best friend's suggestion and is useful in that it helps the person to see that an enemy might be quite happy to see her continue this self-defeating behavior (e.g. 'What would your worst enemy suggest that you do when you know that your friends are out enjoying themselves and you need to study?'). Explore the client's answer and ask her to set a suitable goal at the end of the exploration.

* Therapist suggested options: If none of the above techniques helps to elicit the client's goals on her defined problem, then you as therapist might provide your client with possible goal options. If you do this, it is very important that you give your client an opportunity to discuss those options with you. Your role here is to encourage her to reflect on the advantages and disadvantages of all the provided options as a way of choosing a relevant goal.

Step 4. Dealing with unrealistic and unobtainable goals

It sometimes transpires when you are working with your client to identify her goals with respect to her defined problem that she will nominate goals which are unrealistic or unobtainable. As I pointed out earlier, when your client comes up with such a goal you do need to deal with it, but not necessarily at the precise time when your client discloses it. Thus, whilst making a mental or preferably a written note of this goal, you may choose to wait until you have assessed the client's problem and determined her goal with regard to the assessed problem. When you decide to confront the client on her unrealistic or unobtainable goal must be a matter of clinical judgment and I urge you to discuss such matters with your REBT supervisor. What I will do here is to detail the kinds of client goals which are unrealistic or unobtainable. Then, I will give an example of how to deal with the situation where your client nominates an unrealistic or unobtainable goal in relation to her defined problem.

What are unrealistic and unobtainable goals?

It would be nice if clients set goals for change that were achievable, realistic and involve them changing some aspect of themselves. Suffice it to say, this does not always occur! The following list contains the unrealistic or unobtainable goals that you will most frequently encounter in REBT.

(a) Changing impersonal negative events

Here your client nominates a goal which involves a change in some aspect of the situation (or A) that she is disturbing himself about. Let's suppose King Canute came to see you for counseling. His complaint is that he is unhealthily angry because the tide will not obey him and go back when he orders it to do so. You have accurately defined his problem and go on to ask him for his goal. He replies that he wants you to help him to change the tide so that it goes back at his command. Would you accept this as a legitimate therapeutic goal? Of course you wouldn't. You would explain to King Canute that influencing the tide is outside his control despite the fact that he is a king. You would encourage him instead to set as an achievable goal feeling healthily rather than unhealthily angry about the grim reality that the tide is not compliant with his wishes.

(b) Changing other people

Suppose your client is depressed because she claims that her boss makes, from her perspective, unreasonable demands on her at work. In response to your enquiry concerning her goal for change, she replies: 'I want my boss to stop making unreasonable demands on me.' If you consider this goal carefully, it points to a change in the other person's behavior. Now, on the face of it, this may seem quite reasonable. If her boss is making too many demands on the client what is wrong in her wanting him to change? The answer is both nothing and everything. There is nothing wrong with her goal if we treat it as a healthy desire, i.e. it is rational for her to want her boss to change. However, there is everything wrong with this statement as a therapeutic goal.

It is important for you to note and to encourage your client to appreciate that it is not within her power to change her boss. The client can only realistically hope to change what is in her power to change namely, her thoughts, behavior, feelings etc. Thus, as she cannot *directly* change her boss, you cannot as her therapist profitably accept this as a legitimate goal. Now, of course, your client can influence her boss to change, and these influence attempts may be successful. This means that it is legitimate to accept as your client's goal changes in her attempts to influence her boss because these new attempts are within her control. Accepting your client's new influence attempts as a legitimate goal for change is very different from accepting a change in her boss's behavior as a legitimate goal. The former is within the client's control, the latter is not.

(c) Feeling neutral about negative events

It sometimes occurs in REBT that clients indicate that they want to feel neutral about negative events. Consider Geraldine who was rejected by her boyfriend and felt very hurt about this. Here is an excerpt from my therapy with her which illustrates this unrealistic goal and how I responded to it.

Windy: So, Geraldine, the problem as I understand it is that you feel very hurt about Keith ending the relationship. Have I understood you correctly?

Geraldine: Yes you have.

Windy: What would you like to achieve from counseling on this issue?

Geraldine: I want not to feel anything about it.

Windy: The only way I can help you do that is to help you to develop the belief: 'I don't care whether Keith ended the relationship or not. It is a matter of indifference to me.' How realistic is it for you to believe that?

Geraldine: Put like that it isn't realistic at all. But it hurts so much I just want an end to the pain.

Windy: I understand that you do feel very hurt about the ending of your relationship with Keith and I do want to help you deal with your hurt. But, I want to do so in a way that is realistic and lasting. The trouble with trying to convince yourself that you don't care when, in fact, you care too much is that it is a lie and you just can't sustain that lie. How about this as an alternative? What if I can help you to feel very sorrowful about being rejected rather than very hurt about it? This would mean that you would still care about what happened to you, but you wouldn't care *too* much about it. How does that seem to you as a reasonable goal?

Geraldine: I see what you mean. That would be fine if I could achieve it.

[If Geraldine could not see the difference between hurt and sorrow, I would use a variety of teaching points to clarify this distinction (see Module 5).]

Windy: If you can see the sense of that then I'll do my best to help you achieve it.

(d) Seeking goals which would perpetuate the client's irrational beliefs

Sometimes clients come up with goals with respect to their defined problems which are within their control, but pursuing these goals would serve to perpetuate their irrational beliefs. Let me give a few examples of what I mean.

(i) Defined problem: I find it difficult getting down to studying when I know that my friends are out having a good time.

Goal: To leave my studies and join my friends whenever they go out without feeling guilty.

This would not be an unrealistic goal if the client was studying for long hours and not taking any breaks from her work. However, in this case the client was procrastinating on her studies and was spending her time watching TV when she knew that her friends were out enjoying themselves. Accepting her goal of joining her friends whenever they went out would perpetuate the irrational beliefs that underpinned her procrastination. Here, you could first establish that studying was in your client's best long-term interests and then help her to plan her time so that she spent enough time studying and some time socialising with her friends.

(ii) Defined problem: I'm depressed because my boss makes unreasonable demands on me at work.

Goal: To tell my boss off whenever he makes unreasonable demands on me.

The problem with this goal is twofold. It does not deal with the issue of the client's depression and it encourages the client to develop a new emotional problem — unhealthy anger. Thus, if you accept this goal you will be leaving intact the irrational beliefs underpinning her depression and encouraging the development of unhealthy anger-related irrational beliefs. This is how to proceed. First, encourage your client to consider the benefits of healthy assertion over making unhealthy anger-based rebukes in the light of what she knows about her boss. Review the material on healthy vs unhealthy anger as an aid here (see Unit 15). Second, help your client to see that she will need to deal with her depression before she can assert herself adequately with her boss.

(iii) Defined problem: I feel very hurt about Keith ending our relationship.

Goal: To beg Keith to take me back.

Once again this goal does not help the client to tackle her feelings of hurt about the rejection. Indeed, the client is seeking to deal with the rejection by getting rid of it. In doing so, her begging behavior indicates that she has another problem — a dire need either to have a relationship or a dire need for comfort. Accepting her goal again means that you will bypass her hurt-related irrational beliefs and legitimize whatever irrational beliefs underpin her begging.

(e) Seeking intellectual insight

As we have seen, rational emotive behavior therapy distinguishes between two types of insight: intellectual insight and emotional insight (Ellis, 1963). It defines intellectual insight as a light acknowledgment that one's irrational beliefs are inconsistent with reality, illogical and self-defeating and that the rational alternatives to these beliefs are consistent with reality, logical and self-helping. However, such insight does not, by itself, change how one feels and acts, but is seen as an important prelude to emotional insight. This form of insight is defined as a strong conviction that one's irrational beliefs are inconsistent with reality, illogical and self-defeating and that the rational alternatives to these beliefs are consistent with reality, logical and self-helping. Here, though, this strong conviction does affect how the person feels and acts. In short, when a person has intellectual insight, he or she still experiences unhealthy negative emotions and acts in self-defeating ways when faced with negative As, whereas with emotional insight, he or she responds to these same As with healthy negative emotions and self-enhancing behavior.

When a client responds to your enquiry about goals by saying that he or she wants to understand the target problem, he or she often holds the implicit idea that gaining such insight is sufficient for change to occur.

Unless this idea is identified and confronted, your client will only make limited gains from REBT. Whilst some clients do seek what may be called 'rational emotive behavioral intellectual insight' in that they are genuinely interested in what the approach has to say about the nature of their problems, most clients in my experience are looking for what may be called 'psychodynamic intellectual insight' in that they hope to identify childhood determinants of their problems which when discovered will lead to problem resolution. It follows from what I have said above that neither REBT nor psychodynamic intellectual insight is sufficient for psychological change to take place.

Explaining to your client that intellectual insight has its place, but is insufficient for change to occur, often helps the client to identify a more functional goal. It also helps the client to distinguish between insight as a therapeutic MEANS and a change in psychological functioning as a therapeutic GOAL. This is demonstrated in the following interchange.

Windy: So you find it difficult getting down to studying when you know your friends are out having a good time. What would you like to achieve from counseling on this issue?

Clare: I'd like to understand why I have this problem.

Windy: What information are you looking for?

Clare: Well, there must be something in my childhood that would explain why I have so much difficulty studying when my friends are out.

Windy: Let's suppose there was. What would you hope having this information would do for you?

Clare: It would help me solve this problem.

Windy: And if your problem was solved what would be different?

Clare: I would be able to study even when I knew that my friends were out enjoying themselves.

[Note that this is Clare's real goal. She hopes that psychodynamic intellectual insight will provide the MEANS whereby this GOAL can be achieved. It is important to distinguish between the means and the goal and this is what I address in my next response.]

Windy: Let me put what you've said a little differently. It sounds to me from what you've said that your goal is to be able to study even when you know that your friends are out enjoying themselves. You hope that the way to achieve this goal is by finding a reason in your childhood. Have I understood you correctly?

Clare: Yes.

Windy: Well, I'm happy to work with you towards your goal. However in REBT, we have a different view on the best way that people can achieve their therapeutic goals. Let me outline the REBT position on this issue...

[I would then discuss the REBT view of therapeutic change as it pertains to the role of intellectual and emotional insight.]

Step 5. Assess the defined problem using the ABCs of REBT and come to an agreement with him on this assessed problem.

As I have dealt fully with the issue of assessing clients' problems in Module 6, I will make only a few points that are particularly relevant to the topic of goal-setting here. Remember that the emotional Cs of clients' problems will generally be unhealthy negative emotions. However, don't forget that Cs can also be behavioral.

It is possible to treat behavioral Cs in two ways. First, you can regard behavioral Cs as actual expressions of action tendencies that stem from unhealthy negative emotions. In this case you need to target these unhealthy negative emotions for change. Second, you can regard behavioral Cs as stemming directly from the client's irrational beliefs and as such they can themselves be targeted for change.

As with the defined problem, it is important to agree with your client that your assessment of his problem is accurate. Doing so will help you to set a healthy goal with respect to the assessed problem. Conversely, failing to make such an agreement will lead to difficulties in goal-setting with respect to the inaccurately assessed target problem.

Step 6. Elicit the client's goal with respect to the assessed problem

If you have accurately assessed the specific example of your client's problem, you will have identified an unhealthy negative emotion and, if relevant, a self-defeating behavioral response at C, a critical A and a set of irrational beliefs at B. The next step is for you to elicit your client's goal which is based on your client's assessed problem. This will be in relation to the critical A and will usually involve a negative healthy emotion and a constructive behavioral response. Let me discuss an example based on an assessment of Clare's defined problem as discussed above. If you recall, her defined problem was: 'I find it difficult getting down to studying when I know that my friends are out having a good time.'

My assessment of this problem revealed the following ABC:
A = The unfairness of being deprived of company when I want it.
B = I must have fairness in my life at the moment.
    It's terrible to be deprived in this unfair way.
    I can't bear this unfair deprivation.
    Poor me!
C = Self-pitying depression and procrastination on studying.

Here is how I helped Clare set a realistic and functional goal with respect to the assessed problem. Note, in particular, that in keeping with REBT theory, I assume temporarily that Clare's inferred A is true (see Module 8 for the rationale of so doing). Thus, I help her to set an emotional and behavioral goal in light of the 'unfairness' of the situation.

Windy: So, let's assume that you are in an unfair situation; how is your depression helping you to study?

[Note that here I am drawing on Clare's goal with respect to her defined problem, i.e. 'To be able to study even when I know my friends are out enjoying themselves.']

Clare: It's not. In fact, it's discouraging me.

Windy: Right, so what alternative negative emotion will help you to study?

[I deliberately phrased my question in this somewhat oblique way to encourage Clare to think hard about the issue.]

Clare: What NEGATIVE emotion will help me study? I don't understand.

Windy: Well, think about it? You are never going to like the unfairness of the situation, are you?

Clare: No, I guess not.

Windy: Nor are you likely to be indifferent to it, are you?

Clare: No.

Windy: So, what's left?

Clare: To feel negative about it.

Windy: That's right, but there are two different types of negative emotions. There are what I call unhealthy negative emotions which generally inhibit people from adjusting to a negative life event or from taking constructive action to change it and there are healthy negative emotions which are constructive emotional responses to negative life events and do help people to change these events or make a constructive adjustment if the situation cannot be changed. Now, let's take your feelings of depression about the unfair situation where you need to study when your friends are out enjoying themselves. Is your depression a healthy or unhealthy emotional response?

Clare: Clearly it's unhealthy.

Windy: Why?

Clare: Because it doesn't help me to study.

Windy: Right. Now, given that you are faced with what you consider to be an unfair situation, what would be a healthy negative emotional response?

Clare To be disappointed or sad about it.

Windy: Right, now would that be a realistic-feeling goal for you?

Clare: Yes, I think it would be.

Windy: And would it help you to get down to studying when you knew that your friends were out enjoying themselves?

Clare: Yes, I think it would.

Windy: So let me summarize. When you are faced with the unfairness of your friends going out to enjoy themselves, you want to strive to feel sad or disappointed, but not depressed about this and to get down to doing some studying. Is that right?

Clare: Yes.

Windy: OK, let's both make a note of that goal and let's move on to helping you to achieve that goal...

As mentioned above it is also possible to set a goal in respect of the client's assessed problem, where C is just behavioral. This involves you encouraging the client to set a realistic and adaptive behavioral goal in the face of a negative A. In Clare's case this would be: 'I want to get down to studying even when I am faced with the unfairness of staying in when I know that my friends are out enjoying themselves.'

Unit 50: Setting a Goal With Respect to Your Client's Broad Problem

Let me begin this section by distinguishing between a broad problem and a specific example of a broad problem. A broad problem tends to be general in nature and probably comprises several different examples. A specific example of a broad problem is just that — one concrete instance of a broad problem comprising several similar examples. For example, Clare's broad problem was 'procrastinating over my studies whenever there is something more attractive to do.' A specific example of Clare's broad problem was the one discussed at length above, namely: 'I find it difficult getting down to studying when I know that my friends are out having a good time.'

Many of the issues that I have just dealt with concerning setting goals with respect to specific examples of your clients' broad problems also emerge when you come to set goals in respect to these broad problems. As such I will not repeat myself. What I will do is to provide an example of one client's broad problems and the goals I set with her on the problems.

Problem	Goal
1. Feel anxious about approaching women	1. To feel concerned about approaching women, but not anxious about doing so. To approach them despite feeling concerned
2. Guilty about past wrongdoings	2. To feel remorseful but not guilty about past wrongdoings and make amends where relevant
3. Procrastinate over studies	3. To make a study timetable and keep to it
4. Feel anxious about hosting any kind of gathering in case something goes wrong and therefore avoid being a host	4. To arrange a gathering and feel concerned but not anxious about something going wrong
5. Avoid going to shopping mall because of panic attacks	5. To go to shopping mall and feel concerned but not anxious at first and then to feel comfortable about going after repeated exposure

I want you to note five things about these goals.

(i) All of the goals are within the client's sphere of influence, i.e. they are all achievable.

(ii) All of the goals indicate the presence of an emotional and behavioral state. It is important therefore to avoid setting goals with your clients which involve the diminution or absence of a state. Thus, instead of the goal 'to feel less anxious about...' encourage your client to strive 'to feel concerned, but not anxious about...' Similarly, instead of the goal 'not to feel guilty about...' encourage your client 'to feel remorseful, but not guilty about...'

(iii) Most of the goals contain a negative healthy emotion in response to a negative activating event. You will also note that whilst the presence of a healthy negative emotion is clearly stated, the absence of an unhealthy negative emotion is also made explicit.

(iv) All of the goals contain a piece of functional behavior.

(v) One of the goals (i.e. no. 5) contains an initial healthy negative feeling which then becomes a comfortable feeling state as the result of repeated practice. This last point is important. Whilst it is functional for your client to have a healthy negative emotional response to a negative life event, as a counselor concerned with your client's long-term well-being, you will want her to attempt to change this negative A and increase the number of positive As in her life. This brings us to the third issue concerning goal-setting in REBT.

Unit 51: Moving From Overcoming Disturbance to Promoting Psychological Health

As I mentioned at the beginning of this module, it is possible to think of the goals of psychotherapy as falling into two categories: those to do with overcoming psychological disturbance and those which serve to promote psychological health or growth.

Overcoming disturbance goals (henceforth called OD goals) relates to the problems that clients bring to psychotherapy. Thus, when clients have achieved their OD goals, they experience healthy negative emotions when they confront the negative As about which they previously disturbed themselves and they are able to take constructive action to try and change these negative events.

Psychological health goals (henceforth called PH goals), on the other hand, are related to a number of broad criteria of mental health which are not situation specific. PH goals, then, generally go well beyond OD goals. Although helping clients towards PH goals is beyond the scope of this book, it is important for you to realize that doing so is a legitimate task for REBT therapists. I outline REBT's view of some of the major criteria of mental health in Figure 12.1 to give you some idea of what helping clients to pursue PH goals might involve for clients (for a fuller discussion of REBT's position on these criteria consult Ellis & Dryden, 1997 and Dryden, 1994a).

In general, you will help your client to work toward her OD goals before raising the issue of PH goals. In my experience most of your clients will wish to terminate therapy once they are have achieved their OD goals. In this respect, Maluccio (1979) found that clients were far more satisfied with what they achieved from therapy on termination than were their therapists. So don't be surprised if most of your clients are not interested in working towards psychological health and don't regard this as a failure on your part if this is the case.

1. Enlightened self-interest
Here the person basically puts herself first and puts the interests of significant others a close second. Sometimes, however, she will put the interests of others before her own. Enlightened self-interest is therefore a flexible position and contrasts with selfishness (the dogmatic position where the person is only concerned with her own interests and is indifferent to the interests of others) and selflessness (the position where the person always puts the interests of others before her own).

2. Flexibility

Here the person is flexible in her thinking, open to change, free from bigotry and pluralistic in her view of other people. She does not make rigid, invariant rules for herself and others.

3. Acceptance of uncertainty

Here the person fully accepts that we live in a world of probability and chance where absolute certainties do not and probably will never exist.

4. Commitment to vital absorbing interests

Here the person is likely to be healthier and happier when she is vitally absorbed in something outside herself than when she is not. This interest should be large enough to be involving and allow the person to express her talents and capacities.

5. Long-range hedonism

Here the person tends to seek a healthy balance between the pleasures of the moment and those of the future. She is prepared to put up with present pain if doing so is in her best interests and is likely to lead to future gain.

Figure 12.1. Examples of mental health criteria from an REBT perspective.

Module 13
Eliciting Commitment To Change

Introduction

It is not sufficient to elicit your client's goals. It is also important to elicit his commitment to change and work towards these goals. Therefore, in this module, I will discuss a method which you can use which is helpful in eliciting client commitment to change.

For your client to commit himself to change, it is important for him to see clearly that it is in his best interests to make the change. If your client does not see this, then he is hardly likely to commit himself to work towards his stated goal. You might ask, then, why your client might come up with a goal to which he is not committed. There may be a number of reasons for this. First, your client might identify a goal which others want him to achieve, but which he is either opposed to or ambivalent about. Thus, your client's parents may want him, for example, to become independent whereas he may wish to stay dependent or be in two minds about becoming independent. In order to help your client to commit himself to a goal, it is important to help him first evaluate fully the advantages and disadvantages of both the problem state and the alternative goal state. Over the years I have experimented with a number of ways of doing this. Having made several modifications to my approach of helping clients to weigh up the pros and cons of change, I now use a method which is quite comprehensive. I have devised a form called 'Cost-benefit analysis' which I encourage clients to complete, especially when it is clear that the client is ambivalent about change.

Unit 52: The Cost–Benefit Analysis Form: General Principles

The cost–benefit analysis form which appears in Figure 13.1 is easy to complete and is based on a number of principles.

COST–BENEFIT ANALYSIS
ADVANTAGES/BENEFITS OF
Option 1

SHORT TERM

For yourself	For other people
1:....................	1:....................
2:....................	2:....................
3:....................	3:....................
4:....................	4:....................
5:....................	5:....................
6:....................	6:....................

LONG TERM

For yourself	For other people
1:....................	1:....................
2:....................	2:....................
3:....................	3:....................
4:....................	4:....................
5:....................	5:....................
6:....................	6:....................

DISADVANTAGES/COSTS OF
Option 1

SHORT TERM

For yourself	For other people
1:....................	1:....................
2:....................	2:....................
3:....................	3:....................
4:....................	4:....................
5:....................	5:....................
6:....................	6:....................

LONG TERM

For yourself	For other people
1:....................	1:....................
2:....................	2:....................
3:....................	3:....................
4:....................	4:....................
5:....................	5:....................
6:....................	6:....................

COST–BENEFIT ANALYSIS
ADVANTAGES/BENEFITS OF
Option 2

SHORT TERM

For yourself	For other people
1:....................	1:....................
2:....................	2:....................
3:....................	3:....................
4:....................	4:....................
5:....................	5:....................
6:....................	6:....................

LONG TERM

For yourself	For other people
1:....................	1:....................
2:....................	2:....................
3:....................	3:....................
4:....................	4:....................
5:....................	5:....................
6:....................	6:....................

DISADVANTAGES/COSTS OF
Option 2

SHORT TERM

For yourself	For other people
1:....................	1:....................
2:....................	2:....................
3:....................	3:....................
4:....................	4:....................
5:....................	5:....................
6:....................	6:....................

LONG TERM

For yourself	For other people
1:....................	1:....................
2:....................	2:....................
3:....................	3:....................
4:....................	4:....................
5:....................	5:....................
6:....................	6:....................

Figure 13.1. The cost-benefit analysis form.

1. There is an alternative to the client's problem and it is important for you to help the client to put this in his own words.
2. The problem and the goal both have actual and perceived advantages and disadvantages.
3. These advantages and disadvantages operate both in the short term and in the long term.
4. These advantages and disadvantages are relevant for both your client and others in his life. This relevance is at its most obvious when your client's problem is interpersonal in nature; however, even when the problem does not seem to involve anybody else, it is still worthwhile asking your client to consider the advantages and disadvantages for himself and for others.

It is important to ask your client to complete the cost–benefit analysis form when he is in an objective frame of mind. Otherwise, you will receive an analysis heavily influenced by his psychologically disturbed state. This can best be done as a homework assignment because the form takes quite a while to complete and for you to do it with him in the session is not a cost-effective use of therapeutic time. Once your client has completed the form, ask him to put it away until the next therapy session. Otherwise, he may ruminate on it in an unproductive way.

When you go over the form with your client, first ask him to state what he learned from doing the task. If he states clearly that the goal is more attractive than the problem, you can ask him to commit himself formally to the goal. This may involve him making a written commitment which you could both sign. It could also involve him making a public declaration of some kind indicating his commitment to achieving the goal. Whilst making one or both types of formal commitment is not a necessary part of the REBT change process, these procedures do bring it home to the client that change is a serious business and one that is not to be entered into lightly.

You will note that I do not advocate going over the cost–benefit analysis form in detail with your client when he has stated that his goal is more desirable than the problem state and that he does wish to commit himself to achieving it. However, if you study the form carefully you will frequently gain a lot of information, especially from the 'advantages of the problem' section and the 'disadvantages of the goal' section concerning likely obstacles to client progress. Therefore, it is important that you retain a copy of the client's form and that you have it to hand when you are seeing him. It is also helpful if you encourage your client to keep a copy of the form to hand whenever he comes to therapy and at other times. Later, you will want to ask him to consult it for clues concerning obstacles to his continued progress.

When your client has completed the cost–benefit analysis form and is ambivalent about change or opts for the problem state over the goal state, then you need to go over the form with him in great detail. The purpose of doing this is to discover and deal with so-called advantages of the problem and perceived disadvantages of achieving the goal (I am assuming here that the goal is a healthy one, at least when taken at face value). Unless you deal with these sections of the form and correct the misconceptions you find there, it is not in the interests of either yourself or your client to ask him to commit himself to the goal. To do so under such circumstances is to get the change process off on the wrong foot. The following is an example of how to deal with such a situation. I will first present the client's cost–benefit analysis form (see Figure 13.2), then I will demonstrate how to challenge a client's misconceptions about the 'advantages' of the problem and the 'disadvantages' of achieving the goal. I will call the client in this example Sandra.

As you can see from Figure 13.2, Sandra is ambivalent about giving up 'sulking' (which is her general problem) and opting for the alternative 'communicating my feelings honestly to other people' which is Sandra's stated goal with respect to the general problem of sulking. Whilst you will most often use the cost–benefit analysis method with your client's general problems and goals, you can also use it with specific examples of general problems and related goals.

Unit 53: Responding to Your Client's Perceived Advantages of the Problem and Perceived Disadvantages of Achieving the Goal

As Sandra is ambivalent about change it is important that I, as her therapist, review the form with her and respond in particular to the advantages she sees accompanying 'sulking' (her problem) and to the disadvantages that she sees accompanying 'communicating my feelings honestly to other people' (her stated goal). In Figure 13.3 I outline a summary of the specific arguments I used with Sandra as I challenged the misconceptions on which these 'advantages' and 'disadvantages' appeared to be based. As I will demonstrate later in the chapter, the way I helped Sandra to question her reasoning on this issue was by asking Socratic-type questions. The summary nature of the arguments presented in Figure 13.3 makes it appear that I just told Sandra why she was in error. As you will soon see, this was far from the case.

Unit 54: Using Socratic Questions To Help Your Client Rethink the Perceived Advantages of the Problem and the Perceived Disadvantages of the Stated Goal

You will note that many of the arguments that I used with Sandra are directed at her distorted inferences. Thus, taking the short-term advantage of sulking providing a good way of showing dissatisfaction, I show Sandra that whilst this may be so, there are better ways of doing so. I also show her that sulking may lead to greater problems that she has not considered. Once again, it is very important for you to realize that the arguments presented in Figure 13.3 are summaries. That is why they appear in didactic form. In actuality, I engaged Sandra in a Socratic dialogue on the issue as the following interchange shows.

COST-BENEFIT ANALYSIS
ADVANTAGES/BENEFITS OF SULKING

SHORT TERM

For yourself	For other people
1. 'Safety valve' for anger	1. Lets people know I'm angry
2. Gives me time to think	2. Draws people's attention to a problem or mood
3. Release of frustration behavior does have a negative effect	3. Can jolt people into realising that their
4. Shows dissatisfaction	4.
5. It's a sign of annoyance	5.
6.	6.

LONG TERM

For yourself	For other people
1. None	1. None
2.	2.
3.	3.
4.	4.
5.	5.
6.	6.

DISADVANTAGES/COSTS OF SULKING

SHORT TERM

For yourself	For other people
1. It's a waste of energy	1. It causes an uncomfortable atmosphere
2. It's debilitating	2. It creates tension in my relationship
3. It hides the real problem	3.
4.	4.
5.	5.
6.	6.

LONG TERM

For yourself	For other people
1. It puts me in a bad light with others	1. It causes a lot of misunderstandings
2.	2.
3.	3.
4.	4.
5.	5.
6.	6.

Figure 13.2. Sandra's cost–benefit analysis form.

COST–BENEFIT ANALYSIS
ADVANTAGES/BENEFITS OF COMMUNICATING MY FEELINGS HONESTLY TO OTHER PEOPLE

SHORT TERM

For yourself	For other people
1. Brings problems to a head	1. Brings problems to a head
2. Releases pent-up anger	2. Clarifies matters
3. May help to resolve matters	3. May help to resolve matters
4.	4.
5.	5.
6.	6.

LONG TERM

For yourself	For other people
1. Shows a determination to resolve matters	1. Allows for compromise
2. Represents more mature and positive action	2.
3.	3.
4.	4.
5.	5.
6.	6.

DISADVANTAGES/COSTS OF COMMUNICATING MY FEELINGS HONESTLY TO OTHER PEOPLE
SHORT TERM

For yourself	For other people
1. May say things I may regret	1. Heightens excitability and emotion – alism
2. I may lose relationships	2. They may feel hurt
3.	3.
4.	4.
5.	5.
6.	6.

LONG TERM

For yourself	For other people
1. May become unpopular	1. They may become wary of me
2. I may lose relationships	2. They may decide I'm too unpleasant to be around
3.	3.
4.	4.
5.	5.
6.	6.

Figure 13.2. Continued.

Windy: OK, Sandra. Now you say that a short-term advantage of sulking is that it helps you to show dissatisfaction. Do you see any way of showing dissatisfaction without sulking?

Sandra: Well, letting people know honestly that I am dissatisfied will have the same effect.

SHORT-TERM ADVANTAGES/BENEFITS OF SULKING

For yourself	*Windy's response*
1. 'Safety valve' for anger.	1. Controlled honest communication is a more effective way of channelling anger. It is even more effective if you first challenge your unhealthy anger-creating irrational beliefs and replace them with rational beliefs leading to healthy anger
2. Gives me time to think.	2. You don't need to sulk to give you time to think. There is a difference between withdrawing for yourself in order to give yourself time to think and withdrawal 'against the other' which is what sulking is. In fact, the latter detracts from the quality of your thinking while the former promotes this.
3. Release of frustration.	3. When you communicate honestly, you can release frustration, but in a way which is more likely to resolve problems than sulking.
4. Shows dissatisfaction.	4. While you do show dissatisfaction when you sulk you also show other things too, which are more likely to cause problems than solve them. When you communicate honestly you show dissatisfaction but again in a more constructive way than sulking.
5. It's a sign of annoyance.	5. The above argument is also relevant here. Honest communication is a more reliable and healthy way of communicating annoyance than sulking. In keeping the channel of communication open you are more likely to resolve matters by talking them through than with sulking, which closes down the channel.
For other people	*Windy's response*
1. Lets them know I'm angry	1. Sulking may well let others know that you are angry, but it won't let them know what you're angry about. It is therefore liable to create more problems in this respect than it will solve.
2. Draws people's attention to a problem or mood.	2. Again sulking draws their attention to the fact that you have a problem, but it won't pinpoint the nature of the problem. By communicating honestly and openly you will let other people know exactly what your problem is.

Figure 13.3. Responding to Sandra's misconceptions about the 'advantages' of her problem and the 'disadvantages' of her stated goal.

3. Can jolt people into realising that their behavior does have a negative effect.

3. This may happen, but what is more likely to happen is that you will jolt them into realising that your behavior has a negative effect on them!

LONG-TERM ADVANTAGES/BENEFITS OF SULKING
None stated

SHORT-TERM DISADVANTAGES/COSTS OF COMMUNICATING MY FEELINGS HONESTLY TO OTHER PEOPLE

For yourself

1. May say things I may regret.

Windy's response

1. You are more likely to say things you may regret later when you are unhealthily angry. That is why I recommend that you change the irrational beliefs that underpin your unhealthy anger to rational beliefs that will enable you to be healthily angry instead. Healthy anger is directed at the other's behavior, while unhealthy anger is directed at and puts down the other person.

2. I may lose relationships.

2. You are more likely to lose relationships if you sulk angrily than if you honestly convey your healthy anger in a firm, but caring manner.

For other people

1. Heightens excitability and emotionalism.

1. If this is a disadvantage for other people, then honest communication of healthy anger will reduce the intensity of the emotional atmosphere whereas honest communication of unhealthy anger will increase excitability and emotionalism. That is another reason why I recommend that you first identify and challenge the irrational beliefs that underpin your unhealthy anger and replace it with a set of rational beliefs that will allow you to communicate honestly and firmly, but caringly your feelings of healthy anger.

2. They may feel hurt.

2. Yes, they may feel hurt when you honestly convey your annoyance even if you choose your words carefully. However, they are less likely to feel hurt when you communicate your feelings of healthy anger than if you communicate your unhealthy angry feelings. Also, don't forget that other people may feel hurt when you sulk. There is no way of guaranteeing that others won't be hurt no matter what you do. The more important consideration is whether you want your relationships with others to be based on honest communication or uncommunicative sulking.

Figure 13.3. Continued.

LONG-TERM DISADVANTAGES/COSTS OF COMMUNICATING MY FEELINGS HON-
ESTLY TO OTHER PEOPLE

For yourself	*Windy's response*
1. May become unpopular	1. Yes, you may become unpopular if you honestly communicate your feelings of healthy anger. However, I would argue that in the long term you will be even more unpopular if you sulk or communicate your unhealthy anger. Don't forget either that honest communication also involves expression of positive feelings. If you are open about your good feelings about others as well as your negative feelings about them then you will in all probability increase your popularity.
2. May lose relationships.	2. Again you may lose relationships if you communicate honestly, but if you communicate feelings of healthy anger you will lose less relationships in the long-term than if you sulk or honestly communicate your other-damning unhealthy angry feelings. This will especially be the case if you also communicate your positive feelings to other people.
For other people	
1. They may become wary of me.	1. This is true, but they will probably become equally wary of you when they discover that you sulk. Also expressions of unhealthy anger are more likely to lead to others being wary of you than expressions of healthy anger.
2. They may decide I'm too unpleasant to be around.	2. This seems to be more a disadvantage for you than for others. Even if it is a disadvantage for them, I would argue, as I have done before, that this is more likely to happen if you sulk or show your unhealthy anger than if you show your healthy anger.

Figure 13.3. Continued.

Windy: Right. Incidentally, if you sulk how do you know that in people's minds you are not showing other things too, like unhealthy anger or punitiveness?

Sandra: I guess I don't.

Windy: So which is a more reliable guide to showing dissatisfaction: sulking or honestly communicating your feelings?

Sandra: Honest communication.

Windy: Does that change your view that a short-term advantage of sulking is that it helps you to show dissatisfaction?

Sandra: Yes. It helps me to see that sulking shows a number of things other than dissatisfaction and these other things like unhealthy anger won't be beneficial to my relationships.

Unit 55: Reconsidering the Cost–Benefit Analysis and Asking for a Commitment To Change

After you have helped your client to review the 'advantages' of his or her problem and the 'disadvantages' of the stated goal, it is important that you encourage him or her to reconsider his cost–benefit analysis of the problem and the goal. You can do this in two ways. First, you can have the client take his or her old cost–benefit analysis form and write in a different colour pen the reasons why the problem's perceived advantages are, in fact, not benefits and the reasons why the goal's perceived disadvantages are not, in fact, costs. Second, you can ask your client to complete a second cost–benefit analysis form which, if you have been successful in helping to correct the previous misconceptions, should demonstrate a clear preference for his or her stated goal. If not, you need to proceed as above until a clear preference for one of the two options is demonstrated.

Concerning eliciting a commitment to change let me quote the point I made on this issue on page 198, as it is worth reiterating: 'If he or she (i.e. your client) states clearly that the goal is more attractive than the problem, you can ask for a formal commitment to the goal. This may involve him or her making a written commitment which you could both sign. It could also involve him or her making a public declaration of some kind indicating commitment to achieving the goal. Whilst making one or both types of formal commitment is not a necessary part of the REBT change process, these procedures do bring it home to the client that change is a serious business and one that is not to be entered into lightly.'

You will find, in conclusion, that the disputing process (which is the subject of the following module) will go more smoothly when your client has made a commitment to his stated goal than when he is still ambivalent about change. Trying to dispute your client's irrational beliefs without eliciting such a commitment is like running a race with a ball and chain around one leg. Encouraging your client to make this commitment is the key which removes such an impediment.

Module 14
Disputing Irrational Beliefs: An Introduction

In the following modules on disputing, I will deal with one of the core skills you will need as an REBT therapist — disputing your client's irrational beliefs. In order to help you do this successfully, I will discuss five topics. First, because you need to ensure that you have prepared your client for the disputing process I will begin by considering this issue in this module. Second, I will cover the three major arguments you will need to use in helping your client to question the rationality of her irrational beliefs (Module 15). Third, I will describe the two major disputing styles you will need to master if you are to vary your approach with different clients (Modules 16 and 17) and discuss flexibility in disputing (Module 18). Fourth, I will illustrate some of this material by presenting and commenting on a transcript of Albert Ellis disputing the irrational beliefs of one of his clients (Module 19). Finally, in Module 20, I will show you how you can help your client to bring to the fore her rational beliefs.

Unit 56: Preparing Your Client for the Disputing Process

What are the preparatory steps that you need to take before you dispute your client's irrational beliefs? I have covered most of these issues already in Module 11. Consequently I will only summarize the points here.

Teach the effect of irrational beliefs on psychological disturbance

If you are to engage your client in the disputing process, then you need to help her to understand the central role that irrational beliefs play in the development and maintenance of psychological problems in general.

Assess the client's target problem

If your client is to get the most out of the disputing process, then you need to help her to see the role that her specific irrational beliefs play in the development and maintenance of her specific target problem. You can best do this by carrying out an accurate ABC assessment of this target problem. It is particularly important that your client underscores its accuracy. If she does not do this, re-assess her target problem until she does so.

Identify your client's goal and elicit commitment to change

Ed Bordin (1979) has made a useful distinction between the goals and tasks of psychotherapy. He notes that the purpose of therapeutic tasks is to help clients achieve their therapeutic goals. According to Bordin, then, disputing your client's irrational beliefs is a therapeutic task, the object of which is to help your client achieve her goal. Consequently, as discussed in Modules 12 and 13, helping your client to identify and commit herself to her stated goal for change is an important prerequisite for disputing her irrational beliefs. Unless this is done the disputing process will tend to be directionless.

Helping your client to see the relevance of disputing her irrational beliefs as a primary means of achieving her goal

As well as helping your client to see that her irrational beliefs underpin her target problem, it is equally important that you help her to see that changing these beliefs will help her to achieve her stated goal with respect to this problem. Here is an example of how to do this.

Windy: So, recapping on the ABC of your anxiety, C is your feelings of anxiety, A is the event in your mind that your boss will disapprove of you and B is your irrational belief: 'My boss must not disapprove of me. I am less worthy if he does.' Is that accurate?

Victor: Yes it is.

Windy: From this assessment can you see what largely determines your feelings of anxiety?

Victor: The belief that my boss must not disapprove of me.

Windy: Now let's recap on your goal. What would be a more healthy, but realistic response to receiving disapproval from your boss than anxiety?

Victor: As we said before, to feel concerned but not anxious about it.

Windy: So if your belief that your boss must not disapprove of you leads to your anxiety and your goal is to feel concerned, but not anxious about this possibility, what do we have to help you to change in order for you to achieve your goal?

Victor: We have to change my belief.

Helping your client to understand what disputing involves

As I will discuss in greater detail in Module 16, disputing involves you asking your client a number of questions designed to encourage her to evaluate the rationality of her irrational beliefs and explaining any points about which she is not clear. As such it is useful to help your client understand what you will be doing and why you will be doing it. An example follows from my work with Victor.

Windy: Right, you need to change your irrational belief. The way I can best help you to do this is to encourage you to see why your irrational belief is, in fact, irrational. I will be doing this by asking you a number of questions designed to help you to understand this point. The reason why I will be asking you questions in the first instance is to help you to think about this issue for yourself. This is what Socrates, a famous Greek philosopher, did with his students. He didn't tell them the answers to various difficult philosophical questions. Rather, he asked them a series of questions, the purpose of which was to help them discover the answers for themselves. He helped them with his questions to be sure, but he didn't do the work for them. However, if my questioning doesn't help you to understand any given point I will provide you with an explanation which will I hope clarifies the point. I won't, in other words, leave you up in the air. Does what I say make sense to you?

Victor: Yes. What you're saying is that you will help me to re-evaluate my irrational belief by asking me questions about it. And you'll explain any points that I don't understand.

Windy: Shall we start?

Victor: Go ahead.

Module 15
Disputing Irrational Beliefs: The Three Major Arguments

The noted American REBT therapist, Ray DiGiuseppe, and his trainees listened to numerous audiotapes of Albert Ellis conducting therapy in order to understand better the disputing process (DiGiuseppe, 1991b). As part of their analysis, DiGiuseppe and his trainees discovered that Ellis employed three major arguments while disputing his clients' irrational beliefs.

Unit 57: What Are the Three Major Arguments?

The three arguments that Ellis used were as follows:

1. Empirical Arguments. Empirical arguments are designed to encourage your client to look for empirical evidence which confirms or disconfirms his or her irrational beliefs. The basic question here is this: are your irrational beliefs realistic or consistent with reality?
2. Logical Arguments. Logical arguments are designed to encourage your client to examine whether or not his or her irrational beliefs are logical. The basic question here is this: do your irrational beliefs follow logically from your rational beliefs?
3. Pragmatic Arguments. Pragmatic arguments are designed to encourage your client to question the utilitarian nature of his or her irrational beliefs. The basic question here is this: do your irrational beliefs help you or hinder you as you pursue your stated goals?

Now that I have described the three major arguments, I will outline the points you need to make as you apply these arguments while disputing the four irrational beliefs: musts; awfulizing; low frustration tolerance and self/other downing. As I do so please note that my focus is on the content of the arguments not the way they are presented. I will deal with this latter point in Modules 16 and 17.

Unit 58: Using the Three Major Arguments With Musts

You will recall from Module 1, that musts are absolutistic evaluative beliefs which, according to REBT theory, are at the core of psychological disturbance. From these musts are derived three other irrational beliefs, i.e. awfulizing, low frustration tolerance and self/other downing. Musts are irrational for the following reasons.

Empirical — musts are inconsistent with reality

Let's take Victor's irrational belief: 'My boss must not disapprove of me.' If there was a law of the universe which stated that Victor's boss must not disapprove of him, then it would be impossible for the boss to do so no matter what Victor did. Such a law of the universe would forbid Victor's boss from ever disapproving of him. As it is always possible for his boss to disapprove of Victor, this proves that there is no empirical evidence to support Victor's irrational belief that: 'My boss must not disapprove of me.'

If Victor's irrational belief were true it would mean that Victor's boss would lack free will. He would be deprived of his human right to form a negative opinion of Victor. As the boss does have the freedom to think negatively of Victor, this fact empirically disconfirms Victor's irrational belief.

If Victor's boss did ever disapprove of him, this would contradict Victor's belief. If, under these circumstances, Victor still believed that his boss absolutely should not have disapproved of him, then this would be tantamount to Victor believing: 'what just happened absolutely should not have happened', or 'reality must not be reality' which empirically is nonsense.

Logical — musts do not follow logically from preferences

Victor has a healthy rational belief which is stated in the form of a preference: 'I would prefer it if my boss did not disapprove of me.' However, his irrational belief: 'My boss must not disapprove of me' does not follow logically from his preferential rational belief. Rigid musts and non-dogmatic preferences are not in any way logically connected. So if Victor were to state rationally that it would be preferable if his boss did not disapprove of him and conclude that as a result his boss must not disapprove of him, then his conclusion: 'my boss must not disapprove of me' would not be logically related to his rational belief: 'It would be preferable if my boss did not disapprove of me.' In short it would be an illogical conclusion.

Pragmatic — musts lead to poor psychological results

Victor's irrational demand that his boss must not disapprove of him is likely to lead to poor emotional, cognitive and behavioral results. Thus, if Victor holds this belief in a situation where his boss approves of him, but there is a slight chance that he may incur such disapproval, then he will tend to get anxious and will tend to think and act in certain ways associated with anxiety (see Figure 5.1). In addition, if Victor receives clear evidence that his boss does disapprove of him, then his 'must' will lead him to feel anxiety, depression or anger and again he will tend to think and act in self-defeating ways that relate to whichever unhealthy negative emotion predominates (Figure 5.1).

Victor's irrational demand that his boss must not disapprove of him will interfere with his stated goal. For example, if he wants to be healthily concerned about the prospect of being disapproved of by his boss, but not anxious about this, then his must will constitute a major obs-tacle to Victor achieving this goal.

Unit 59: Using the Three Major Arguments With Awfulizing

According to REBT theory, awfulizing is an irrational derivative of a primary must. It represents the tendency to evaluate events in grossly exaggerated, dogmatic ways. Awfulizing is irrational for the following reasons.

Empirical – 'nothing is awful in the universe'

Ellis defines the term 'awful' when used in its absolute disturbance-creating sense as more than 100% bad, worse than it absolutely must be. As such, because you can never reach awful, it empirically does not exist. As I have already noted, Smokey Robinson's mother's advice to her son aptly illustrates this idea: 'From the day you are born, 'til you ride in the hearse, there's nothing so bad that it couldn't be worse.' Thus, awfulizing is not a property of the natural world; rather, it is a concept that constitutes a creation of the human mind.

Consequently, when Victor concludes: 'It would be awful if my boss disapproved of me', he is making an empirically unsupportable statement because he can presumably think of many occurrences that would be worse than being disapproved of by his boss.

Logical – awfulizing represents an illogical over-generalisation from non-dogmatic ratings of badness

It would be healthy for Victor to conclude that it would be bad if his boss disapproved of him. However, if he were to conclude that it would be awful if his boss disapproved of him, his awfulizing belief would not follow logically from his healthy evaluation of badness. Evaluations of badness lie on a continuum from 0–99.99% badness, whereas awfulizing lies on a magical continuum from 101%–infinity. As you can see there is no logical connection between the two continua.

Pragmatic – awfulizing leads to poor psychological results

Victor's irrational belief that it would be awful if his boss disapproved of him is likely to lead to poor emotional, cognitive and behavioral results. Thus, if Victor holds this belief in a situation where his boss approves of him, but there is a slight chance that he may incur such disapproval, then he will again tend to get anxious and to think and act in ways associated with anxiety (see Figure 5.1). In addition, if Victor receives clear evidence that his boss does disapprove of him, then his awfulizing belief will lead him to feel anxiety, depression or unhealthy anger and again he will tend to think and act in self-defeating ways that relate to whichever unhealthy negative emotion predominates (see Figure 5.1).

Victor's belief that it would be awful if his boss disapproved of him will interfere with his stated goal. Thus, if he wants to be healthily concerned about the prospect of being disapproved of by his boss, but not anxious about this, then his awfulizing will constitute a major obstacle to Victor achieving this goal.

Unit 60: Using the Three Major Arguments With Low Frustration Tolerance

According to REBT theory, low frustration tolerance is another irrational derivative of a primary must. It represents the position that one cannot tolerate frustrating or uncomfortable situations. This belief is irrational for the following reasons.

Empirical — you can bear the so-called unbearable

If it were true that you couldn't tolerate a frustrating or uncomfortable situation then you would literally die or you would never experience any happiness for the rest of your life, no matter how you thought about the situation in question. Thus, if it were true that Victor couldn't tolerate being disapproved of by his boss, as he believes, then if this disapproval occurred Victor would have to die or forfeit any chance of future happiness. Obviously, neither of these two things would happen. The ironic thing about a philosophy of low frustration tolerance is that even when Victor tells himself that he can't stand his boss's disapproval he is standing it. Now he could tolerate it better and you can help him to do so. But the point is that he is tolerating it even when he is doing so poorly. Thus, it is completely anti-empirical to believe that you can't stand something even when it is very difficult to bear.

In this context, I ask clients who believe they cannot stand something whether they could stand it if it meant saving the life of a loved one. They invariably say 'yes'. This proves that the 'I can't stand it' statement is again anti-empirical because, if it were true that they couldn't stand the relevant situation, they would not be able to stand it under any circumstances.

Logical — it makes no logical sense to conclude that you can't stand something because it is difficult to tolerate

Once again it is healthy for Victor to believe that it would be difficult for him to tolerate his boss's disapproval. However, it would be illogical for him to conclude that because this would be hard to bear, it would therefore be unbearable. If something is difficult to bear, it is still bearable; thus Victor's conclusion is really this: because I am tolerating my boss's disapproval, it is therefore intolerable. This is clearly illogical nonsense.

Pragmatic — low frustration tolerance leads to poor psychological results

The points that I made with respect to the pragmatic consequences of holding musts and awfulizing beliefs are also relevant to low frustration tolerance beliefs. Victor's irrational belief that he could not stand it if his boss disapproved of him is likely to lead to poor emotional, cognitive and behavioral results. Thus, again if Victor holds this belief in a situation where his boss approves of him, but there is a slight chance that he may incur such disapproval, then he will tend to get anxious and to think and act in ways associated with anxiety (see Figure 5.1). In addition, if Victor receives clear evidence that his boss does disapprove of him, then his LFT belief will lead him to feel an-xiety, depression or unhealthy anger and again he will tend to think and act in self-defeating ways that relate to whichever unhealthy negative emotion predominates (see Figure 5.1).

Furthermore, Victor's belief that he could not stand it if his boss disapproved of him will interfere with his stated goal. Thus, if he wants to be healthily concerned about the prospect of being disapproved of by his boss, but not anxious about this, then his LFT belief will constitute a major obstacle to Victor achieving this goal.

Unit 61: Using the Three Major Arguments With Self/Other Downing

According to REBT theory, self/other downing is yet another irrational derivative of a primary must. It represents the position that the worth or value of a person varies according to changing conditions. The common factor linking self-downing and other-downing is the philosophy of downing. As such, I will concentrate my discussion on self-downing. However, similar points could be made for the concept of other-downing. Self-downing is irrational for the following reasons.

Empirical — it is empirically untenable to rate the 'self'

Self-downing is known in common parlance as low self-esteem (LSE). Most clients with LSE wish to have HSE (high self-esteem). However, both rest on the idea that it is possible to rate (i.e. esteem) the 'self'. Is this in fact possible? To answer this question we need to define what we mean by the 'self'. Paul Hauck's (1991) definition of the self is as good as any (and better than most) so I will use it to construct my argument that it is empirically untenable to rate the 'self'. Hauck (1991), then, defines the 'self' as 'every conceivable thing about you that can be rated' (p. 33). As such, your 'self' is too complex to be given a single rating. Such an evaluation would be possible if you were a single-cell amoeba; but you are a human organism who has millions of thoughts and feelings, has acted in countless ways and has very many traits and characteristics. Consequently, you cannot give your 'self' a legitimate rating. You can and probably do give your 'self' an illegitimate rating, but this evaluation has nothing to do with the reality of who you are.

Even if it were possible to give your 'self' a single rating with the help of a computer so powerful that it hasn't been invented yet, such an evaluation would be out of date as soon as it was made. Why? Because you are not static, but constantly in flux. A rating, once made, is a static thing and thus cannot do justice to an ongoing, ever-changing organism.

Thus if Victor concluded that he was a bad person if his boss disapproved of him then he would be making an unempirical statement. If it were true that Victor were a bad person then everything about him would have to be bad now, in the past and in the future. This is hardly likely.

Logical — whilst you can legitimately rate single aspects of your 'self', it does not follow logically that you can rate your whole 'self'.

It makes logical sense to rate given aspects of your 'self' because doing so helps you to determine whether or not these aspects aid you in the pursuit of your basic goals and purposes. Having rated a given aspect, however, it is illogical then to proceed to rate your entire 'self'. Doing so involves making the logical error of over-generalisation or what is known as the part–whole error. Here you assign a rating to your entire self on the basis of your evaluation of a part of your self. Another name for this illogicality is prejudice.

Thus, if Victor concluded that he was a bad person if his boss disapproved of him then he would be making an illogical statement. He would take a negative situation (i.e. his boss's situation) and conclude on the basis of this that his whole 'self' was bad — a clear over-generalisation.

Pragmatic — self-downing leads to poor psychological results

Victor's irrational self-downing in the face of his boss's disapproval is likely to lead to poor emotional, cognitive and behavioral results before the fact of the disapproval and after that fact. The same points that I made about the pragmatic consequences of musts, awfulizing and LFT beliefs also apply to self-downing beliefs.

I made the point earlier that rating a specific aspect of yourself is useful in that doing so helps you to determine whether or not this aspect aids you in your pursuit towards your long-term goals and, thus, whether you need to change it. However, rating your 'self' over and above the rating you assign to that given aspect does not give you added benefit as you strive to determine whether or not the aspect is goal-enhancing. Indeed, rating your 'self' will hamper you in your deliberations about the usefulness of the specific aspect of yourself. In this situation, while you are trying to think about the usefulness of the specific aspect, you simultaneously give your 'self' a single (often negative) rating. Trying to do two things at once will interfere with your major task — judging the utilitarian value of the aspect under consideration.

Unit 62: The Importance of Order in Disputing

Before completing this module, I want to stress one important point. When you dispute your client's irrational belief it is best for you to do so one at a time and to use one argument at a time. Otherwise, you will 'bounce around' from one belief to the next and from one argument to the next. Let's suppose that you have chosen to target your client's must for change and to employ an empirical argument first. As this is your chosen strategy persist with it until your client has grasped the point or shows signs that he or she is unlikely to understand that there is no empirical evidence for the existence of a must. In which case, switch to employing, say, a logical argument to dispute the same must. Persist with this tack until your client has again understood the illogical nature of his or her 'must' or is unlikely to grasp your meaning. Then, switch to using the remaining argument (in this case, the pragmatic one) until one of the two criteria for stopping disputing has been met. Then use the same three arguments, one at a time, with one or more of the client's irrational belief derivatives of her primary must.

Figure 15.1 shows a good sequence of disputing as demonstrated in the work of Therapist A. Here the first twenty responses made by Therapist A were analyzed response by response by looking at which type of irrational belief was targeted for change and which of the three major arguments was employed. Then the first twenty responses of Therapist B were analyzed in the same way. This therapist's work shows a poor sequence of disputing. Of course a therapist's responses will be influenced by the client's prior response and it is likely that Therapist B had to deal with a client who was less ordered. However, it is your responsibility as an REBT therapist to help to structure your client's thinking rather than follow his chaos as Therapist B did. In clinical practice it is impossible to achieve perfect sequencing on a consistent basis, so don't become perfectionistic on this issue. One way to discover how much order you are bringing to your disputing work with clients is to tape record your sessions and apply the same analysis on your disputing work that I have demonstrated in Figure 15.1. As long as there is a discernible

Therapist A			Therapist B		
Response	Belief	Argument	Response	Belief	Argument
1	Must	Empirical	1	Must	Empirical
2	Must	Empirical	2	Must	Pragmatic
3	Must	Empirical	3	Awfulizing	Pragmatic
4	Must	Empirical	4	LFT	Logical
5	Must	Pragmatic	5	LFT	Logical
6	Must	Pragmatic	6	Must	Logical
7	Must	Logical	7	LFT	Empirical
8	Must	Logical	8	LFT	Pragmatic
9	Must	Logical	9	Awfulizing	Empirical
10	Must	Logical	10	Must	Empirical
11	Must	Logical	11	Awfulizing	Logical
12	Must	Logical	12	Must	Logical
13	LFT	Empirical	13	Must	Logical
14	LFT	Empirical	14	Must	Empirical
15	LFT	Pragmatic	15	LFT	Empirical
16	LFT	Pragmatic	16	Awfulizing	Empirical
17	LFT	Logical	17	Awfulizing	Logical
18	LFT	Logical	18	LFT	Logical
19	LFT	Logical	19	LFT	Empirical
20	LFT	Logical	20	Must	Empirical

Figure 15.1. Analysis of two therapists' disputing responses by belief target and argument employed.

degree of order in your work, you are probably doing well enough. If there is the chaos characteristic of the work of Therapist B, then seek help from your REBT supervisor and/or trainer.

Having considered the three main arguments you can use while disputing your client's irrational beliefs and having applied these arguments to the four main irrational beliefs, I will now move on to consider the two major styles of disputing. As a beginning practitioner of rational emotive behavior therapy, you need to develop competence in both major styles of disputing: Socratic and didactic. Clients will differ in the value they derive from these different styles, so you may need to make predominant use of Socratic disputing with one client and didactic disputing with another. You will discover, though, that you frequently need to use both with a given client. Whichever style of disputing you use the purpose of each style is the same — to help the client gain intellectual insight into the irrationality of his or her irrational beliefs and the rationality of his or her alternative rational beliefs, using the kind of arguments I discussed in the previous section.

Module 16
Socratic Disputing of Irrational Beliefs

As I briefly showed earlier, Socrates educated his students by asking them open-ended questions designed to encourage them to think critically about philosophical problems. He knew the answers to these problems, but he saw that there was little to be gained by telling his students the solutions. Rather, his goal was to help his pupils, through his questioning procedure, gain a way of thinking about philosophical problems which they could then apply to a broad range of questions and, most importantly, which they could use in his absence. This is similar to the sage who said that if you plant a crop for hungry people you help them now, but if you teach them how to plant crops you help them to help themselves now and in the future. Thus, when you employ Socratic-type questions while disputing your client's irrational beliefs, you are not only helping him or her to question the rationality of these beliefs in the present, but you are also helping him or her to develop a methodology for questioning the rationality of irrational beliefs in the future.

When you ask a Socratic-type question in disputing, it is important to take great care to evaluate your client's response. In particular, you need to monitor four likely responses: (i) the client has answered your question correctly; (ii) the client has answered your question incorrectly; (iii) the client has misunderstood your question and has provided an answer to a different question; (iv) the client has changed the subject.

Let me deal with each of these situations in turn.

Unit 63: Socratic Disputing When Your Client Has Answered Your Question Correctly

When your client has answered your question correctly, it is important to assess the status of her answer. Has she given you the correct answer because she thinks it is what you want to hear? If so, does she also see the sense of it or is she looking for your approval? You need to examine these issues and deal with them (Socratically if possible) until your client sees for herself the correctness of her answer and provides it for no other reason than that it is the correct answer.

For example:

Windy: So where is the evidence that you must pass your exams?

Fiona: There isn't any.

Windy: Why isn't there?

Fiona: Because if there was such a law I could not fail.

Windy: Do you believe that because you're convinced of it or because it is the answer you think I want to hear?

Fiona: ...(pause)...Well, to be frank because it's the answer I think you want to hear.

Windy: What if I wanted to hear the opposite answer?

Fiona: Well...I would still believe it.

Windy: Even if I was disappointed?

Fiona: Yes.

Windy: Why?

Fiona: Because it is true.

Windy: How would you defend it to a friend then?...

Unit 64: Socratic Disputing When Your Client Has Answered Your Question Incorrectly

When your client has answered your question incorrectly, you need to use her answer to formulate another Socratic question. Keep doing this until your client has understood the rational point. For example:

Windy: So where is the evidence that you must pass your exams?

Fiona: Well, if I don't I'll find it harder to get a job.

[Here the client has provided evidence why not passing her exams would have disadvantages for her. She has not, though, provided evidence in support of the idea that she must do so.]

Windy: Is finding it harder to get a job evidence for the idea that you must pass your exams or for the idea that it is undesirable if you fail?

Fiona: Put like that, it's evidence for it being undesirable.

Windy: Do you have any other evidence in support of your belief that you must pass your exams?

Fiona: Well, my parents will be very upset if I fail.

Windy: Again, is that evidence in support of the idea that it is undesirable if you fail or that you absolutely must pass?

Fiona: It's undesirable.

Windy: Any other evidence in support of the idea that you must pass?

Fiona: I guess not.

Windy: What do you conclude from that?

Fiona: That I want to pass my exams, but there is no law that states that I have to do so.

Unit 65: Socratic Disputing When Your Client Has Misunderstood Your Question and Answers a Different Question

What do you do when your client thinks you have asked her a different question? If this is the case bring this to her attention as Socratically as you can, although you probably cannot avoid making an explanatory statement during this process. For example:

Windy: So, where is the evidence that you must pass your exams?

Fiona: I know exams are not a good way of assessing people, but they do need to be taken you know.

[Here it is clear that the client is responding to a very different question.]

Windy: Did you think I asked you why you consider exams to be a good way of assessing people or where is the evidence that you must pass yours?

Fiona: Oh. Did I hear you wrongly? Let me see...Sorry, can you ask me the question again?

Windy: Where is the evidence that you absolutely must pass your exams?

Fiona: I guess there is none...

Unit 66: Socratic Disputing When Your Client Changes the Subject

Finally, how do you respond when your client changes the subject? Here you have a number of options. First, you may consider that the client is following her train of thought rather than yours. In ordinary conversation, people do suddenly change the direction of a conversation because something the other person has said sparks off a thought in the person's mind which she then articulates. If you think this is the case, this is how you might respond:

Windy: So where is the evidence that you must pass your exams?

Fiona: You know my friend Jane is coming down this weekend.

Windy: Sorry, I'm a bit confused. Can you help me understand the connection between looking for evidence for the belief that you must pass your exams and your friend Jane visiting you this weekend?

Fiona: I'm sorry. You asking me that question reminded me that Jane's exams finish on Friday and she promised to come down as they were over.

Windy: So you are looking forward to seeing her. But do you think you will be able to concentrate on challenging your belief about having to pass your exams if we go back to it?

Fiona: I'm sure I will.

Windy: So where is the evidence that you must pass your exams?...

At other times you will recognize that your client's change of topic while you are disputing her irrational belief is probably related to other, less benign factors. First, your client may have difficulty in keeping her attention on what you are both discussing. In this instance, ask your client for permission to interrupt her when she deviates from the issue and bring her back to the disputing sequence. If this doesn't work and you notice that it happens frequently no matter what you are discussing, it is probably a good idea to refer your client for a neuropsychological assessment or in cases of more profound attentional impairment for a neurological examination.

Second, you may suspect that your client finds your Socratic questions threatening in some way and thus she deals with the threat by avoiding the issue. If this is the case, it may be that your client finds the content of your questions threatening. For example, Fiona may change the subject because she does not want to face up to the issue that she has a problem with her exams or she does not want to confront the fact that she may be thinking irrationally about this issue. If correct, these constitute evidence that the client may have a meta-emotional problem which warrants exploration and intervention. You may need to switch focus and do this if it is the case. Alternatively, your client may find the process of Socratic questioning difficult and she may change the subject to cope with her discomfort. If this is the case, you may wish to be more didactic or, if you deem it important, you may wish to encourage her to tolerate her feelings of discomfort and persist with the Socratic questioning. Here is an example of dealing with one of these scenarios:

Windy: So where is the evidence that you must pass your exams?

Fiona: You know my friend Jane is coming down this weekend.

Windy: Fiona, you seemed to change the subject again when I asked you for evidence for your belief. Is there anything that you find uncomfortable about the question?

Fiona: Well...your question reminds me that I'm not handling this situation well.

[This is a clue that the client may have a hitherto undiscovered meta-emotional problem.]

Windy: And as you focus on the fact, and let's assume for the moment that it is a fact, that you aren't handling the situation well, how do you feel about that?

Fiona: Ashamed.

Windy: Given that you feel ashamed every time I question you about your demand that you must pass you exams, does that explain why you change the subject?

Fiona: Yes it does.

Windy: So shall we stick with challenging your demand to pass your exam or shall we deal with your feelings of shame first?

Fiona: I think we need to deal with the shame first.

This example demonstrates something interesting. Even though you may have worked carefully in the assessment phase of therapy to identify a meta-emotional problem, it may only be at the disputing phase that you discover that one exists and that it interferes with the work you are doing on your client's primary target problem. Sometimes you will only learn of the presence of a meta-emotional problem when your client acts to avoid discussing issues that he finds personally threatening (see Dryden, 1994b).

Unit 67: Examples of Socratic Questions

In module 19 I present disputing strategies carried out by Albert Ellis which illustrate the kind of Socratic questions that he asks. But, first, I will list some Socratic-type questions for each of the three major arguments discussed earlier; the target of the questions will be a must.

Empirical

*   Where is the evidence that you must...?
*   Is there any evidence that you must...?
*   Where is the law of the universe which states that you must...?

* Is there a law of the universe which states that you must...?
* If there were a law of the universe which stated that you must, how do you account for the fact that you didn't do what the law dictated that you do?
* Would a scientist think that there was evidence in support of your must?

Logical

* Where is the logic that you must...?
* Is it logical to believe that you must...?
* Does it logically follow that because you want to...therefore you must...?
* Does that must logically follow from your preference?
* Is it good logic to believe that because you want...therefore you must...?
* Would a philosopher think that it was good logic to believe that because you want to...therefore you must...?

Pragmatic

* Where will it get you to believe that you must...?
* What are the emotional and behavioral consequences of believing that you must...?
* Will that must give you good results?
* Is it healthy for you to believe that you must...?
* How is believing that you must...going to help you achieve your (long-term/healthy) goals?
* Is believing that you must...going to help or hinder you in the pursuit of your (long-term/healthy) goals?

Module 17
Didactic Disputing of Irrational Beliefs

The term 'didactic disputing' is actually something of a misnomer because when you are being didactic in REBT you are teaching the client by telling him why irrational beliefs are irrational and why rational beliefs are rational. So the essence of didactic disputing is teaching rational principles by explanation, using the same three major arguments that have been reviewed earlier in this book, i.e. empirical, logical and pragmatic.

What I will do in this module is outline several criteria for good practice when disputing didactically. In doing so, I will also alert you to the most common problems that novice REBT therapists experience when using didactic disputing methods.

Unit 68: Keep Your Didactic Explanations As Short As Possible

When you are challenging your client's irrational beliefs by providing her with information designed to cast doubt on the empirical, logical and pragmatic status of these beliefs, it is important that you keep your explanations as brief as possible. Otherwise you will provide your client with too much information to process adequately. Of course, clients will vary quite considerably with respect to how much information they can process at a given time and you will want to take this issue into account when deciding how much information to provide your client with. If you are in doubt here, err on the side of caution and provide your client with less information than you believe she can digest.

As a training exercise, tape record your therapy sessions and listen particularly to your didactic explanations. Write out ways in which you could have shortened your explanations and show these to your REBT trainer or supervisor. Also play them the relevant taped segment so that they can compare what you said to your client with the proposed shortened version.

Unit 69: Periodically Check Your Client's Level of Understanding of the Points You Are Didactically Presenting to Her

The purpose of presenting your client with information in a didactic manner is to help her to LEARN rational principles which she can later apply in her everyday life. I have emphasized the word LEARN here because many novice REBT therapists think that the goal of didactic disputing is to teach rather than to encourage the client to learn. As the emphasis here is on client learning rather than on therapist teaching, you need to ensure, in the first instance, that your client understands the points you are didactically presenting to her. You can best do this by periodically asking her questions like: 'I'm not sure that I'm making myself clear, can you put into your own words what you've heard me say?'

Note, in particular, two points about this question:

(i) It puts the burden on the therapist to make herself clear rather than on the client to understand.

(ii) It encourages the client to be an active rather than a passive learner by asking her to put her understanding of what you have said into her own words. If your client still uses the same words as you employed, gently encourage her to reformulate her understanding of your points in different language.

If in doing so your client makes errors of understanding, correct these prefacing your remarks by saying something like: 'I don't think that I phrased my explanation very well. Let me see if I can put it another way.'

This again shows that you are taking primary responsibility for your client understanding the rational message. If you don't do this your client may well blame herself for her failure to comprehend what you have been saying. Having prefaced your remarks in this way, make your point again and once more elicit your client's understanding. Proceed in this manner until your client has understood the point you have been making.

Unit 70: Once Your Client Has Understood a Substantive Rational Point, Ask Her for Her Views on It

Just because your client has understood a rational point, it does not follow that she agrees with it. Thus, after your client has understood the substantive point you have been making, ask her for her views on it. Does she agree or disagree with it? Does she think that the point has some practical value for her? Don't be afraid to debate an issue with your client or to correct any misconceptions that she might reveal. However, do so in a non-defensive way and without attacking your client in any way.

Module 18
Flexibility in Disputing

As you learn more about disputing, you will discover that it is a difficult skill that needs to be used flexibly. Whilst a full discussion of this point is beyond this book, I will give you an example of the flexible use of disputing. (For a fuller discussion of the complexity of disputing see DiGiuseppe, 1991b.)

Unit 71: Using the Two Styles of Disputing Conjointly

Having introduced the two disputing styles, how are you to know which style to use with which client? Whilst this is a difficult and complex question to answer fully, let me give you this rule of thumb. Some clients will resonate to a predominantly Socratic style of disputing. These will basically be intelligent clients who are accustomed to thinking for themselves. For other clients who are less intelligent and are less used to reflecting on their own cognitive processes, a more didactic style is indicated.

However, as I mentioned briefly earlier, you will probably need to use both disputing styles with most of your clients. What happens most often in REBT is that you will start with Socratic disputing and use didactic explanations to supplement your work. Here is a typical sequence of disputing that you will hear in the work of Albert Ellis, the founder of REBT (Yankura & Dryden, 1990).

Client: I must do well in my exams.

Therapist: Why do you have to do well?

[Socratic question]

Client: Because if I don't, my parents will feel let down.

Therapist: That's why it's unpreferable. But just because it is unpreferable if you don't do well, how does it follow that you must do well?

[A very brief didactic point followed by another Socratic question]

Client: Because I won't get a very good job later.

Therapist: But again that proves that it would be undesirable if you don't do well. You're saying, though, that you must do well. Now if there was a law of the universe that said that you had to do well, you would have to do well because you would have to follow that law of the universe. Now does that law of the universe exist?

[The therapist realizes that the client isn't grasping the point when it is presented Socratically so he or she makes greater use of didactic explanation. However, note that at the end of the intervention, the therapist asks another Socratic question to encourage the client to reflect actively on the point that was presented didactically.]

Module 19
Examples of Albert Ellis's Disputing Work

In this module, I will provide and comment on therapeutic work carried out by Albert Ellis disputing the irrational beliefs of three of his clients. Each sequence focuses on a particular argument.

Unit 72: Using Empirical Arguments

In this sequence Ellis is disputing the irrational belief of a client who insists that she absolutely must succeed in her career using primarily empirical arguments.

Ellis: Why MUST you have a great career?

Client: Because I very much want to have it.

Ellis: Where is the evidence that you MUST fulfil this strong desire?

Client: I'll feel much better if I do.

Ellis: Yes, you probably will. But how does your feeling better prove that you must succeed?

[So far, Ellis has been using Socratic-type questions. Note how he takes the client's answers to his questions which represent evidence in support of her rational belief (i.e. 'I want to have a great career, but I don't have to have one') and asks whether or not such evidence supports her irrational belief.]

Client: But that's what I want more than anything else in the world.

Ellis: I'm sure you do. But if we take 100 people like you, all of whom want a great career, want it more than anything else in the world, and would feel much better if they achieved it, do they all HAVE to succeed at it?

[Here Ellis probably realizes that he has to use a different type of argument with this client. So he asks whether or not it is empirically true that 100 people who have the same strong preference as the client would all change this into a must.]

Client: If they are to have any joy in life, they have to do so.

[The client still does not get the point that Ellis is implying through his Socratic-type questions.]

Ellis: Really? Can't they have ANY pleasure if they fail to get a great career?

[Taking the lead from the client's last response, Ellis changes the focus of his argument again. If 100 people all must have a great career, none of them will have any pleasure if they don't achieve it. Ellis then questions whether this is empirically the case.]

Client: Well, yes. I guess they can have SOME pleasure.

[This is the first time that the client shows any sign that she can think rationally about the issue at hand. Note how Ellis capitalises on this.]

Ellis: And could some of them have a great deal of pleasure?

Client: Um. Probably, yes?

Ellis: Probably?

Client: Well, highly probably.

Ellis: Right. So, no matter how much people greatly want success and would feel better about gaining it, they don't have to get it. Right?

[Here Ellis summarizes the rational point and asks for agreement. I might have asked, 'What do you think of this idea?', in order to encourage the client to be more independent in her thinking.]

Client: Well, yes.

Ellis: Reality is that way — isn't it?

Client: It seems so.

Ellis: Back to you. Does YOUR great desire for a successful career mean that you ABSOLUTELY MUST achieve it — that the world HAS TO fulfil this desire?

[Having got the rational point over in an abstract way, Ellis then seeks to apply it to the client's own specific set of personal circumstances.]

Client: I see what you mean. Reality is the way it is, no matter how unpleasant I find it to be.

[The client shows signs of really understanding Ellis's point.]

Ellis: Exactly. Make a note of that Effective New Philosophy you just arrived at and keep thinking that way until you thoroughly believe it!

Unit 73: Using Logical Arguments

In this segment Ellis is disputing the irrational beliefs of a client who insists that because he treated his friend very nicely and fairly, this friend ABSOLUTELY SHOULD treat him the same way. He does so using primarily logical arguments.

Ellis: Let's suppose that you're describing the situation with your friend accurately and that he treats you shabbily and unfairly after you consistently treat him well. How does it follow that because of your good behavior he has to respond in kind?

Client: But he's unfair if he doesn't!

Ellis: Yes, we're agreeing on that. He IS unfair and you are fair. Can you jump from 'Because I'm very fair to him, he HAS TO BE fair to me?'

Client: But he's wrong if he isn't fair when I am.

[At this point Ellis and the client appear to be at cross-purposes. Ellis keeps asking the client why his friend MUST be fair to him and the client keeps replying that his friend is wrong and unfair which Ellis is not questioning.]

Ellis: Agreed. But because you are fair, and presumably right, and because he takes advantage of your fairness, does it STILL follow that he has to be right and to treat you fairly?

Client: It logically follows.

Ellis: Does it? It looks like a complete *non sequitur* to me.

Client: How so?

[This is a typical Ellis change of emphasis. He asserts that the client's belief is illogical and waits for the latter to ask why before expanding on his theme. He wants to get his client into an enquiring, 'Why do you say that?' mode.]

Ellis: Well, it's logical or consistent that he preferably should treat you fairly when you treat him well. But aren't you making an illogical — or 'magical' — jump from 'Because he PREFERABLY should treat me fairly he ABSOLUTELY HAS TO do so?' What 'logical' law of the universe leads to your 'He absolutely has to do so?'

Client: No law, I guess.

Ellis: No, in logic we get necessitous conclusions, such as 'If all men are human and John is a man, John must be human.' But your 'logic' says, 'People who get treated fairly, often treat others fairly; I treat my friend fairly; therefore it is absolutely NECESSARY that he treat me similarly.' Is that a logical conclusion?

[This is another typical Ellis strategy. He begins by making a point in didactic fashion. As occurs here, this point illustrates a rational idea (in this case a logical idea). He then contrasts this with the client's irrational idea (in this case an illogical idea), but does not tell the client that his idea is illogical. Rather he encourages the client to think for himself by asking, 'Is that a logical conclusion?'. It is worth studying this sequence in detail because it is so typical of Ellis's effective disputing work.]

Client: I guess not.

Ellis: Moreover, you seem to be claiming that because you act fairly and your friend behaves unfairly, his ACTS make him a ROTTEN PERSON. Is that logical thinking?

[Ellis infers other-downing from his client's must. He is probably correct; however, my practice is to check my hunch with the client before proceeding.]

Client: Why not?

[As you will see, Ellis immediately answers the client's question. I would have encouraged the client to make a stab at answering his own question before going into didactic mode.]

Ellis: It's illogical because you're over-generalising. You're jumping from one of his rotten BEHAVIORS — or even one of his TRAITS — to categorising HIM, his totality as 'rotten'. How does that over-generalisation follow from a few of his behaviors?

[Here Ellis states the logical error that the client is making, shows him in what way the error is present in his belief about his friend and finally questions him about the logicality of that belief.]

Client: I can see now that it doesn't.

Ellis: So what could you more logically conclude instead?

[Here, Ellis encourages the client to be active in his thinking.]

Client: Well, I could think that he isn't one of his main behaviors. He is a person who often, but not always, acts rottenly.

Ellis: Good! Alfred Korzybski and his followers in General Semantics would approve of your new conclusion!

Unit 74: Using Pragmatic Arguments

In the following piece of work, the client insists that if she believes that she must do well, she will succeed better at school and win others' approval. Ellis shows her that her irrational belief will in all probability produce poor results.

Client: If I am anxious about doing poorly at school because, as you say, I think that I must do well, won't my must and my anxiety motivate me to do better?

Ellis: Yes, in part. But won't they also defeat you?

[Here Ellis gives a straight answer to the client's straight question. But he then follows up by asking a question to encourage the client to think about the issue for herself. This is another typical Ellis disputing strategy.]

Client: How so?

Ellis: If you keep making yourself very anxious with 'I must do well! I must perform perfectly!' won't you preoccupy yourself so much that you DETRACT from the time and energy you can give to studying?

[Yet another typical Ellis intervention. Here Ellis is really making a statement in the guise of a question. The question format is to encourage the client's active participation, but the rational point that Ellis is making is clear.]

Client: Maybe. But I'll still feel quite motivated.

Ellis: Mainly motivated to obsess! You'll be DRIVEN to study. And while you drive yourself, you'll keep thinking, 'But suppose I fail! Wouldn't that be AWFUL?' You'll worry about what your texts will be like, how you will handle them, how you will subsequently perform, etc. How will keeping the future so much in mind help you focus on the PRESENT studying?

[This intervention comprises a number of didactically made points with the question twist at the end.]

Client: It may not help.

Ellis: No, it's much more likely to sabotage. Moreover, even if you somehow succeed in your courses, do you want to be miserably anxious and depressed, WHILE you are succeeding?

Client: Frankly, no.

Ellis: And do you want to be SO absorbed in worrying about school that you have little time for relationships, sports, music and other enjoyments?

[Having succeeded in getting the point across to the client that her irrational belief will do her more harm than good, Ellis spends time — cf. his last two interventions and much of his following responses — underscoring this important point.]

Client: I don't think so. I passed my courses last term but was able to do little else.

Ellis: See! And what about the physical results of your constant worry and perfectionism?

Client: My physician thinks they are making my digestive tract hyperactive.

Ellis: I'm not surprised. And when you constantly worry, how do you feel about YOU for being such a worrier?

Client: Pretty shitty.

Ellis: Is THAT feeling worth it? But even if you felt bad about your anxiety and didn't put YOURSELF down for having it, you would still bring on endless frustration and disappointment by indulging in it.

Client: You may be right.

Ellis: Don't take my word for it. Look for yourself at the results you get from your perfectionistic demands and figure out what you could say to yourself to replace them.

[Ellis often urges his clients not to take his word for it. However, his didactic style does encourage clients not used to thinking for themselves to do just that. Greater extended use of Socratic disputing would achieve this result more effectively.]

Client: Well, I could tell myself, 'It's great to do well at school, but I DON'T HAVE TO BE PERFECT. Even if my anxiety sometimes helps me to get good marks, it, too, has too many disadvantages and it isn't worth it.'

Ellis: Good! That's a much better way to think.

Module 20
Helping Your Client To Understand the Rationality of His Rational Beliefs

In addition to helping your client understand the irrationality of his irrational beliefs, you need to encourage him to understand the rationality of his rational beliefs. By Socratic or didactic means you need to help him to acknowledge the following.

Unit 75: Preferences

Empirical Argument: Your client's rational preferences are consistent with the internal reality of what she wants. To judge whether or not a person has a preference, look at what she says and how she acts. If a preference exists, for example, it will motivate her to approach certain things and to avoid others and this can be observed empirically. Holding a preference is also consistent with reality because it does allow for the person not getting what he wants.

Thus, Victor can provide evidence for his healthy preference: 'I would prefer my boss not to disapprove of me, but there is no reason why he must not do so'. It is consistent with the internal reality of what he wants and you can determine if this is the case by studying how he thinks, talks and acts. Also his rational belief is consistent with reality because it allows for the possibility that his boss may disapprove of him.

Logical Argument: Your client's specific preference follows logically from her general philosophy of preferring to get what she wants. Thus, Victor's specific preference for not having his boss's disapproval follows logically from his general preference of getting what he wants.

Pragmatic Argument: Your client's preferences are more likely to help her to achieve her goals and less likely to lead to psychological disturbance than her musts. Thus, Victor's preference about not having his boss's disapproval will more likely result in him achieving his goal of feeling concerned but not anxious about such disapproval than will his must.

234

Unit 76: Anti-Awfulizing

As mentioned in Module 1, an anti-awfulizing philosophy involves your client making flexible evaluations (from 0%–99.99%) on a continuum of badness.

Empirical Argument: You can prove that something is bad by looking at the actual or likely consequences for the person concerned. In addition, you can prove that something exists on a continuum of badness by discovering an event that can be worse. Thus, Victor can provide evidence for his anti-awfulizing belief: 'It is bad, but not terrible if my boss disapproves of me.' He could argue with justification that if his boss disapproves of him, he is more likely to dismiss Victor and less likely to promote him than if he approves of Victor. Also, Victor can prove his anti-awfulizing belief by pointing to situations that would be worse for him than being disapproved of by his boss.

Logical Argument: A person's specific anti-awfulizing beliefs make sense in that they point to what the person values and they are also logically related to the broader concept of his general anti-awfulizing philosophy. Thus, if Victor believes that it is bad, but not awful when he does not get what he wants (general belief), then it is perfectly logical for him to say that it would be bad, but not awful if his boss disapproved of him (specific belief).

Pragmatic Argument: Anti-awfulizing beliefs promote goal achievement. Victor's belief that it is bad, but not awful if his boss disapproves of him will help him to feel concerned, but not anxious about such disapproval. It will also help him to work effectively at his job, thus helping to minimize the chances that he will incur his boss's disapproval.

Unit 77: High Frustration Tolerance (HFT)

HFT beliefs involve the person believing that she can tolerate difficult life situations and that it is in her interests to do so.

Empirical Argument: HFT beliefs are consistent with reality. It is realistic for Victor to say that he can stand being disapproved of by his boss even though this situation would be difficult for him to tolerate. Indeed, empirically he can prove that he can stand his boss's disapproval even when he irrationally tells himself that he cannot do so. Because, even when he has such an LFT belief, he is standing the situation in that he has neither died nor has he forsaken the possibility of future happiness.

Logical Argument: HFT beliefs are logical. A person's specific HFT beliefs make sense in that they point to what she values and they are also logically related to her broader HFT philosophy. Thus, if Victor believes that he can stand negative events in general, even though he finds it difficult to tolerate them, then it is logical for him to say that whilst he would find it difficult to tolerate, he could stand the specific situation of being disapproved of by his boss.

Pragmatic Argument: HFT beliefs aid goal achievement. If Victor shows himself that he can stand his boss's disapproval even though it would be difficult for him to do so, this belief will help him to feel concerned but not anxious, which is his goal. In addition, his HFT belief will help him to concentrate on his job performance, thus decreasing the chances of him incurring his boss's disapproval.

Unit 78: Self/Other Acceptance

Accepting oneself and others as fallible human beings is the healthy alternative to self/other-rating. I will outline the empirical, logical and pragmatic reasons for encouraging clients to endorse self/other-acceptance by taking the example of self-acceptance, although the same arguments can be applied to other-acceptance.

Empirical Argument: Accepting oneself as a fallible human being is consistent with reality. Victor can prove that he is human and fallible with positive, negative and neutral aspects. His essence does not change whether his boss approves or disapproves of him.

Logical Argument: It makes sense for Victor to accept himself as a fallible human being even when his boss disapproves of him. It is perfectly logical, therefore, for him to evaluate this disapproval as negative whilst refraining from giving himself a single rating, as in doing so he is rating a part of his experience without rating his whole person. He does not, thus, make the part–whole error.

Pragmatic Argument: Self-acceptance promotes goal achievement. If Victor accepts himself as a fallible human being even though his boss may disapprove of him he is likely to be concerned, rather than anxious about this disapproval. His self-accepting belief will also encourage him to focus on what he is doing at work rather than on what his boss is thinking of him. This will improve his chances of doing well at work which in turn will decrease the chances of his boss disapproving of him.

Whilst I have presented these arguments didactically, I do want to stress that you can help your client to understand these points Socratically as well as didactically.

In conclusion, the purpose of disputing your client's irrational beliefs is to help her to gain intellectual insight into the fact that her irrational beliefs are inconsistent with reality, illogical and lead to poor psychological results, whereas rational beliefs are empirically based, logical and constructive. Don't expect that once she sees this, she will also have corresponding emotional insight. She won't — yet. In order for her to integrate these concepts so that they make a significant difference to the way she feels and acts, she will need to put them into practice in her everyday life and do so repeatedly using a number of homework assignments. This is the subject of Modules 21 and 22.

Module 21
Negotiating Homework
Assignments

As I mentioned at the end of the previous module, it is important for your client to put into practice in her everyday life what she learns in therapy sessions. In this module, I will discuss several issues that need to be considered when encouraging your client to develop her in-therapy insights.

Unit 79: What's in a Name?

Traditionally, REBT therapists call the formal work that clients agree to do between therapy sessions 'homework assignments'. However, it is not envisioned that your client will only do this work 'at home'. Rather, your client will carry out such assignments in whatever extra-therapy context is deemed to be relevant. Thus, the term 'homework assignment' means work that the client agrees to do between therapy sessions. Whilst most of your clients will be happy to use the term 'homework assignment' when discussing with you the work they are prepared to do on themselves between sessions, it is important for you to appreciate that some clients will find this term off-putting.

The main reason for such antipathy concerns the associations that the term 'homework assignment' has with school. In my experience, such clients have negative memories of school in general or homework in particular. For example, one of my clients, Geraldine, associated homework assignments with being locked in her room by her tyrannical mother until she had finished her school homework before being allowed to eat her supper. Not surprisingly, Geraldine reacted negatively to the term 'homework assignment' the first time I used it in counseling. Indeed, she winced visibly at the very mention of the term.

Whilst there has been no research on the relationship between clients' reactions to the term 'homework assignments' and the extent to which they actually carry out such between-session tasks, my clinical experience has been that clients are more likely to carry out such tasks when they use positive (to them) terms to denote these tasks. Given that at least some of

your clients will have negative reactions to the term 'homework assignment', it is important that you develop with them terms that have positive
connotations.

As a training exercise, pair up with a trainee colleague and develop a
list of terms, other than 'homework assignment', that describe the work
that your clients need to do between therapy sessions if they are to get the
most out of REBT. Do this task before you read the next paragraph.

Here is a brief list of terms that I have used with a sample of my clients
who reacted negatively to the term 'homework assignment':

* between-session task;
* change work;
* improvement task;
* goal-achievement task;
* self-help assignment;
* progress assignment.

Having made the point that it is important to use a term that enables your
client to construe between-session work positively, I will use the term
'homework assignment' in the remainder of this module for ease of communication.

Unit 80: Discussing the Purpose of Homework Assignments

Bordin (1979) has made the important point that therapeutic tasks need
to be goal-directed if their therapeutic potency is to be realized. As discussed in Module 2, one of the most important tasks that your client has
to perform in REBT is putting into practice outside therapy what she
learns inside therapy. As I have shown above, the best way that she can
do this is by carrying out homework assignments. However, as Bordin
rightly notes, your client will be unlikely to carry out such assignments if
(i) she does not clearly understand the point of doing so in general and
(ii) if she does not clearly understand the specific purpose of specific
assignments. As I have already dealt with the issue of helping clients
understand the importance of carrying out homework assignments in
general earlier in this book (see Module 11, Unit 47), I will concentrate
here on the importance of helping your clients to understand the specific purpose of given homework assignments.

The most obvious way of doing this is by keeping to the fore of the
therapeutic discussion your clients' goals. Here is an example of how to
do this.

Windy: So, Barry, can you see that as long as you believe that you must
never be rejected you will never ask a girl out for a date?

Barry: Yes, that's self-evident.

Windy: So what's the rational alternative to this belief?

Barry: That I'd rather not be rejected, but there's no reason to assume that I must not be rejected.

Windy: Right. Now, how can you strengthen this belief?

Barry: By asking women out for dates.

Windy: While practicing which belief?

Barry: The rational belief that I've just mentioned.

Windy: So do you think it would be a good idea to ask a woman out for a date between now and next week to strengthen this belief?

Barry: OK.

Windy: Will you agree to do this?

Barry: Yes, I will.

Windy: What's the purpose of doing so?

Barry: To get over my anxiety about asking women out on dates and to get used to rejection if it happens.

Windy: That is in fact one of the goals that you mentioned when we discussed what you wanted to gain from counseling. Now, do you think that it would be a good idea to make a note of the homework assignment and the reason why you are going to do it?

Barry: Yes, I do.

Unit 81: Different Types of Homework Assignments

There are different types of homework assignments that you can suggest to your client. I will mention several here, but for a fuller discussion, consult Walen, DiGiuseppe and Dryden (1992).

Cognitive assignments

Cognitive assignments are primarily those which help your client to understand the REBT model and the role that beliefs play in human disturbance and health. They also provide clients with a means of identifying and changing irrational beliefs. Many cognitive assignments are thus structured in a way to help clients use the ABCs of REBT to assess their own problems and use disputing techniques to challenge and change their irrational beliefs. Normally, on their own, such assignments help clients to gain intellectual insight rather than emotional insight into rational principles. They thus serve a very important role in the initial and early-middle stages of therapy.

Many of the assessment techniques that I covered in Modules 8 and 15–18 can be adapted or tailored for client self-help use. Given this, I will illustrate only two types of cognitive techniques here.

Reading assignments

Reading assignments are mainly cognitive in nature in that your client will gain cognitive understanding from such material. Such assignments are frequently known as bibliotherapy. There is a plethora of self-help books that cover different client problems from an REBT perspective. Initially, you will want to suggest that your client reads a text which introduces basic REBT principles. This may be best done after you have taught your client the ABCs of REBT (see Module 4).

Howard Young (in Dryden, 1989) noted that clients are generally impressed if you suggest that they read a text or an article that you have written yourself and he thinks that doing so increases the chances that they will read the material. Whilst this awaits empirical investigation, it does make sense and for this reason I frequently suggest that my clients read *Think Your Way to Happiness* which outlines the basic principles of REBT and how these can be applied to common emotional problems (Dryden and Gordon, 1990). If my client expresses alarm at the thought of reading an entire book then I will suggest that he starts with the first chapter or that he reads a condensed booklet version entitled *Think Rationally: A Brief Guide to Overcoming Your Emotional Problems* (Dryden & Gordon, 1992).

Of course, different clients will benefit from reading different introductory material and it is worthwhile becoming familiar with different introductory self-help REBT material so that you can suggest suitable reading material. These range from the simple, e.g. *A Rational Counseling Primer* by Howard Young (1974), to the linguistically complex, e.g. *A New Guide to Rational Living* by Albert Ellis and Bob Harper (1975), which is written in E-prime where no form of the verb 'to be' is employed.

Later you might suggest that your client reads books or articles that are devoted to his specific emotional problems. Paul Hauck has specialized in books on specific themes which are clear and easy to read. He has written books on anger (Hauck, 1980), assertion (Hauck, 1981a), depression (Hauck, 1974) and anxiety (Hauck, 1981b) amongst others. I have written specific books on sulking (Dryden, 1992), guilt (Dryden, 1994c), anger (Dryden, 1996) and shame (Dryden, 1997).

Another way of approaching rational-emotive bibliotherapy is to suggest that your client reads a book on one or both of the two major forms of

psychological disturbance (i.e. ego disturbance and discomfort disturbance). Hauck (1991) has written a book on ego disturbance issues entitled *Hold Your Head Up High* and Jack Gordon and I have written a book
devoted to discomfort disturbance issues entitled *Beating the Comfort
Trap* (Dryden and Gordon, 1993).

Whichever books or articles you recommend to your client, it is important to note that the purpose of bibliotherapy is to encourage your client to
develop intellectual insight into rational principles. Many clients believe
that if they read and re-read articles and books on REBT then they will not
only understand these principles but will automatically be able to internalize them into their behavioral and emotional repertoire. As I discussed in
Module 11, Unit 47, it is very unlikely that this will happen, as internalization of rational beliefs will usually only occur as a result of repeated cognitive, emotive AND behavioral practice.

Here are three training exercises that will help you to make effective
use of bibliotherapeutic materials.

1. Suggest to your trainee colleagues that you each review three different
   REBT self-help books. In doing so, briefly summarize the content of
   these books and develop a list of indications and contra- indications for
   their use. This exercise will allow you and your colleagues (a) to com-
   pile a growing list of REBT reading resources and when they can best
   be used and (b) to develop your powers of criticism in relation to this
   material.
2. Begin to write your own REBT self-help material. This will enable
   you to increase your credibility with your clients as well as helping
   them to 'hear your voice' in the material that they read. I have found
   that when my clients say that they can 'hear my voice' in the books
   that I have written, then this helps to reinforce their within-therapy
   learning.
3. Pair up with a trainee colleague and as therapist help your 'client' to
   understand the purposes of reading assignments and, as importantly,
   the limits of bibliotherapy. As elsewhere, tape record the interchange
   and play it to your REBT trainer or supervisor for feedback.

Listening assignments

Reading assignments obviously involve your client using his or her visual
mode of experience. Some clients, however, may not process information
readily using this mode. Others may be blind or find reading the small print
of self-help books or articles difficult because of failing eyesight. Given
these points you will need to offer such clients a plausible and effective
alternative mode of communication whereby important rational principles
are conveyed.

Using the auditory mode of communication is the obvious alternative
here and there are two major types of listening assignments that you can

suggest your client does between sessions. First, you can suggest that your client listen to one or more of the numerous audiotapes that are put out by the Albert Ellis Institute for Rational Emotive Behavior Therapy (for a catalogue write c/o 45 East 65th Street, New York, NY 10021, USA). Most of these tapes are in the form of lectures on client problems (such as anxiety, unhealthy anger, depression and procrastination) and how these can be tackled using the principles of REBT.

Second, you can suggest that your client listens to an audio-recording of her therapy sessions. Numerous clients report that they find listening to such recordings helpful. They frequently say that points that they did not quite understand during a therapy session became quite clear on later auditory review. There are three reasons why this might be the case. As a training exercise see if a small group of your trainee colleagues can identify them. You may well discover additional reasons. Do this exercise before reading further.

I hope that you were able to discover the three reasons which I will now discuss.

(i)   During therapy sessions, your client may be distracted by her own thoughts and feelings related to the problem that she is discussing with you. Such thoughts and feelings will interfere with her ability to process adequately the points you are trying to convey to her using Socratic or didactic means. On later review and freed from the distracting nature of these thoughts and feelings, your client may well be more able to focus on what you were saying than when you said it at the time.

(ii) During therapy sessions, your client may be reluctant to tell you that she does not understand what you are trying to convey to her. Even when you ask her for her understanding of the points you have been making*, her correct response may belie her true understanding. On later review, and freed from the self-imposed pressure to understand what you are saying, she may, paradoxically, understand more fully than at the time the rational principles you were explaining.

(iii) When your client comes to listen to the recording of her therapy session, she can replay the entire session or segments of it as many times as she chooses. Unless she asks you to repeat points several time in the session (which the vast majority of clients will not do), your client only gets to hear once what you say in the therapy session. Repeated review of the entire session or salient segments of the session will often facilitate client understanding of rational principles.

Whenever I suggest that clients review recordings of therapy sessions, I suggest that they make written notes as this encourages them to be active

---

*If you recall, I have urged you to do this especially when you have been presenting points didactically (see Module 17).

in the reviewing process. I particularly ask them to note points that they found most salient and points which they could not understand even after repeated review. I stress that this is most probably attributable to my deficits as a communicator rather than their deficits in understanding what I was trying to convey.

Another benefit of encouraging clients to listen to recordings of their therapy sessions is that it helps them to re-orientate the therapy. Clients sometimes say, for example, that on reviewing the session they realized that they were not discussing what they really wanted to discuss or that they had omitted important information while discussing salient issues. In this way, your client may well help you to get therapy back on the most important track.

Of course, not all clients will find such listening assignments valuable. In particular, your client may well say that she felt worse after listening to a therapy session than before reviewing it. If this happens regularly, it may well be a sign that you need to suspend the use of this type of homework assignment. Common reasons for clients feeling worse after listening to recordings of therapy sessions usually centre on self-downing issues. Clients may say such things as:

* 'I hated the sound of my voice' (and implicitly — I put myself down for the way I sounded);
* 'I hated myself for sounding so pathetic';
* 'I couldn't believe how stupid I was for not understanding what you were saying'.

Whilst you may be able to encourage your client to practice self-acceptance while listening to facets of herself that she didn't like, most often you will find it more profitable to suspend 'audiotherapy' until your client has made more progress on her self-downing issues. Here as elsewhere in REBT it is important to be flexible.

Imagery assignments

When your client uses imagery assignments, she makes use of both her cognitive and affective modalities. Imagery assignments are obviously cognitive, although they draw on a different part of the brain to that which processes verbal information. They are also affective in nature because visual images, particularly clear images, are affect laden when they embody inferences that are central in the client's personal domain (see Dryden, 1994b)

Imagery assignments can be used by your client between sessions as an assessment tool to identify irrational beliefs that are likely to underpin her predicted disturbed feelings in forthcoming situations. They can also be used by your client as a way of gaining practice in changing unhealthy negative feelings to their healthy counterparts by changing her irrational beliefs to rational beliefs. The important point that your client needs to bear in mind here is keeping the A constant. Otherwise she may learn that she can change her feelings by changing the actual or inferred A. As I showed earlier, belief-based change is regarded in REBT as more enduring than inference-based or environmental change.

A third way that your client can employ imagery assignments is as a form of mental rehearsal before carrying out behavioral assignments. Here your client is advised to practice seeing herself in her mind's eye perform poorly as well as adequately. The purpose of encouraging your client to picture herself performing poorly is to help her to think rationally about such an eventuality. Preparing clients for failure as well as success is a typical REBT strategy.

Whilst clients differ markedly in their ability to visualise clearly, a more important factor than image clarity in determining the employment of imagery assignments is the presence of client affect accompanying their use. In my view, such assignments are less useful with clients who experience no affect while picturing themselves in situations where they would in reality feel a lot of emotion than with clients who do experience affect while using imagery.

Behavioral assignments

Behavioral assignments involve your client doing something to counter-act his irrational beliefs and to consolidate his rational beliefs. They are assignments which encourage your client to act on his preferences. Given this, behavioral assignments are often used simultaneously with cognitive assignments which provide your client with an opportunity to challenge and change his irrational beliefs. The main purpose of behavioral assignments, then, is to strengthen his conviction in his rational beliefs.

Emotive assignments

Emotive assignments are therapeutic tasks that fully engage your client's emotions. As such, as long as they meet this criterion, certain cognitive and behavioral techniques can be regarded as emotive assignments.

Thus, Ellis regards certain cognitive techniques as emotive in nature when they are employed by the client with force and energy and he sees certain behavioral techniques such as 'shame-attacking exercises' as emotive because the client is encouraged to do certain 'shameful' things and simultaneously 'attack' his shame by disputing the irrational beliefs that underpin this emotion. In addition, certain imagery methods, such as rational-emotive imagery, can be classified as emotive assignments because they attempt to engage fully the client's emotions. As with behavioral assignments, the major purpose of emotive assignments is to help your client to turn his intellectual conviction in his rational beliefs into emotional conviction (see Module 11, Unit 47).

Unit 82: The Importance of Negotiating Homework Assignments

The field of behavioral medicine has focused much attention on the factors associated with patient compliance with prescriptive medical treatment. However, the term 'compliance' is an unfortunate one when used in counseling and psychotherapy as it conjures up the image of an all-knowing therapist telling the ignorant client what to do, with the client either complying or not complying with these instructions. Whilst it is debatable whether this image is even appropriate in the field of medicine, it is certainly unsuitable in the field of psychotherapy in general and REBT in particular.

On the other hand, the image of equal collaboration between therapist and client is also not appropriate in REBT. Whilst the egalitarian-collaborative model of the therapeutic relationship is appealing to therapists who view their main role as encouraging the client to use his or her own resources, it is viewed as dishonest by REBT therapists. It ignores, for example, the fact that as an REBT therapist you know more than your client about (i) the nature of psychological disturbance; (ii) how clients, in general, perpetuate their psychological problems and (iii) the processes of therapeutic change and how to facilitate it. Having this knowledge does not entitle you to view yourself as an all-knowing guru and act accordingly, but neither should it lead you to deny that you have such knowledge in the spirit of well-meaning, but ultimately misguided egalitarianism.

As I argued earlier, REBT theory holds that you and your client are equal in humanity, but unequal in your knowledge and understanding of human disturbance and its remediation. This view of the therapeutic relationship in REBT underpins the importance of negotiating homework assignments with your client. This means that you neither unilaterally tell your client what he will do for homework, nor do you wait for him to tell you what he is going to do between sessions. It means that you will have an informed view concerning the best homework assignment for him at a given time, that you will express this view honestly with your client, but you will very much respect his opinion on the matter and will discuss with him your respective views with the purpose of agreeing a homework assignment to which he will commit himself.

Let me illustrate the differences between the three approaches to homework assignments that I have described. I will first set the scene and then vary the dialogue to highlight these differences.

Windy: So, Norman, you can now see that your anxiety about speaking up in class stems from two beliefs: first, the belief that you must know for certain that you won't say anything stupid and, second, that if you do say something stupid then other people will laugh at you which would prove that you would be stupid through and through. Right?

Norman: Right.

Windy: And the healthy rational alternatives to these two irrational beliefs are?

Norman: That I'd like to be certain that I don't say something stupid, but I don't need this certainty. And I can accept myself as a fallible human being in the event of saying something stupid and people laughing at me.

Windy: Now you also understand that if you want to really believe these two ideas, you need to ...?

Norman: Practice acting according to these two ideas.

1. REBT therapist as unilateral expert: telling a client what he will do for homework

Windy: OK, so what I want you to do between now and next week is to speak up five times in class, and practice your two rational ideas before, during and after doing this. Agreed?

Norman: ...(pause)...(very hesitantly)...A-A-Agreed.

[As you can see, here I have unilaterally decided what is good for my client and I have told him what I want him to do. As the very hesitant response of my client shows, he is most unlikely to do this homework or, if he does, it will be out of fear.]

2. REBT therapist as laissez-faire egalitarian: waiting for your client to tell you what he will do for homework

Windy: So, Norman, what can you do between now and next week to practice and strengthen these two ideas?

Norman: Well, I suppose I can think about the ideas once a day.

Windy: OK, fine.

[Here, because I am overly keen to encourage my client to use his own resources, I do not query his own suggestion. Whilst the client may well carry out this assignment, he will not derive much benefit from it, primarily because it is not a behavioral task.]

3. REBT therapist as authoritative egalitarian: negotiating a homework assignment with your client

Windy: Now, Norman, let me make a suggestion about what you can do to strengthen these beliefs and then we can discuss it. OK?

Norman: Fine.

Windy: First of all, it is important to do something active to get over your fear. Can you see why?

Norman: Because if I don't, I won't overcome it.

Windy: Right, so how about speaking up in class while showing yourself before, during and after you do so that you'd like to be certain that you don't say something stupid, but you don't need this certainty. And that you can accept yourself as a fallible human being in the event of saying something stupid and people laughing at you?

Norman: OK, that sounds reasonable.

Windy: How about speaking up every college day between now and then?

Norman: That's five days! That seems a bit steep.

Windy: What would you suggest?

Norman: Twice?

Windy: How about a compromise of three or four?

Norman: Three it is then.

[Note that here I have taken an authoritative stance by selecting for Norman a relevant behavioral task. However, I am egalitarian in that I ask him for feedback on my suggestion and I am prepared to negotiate a compromise. I thus show that I respect his opinion, but I also ask him to respect mine. My hypothesis is that the client is more likely to carry out this task than he would in the first scenario discussed above when I unilaterally told him what he was to do for homework.]

Unit 83: The "Challenging, but Not Overwhelming" Principle of Homework Negotiation

Albert Ellis (1983) has been openly critical of many popular behavior therapy techniques that are based on the principle of gradual desensitisation.

Ellis argues that the use of such techniques is inefficient in that it needlessly prolongs the length of therapy and that it tends to reinforce clients' philosophy of low frustration tolerance. By using gradual desensitisation methods it is as if the therapist is implicitly saying to the client: 'You really are a delicate flower who can tolerate virtually no anxiety or discomfort and that is why we will have to take things very gradually.'

Given this, Ellis argues that clients can help themselves best by doing homework assignments based on the principle of flooding or full exposure. Here, your client would practice strengthening his rational beliefs by seeking out situations in which he would be most anxious. He would then stay in these situations until he has strengthened his rational beliefs to the extent that he no longer feels anxiety. He would then do this frequently and repeatedly until he has overcome his problem. Ellis (1985) describes a case where he helped a woman overcome her lift phobia by full exposure methods. The woman agreed to travel repeatedly in lifts in a short period of time until she could travel in them without anxiety. It goes without saying that the client needs to be very motivated to do this. Thus, Ellis's client had just been offered a desired job at the top of a New York skyscraper. Because it was impossible for her to take the stairs, she was faced with the choice of declining the position or travelling in the lift to her new office.

When clients have such motivation and are prepared to tolerate the high levels of discomfort to which flooding methods lead, you should encourage them to undertake homework assignments based on the principle of full exposure. However, in my experience, most clients will not agree to carry out such assignments. In such instances, is there a better alternative to homework assignments based on gradual desensitisation? The answer is yes and these are assignments based on the principle that I have called 'challenging, but not overwhelming'. Such assignments occupy a middle ground between flooding and gradual desensitisation methods. They constitute a challenge for the client, which if undertaken would lead to therapeutic progress, but would not be overwhelming for the client (in his judgment) at that particular time. Here is an example of how I introduce this concept to clients.

Windy: Now, Norman, how quickly do you want to overcome your fear of speaking up in class: very quickly, moderately quickly or slowly?

Norman: Very quickly.

Windy: And how much discomfort are you prepared to face in overcoming your problem: great discomfort, moderate discomfort or no discomfort?

Norman: Well, ideally no discomfort.

Windy: So you'd like to overcome your problem very quickly and without discomfort. Right?

Norman: Right.

Windy: Well, I'd really like to help you to do that but, unfortunately, I can't. Let me explain. If you want to overcome your problem very quickly, you will have to speak up in class very frequently and this will involve you tolerating much discomfort. Here you will have to do assignments based on the principle of full exposure. However, if you want to experience minimal levels of discomfort, then it follows that you will have to go very slowly. Here you will do assignments based on the principle of gradual desensitisation. A middle ground between these two positions is based on the principle that I call 'challenging, but not overwhelming'. Here you will choose to do homework assignments that are challenging, but not overwhelming for you at any point in time. This would involve you tolerating moderate levels of discomfort and would lead you to make progress moderately quickly. Is that clear?

Norman: Yes. You're saying that I can go slowly, moderately quickly or very quickly. The quicker I decide to go, the more discomfort I will have to tolerate.

Windy: That's exactly right. So, how would you like to proceed?

Norman: According to the 'challenging, but not overwhelming' principle.

Windy: Then let's see what you can do between now and next week that will allow you to practice strengthening your rational beliefs in a way that is challenging for you...

Let me make two concluding remarks on this issue.

1. I tend to dissuade any clients who say that they wish to follow the 'gradual desensitisation' route. I point out to them that doing so will be counterproductive in that taking this route will tend to reinforce their philosophy of low frustration tolerance. However, I do not insist that such clients begin with 'challenging, but not overwhelming' homework assignments. If the worst comes to the worst, I would start with the 'gradual desensitisation' route, hoping to 'transfer' them to the 'challenging, but not overwhelming' route as quickly as possible.
2. A number of clients who begin by carrying out 'challenging, but not overwhelming' homework assignments do switch to flooding-type assignments after they have made some progress and they get accustomed to tolerating moderate levels of discomfort.

In the following units, I want to mention a number of principles that you can follow to increase the chances that your client will carry out his jointly negotiated homework assignment. Please note, however, that none of these methods will guarantee that he will actually do the assignment. Assuming that you have carried out the following steps, it is important not to lose sight of the fact that your client is ultimately responsible for whether or not he will do his homework. Thus, whether he does so or not, it is not a measure of your worth as a therapist (or even as a person!).

Unit 84: Teach Your Client the "No-Lose" Concept of Homework Assignments

The 'no lose' concept of homework assignments is designed to give your client additional encouragement to agree to carry out an assignment. While introducing the concept to your client you need to stress that there is no way that your client can lose if he agrees to undertake the homework task, and you need to emphasize three points as shown in the following dialogue.

Windy: So to recap, Norman, you have agreed to speak up in class on three occasions while showing yourself (i) that you don't need to be certain that you won't say anything stupid before you speak and (ii) that if you do say something stupid you can still accept yourself as a fallible human being even if people in your seminar group laugh at you. Is that right?

Norman: Well, I'm still a bit doubtful about it.

Windy: I can appreciate that, but let me put it this way. If you undertake to do the assignment, then there is no way you can lose. Do you know why?

Norman: No, why?

Windy: Well, let me put it like this. First, if you agree to do the assignment and you actually do it and it works out well, then that's good because you have made a big stride forward in meeting your goals. Right?

Norman: Yes, I can see that.

Windy: Second, if you agree to do the assignment and you actually do it, but it doesn't go well, then that's valuable because we can analyze what happened and you can learn from the experience. Do you see that?

Norman: Yes, I do.

Windy: And finally, if you undertake to do the homework assignment, but you don't do it, then that is also valuable. Do you know why?

Norman: ...Because we can find out how I stopped myself from doing it?

Windy: That's right. We can discover obstacles which neither of us knew about and then we can help you to overcome them. So, can you see why if you agree to do the assignment, you can't lose.

Norman: Very good. You should be a salesman!

Windy: I am. I'm trying to sell you on the concept of mental health and how you can achieve it!

Unit 85: Ensure That Your Client Has Sufficient Skills To Carry Out the Homework Assignment

It is important that your client has the skills to carry out the negotiated homework assignment. For example, if you have suggested that he complete a written ABC form, it is important that you first instruct him in its use. He is more likely to do the assignment if he knows what to do than if he doesn't.

Unit 86: Ensure That Your Client Believes That He Can Do the Homework Assignment

Self-efficacy theory (Bandura, 1977) predicts that your client is more likely to carry out a homework assignment if he believes that he can actually do it than if he lacks what Bandura calls an 'efficacy expectation'. Given this, it is important to spend some time helping your client to see that he is able to carry out the homework task. One way to do this is to suggest that your client uses imagery techniques where he repeatedly pictures himself carrying out the assignment before he does so in reality.

It is important to distinguish between an efficacy expectation and the more objective question of whether or not your client has a particular skill in his repertoire. It is possible that your client has a skill in his repertoire but subjectively believes that he is unable to use this skill in a particular setting. Thus, it is insufficient to teach your client a skill such as filling in a written ABC form (see point 1 above). You also need to help him to develop the relevant efficacy expectation.

Windy: So do you think you can speak up in class while showing yourself that you don't need to be certain that you won't say anything stupid and that you can accept yourself as a fallible human being if you do?

Norman: I'm not sure.

Windy: Well let's see. Close your eyes and picture yourself in class. Have you got that image in mind?

Norman: Yes, I have.

Windy: Good. now see yourself showing yourself that you don't need to be certain that you won't say anything stupid and that you can accept yourself as a fallible human being if you do. Have you got that?

Norman: Yes.

Windy: Now keep those two beliefs in mind and see yourself speaking up in class. Can you do that?

Norman: Yes, I can picture that.

Windy: So does this show you that you can do this assignment in reality?

Norman: Yes, it does.

Unit 87: Give Yourself Sufficient Time To Negotiate a Homework Assignment

I have listened to many therapy sessions conducted by beginning REBT therapists over the years and I have been struck by how little time such therapists allocate to negotiating homework assignments with their clients. They frequently leave the issue of homework to the very last minute with the result that they end up by telling their clients what they want them to do between sessions. Because negotiating a suitable assignment takes time, I suggest that you allocate ten minutes to this activity. This will enable you to incorporate all of the issues that I have discussed in this module which, I argue, will increase the chances that your client will execute the homework task successfully.

If you have negotiated a suitable homework assignment in the early or middle part of a therapy session you will not need to devote ten minutes to this task at the end of a session. However, it is still worthwhile allocating a few minutes to recap on the homework, otherwise your client may forget what his homework is. This latter point emerged from a book that my colleague, Joseph Yankura, and I did on the therapy work of Albert Ellis entitled *Doing RET: Albert Ellis in Action* (Yankura and Dryden, 1990). We noted that Ellis did not consistently negotiate specific homework assignments with his clients at the end of a session. Ellis replied that he often makes homework suggestions during a therapy session. The important point here is not whether a therapist did or did not negotiate a homework assignment, but whether her clients remember the homework. When we interviewed several of Ellis's clients for the book we came away with the impression that Ellis's clients did not recall that he consistently suggested specific homework tasks. One way to ensure that your client remembers that homework has been negotiated, particularly when this has been discussed in the main body of the session, is to review it at session's end.

Another way of encouraging your client to remember his homework is to suggest that he keeps a written record of the assignment. I will discuss this further in Unit 92 below.

Unit 88: Ensure That the Homework Assignment Follows Logically From the Work You Have Done With Your Client in the Therapy Session

Much of the work you will do in a therapy session will be focused on one of your client's target problems. Towards the end of the session, you should negotiate a homework assignment with your client that logically follows from the work you have done with him on the target problem. The following is a rough guide of when to negotiate which type of homework assignment.

(a) Negotiate a reading assignment when the work you have done with your client has centred on helping your client to understand the relationship between her unhealthy negative emotion and her irrational beliefs.

(b) Negotiate a written homework assignment (e.g. an ABC form) when the session work has centred on helping your client to identify and dispute her irrational beliefs and when you have trained your client in the use of the relevant written form.

(c) Negotiate an imagery assignment when the session work has focused on beginning to strengthen rational beliefs, but your client is not ready to undertake a behavioral assignment.

(d) Negotiate a behavioral assignment (along with a relevant cognitive disputing technique) when the session work has prepared your client to strengthen her rational beliefs by 'acting on her preferences'.

(e) Negotiate an emotive assignment when the session has been devoted to discussing how your client can deepen her conviction in her rational beliefs other than through the use of behavioral assignments.

To reiterate, whatever type of homework assignment you negotiate with your client, ensure that it is relevant to the work you have done with her in the session.

Unit 89: Ensure That Your Client Understands the Nature and Purpose of the Homework Assignment

I have mentioned this point in Unit 40, but it is so important I wish to reiterate it here. At the end of the process of homework negotiation, it is useful to ask your client to summarize the homework assignment and its rationale. It is particularly important to ensure that your client has understood the reason why he has agreed to carry out the assignment. My clinical experience has shown me that the more a client keeps the purpose of a negotiated homework assignment at the forefront of his mind, the more likely it is that he will do the agreed assignment.

Windy: So let's recap. What are you going to do between now and next week?

Norman: I'm going to speak up in class and practice my new rational beliefs.

Windy: And what's the purpose of speaking up in class while showing yourself that you don't need to be certain that you won't say anything stupid and that you can accept yourself as a fallible human being if you do?

Norman: Well, it will help me to be able to speak up in class whenever I want to say something without feeling anxious.

Unit 90: Help Your Client To Specify When, Where and How Often She Will Do the Homework Task

If you can help your client to specify the number of times he will carry out the negotiated homework assignment, when he will do it and in what setting, then he is more likely to do it than if no such agreements are made.

Windy: Now, Norman, how many times between now and next week will you agree to speak up in class while practicing your rational beliefs? I was thinking that four times might be a challenging number, but I don't want to suggest this if it is too overwhelming for you at this point.

[Review the 'challenging, but not overwhelming principle' in Unit 83.]

Norman: Well, that's sounds a bit steep. How about twice?

Windy: Shall we compromise on three?

Norman: OK then.

Windy: And where will you do this?

Norman: Well, I've got four seminars next week. I can do it in three of those.

Windy: Let's be really specific here.

Norman: Well, I can do it in the Monday seminar at 3 pm, in the Wednesday seminar at noon and in the Friday seminar at 10 am.

Windy: Good, now let's talk about when in the seminars you will do this. In my experience it is better to do the homework early in the seminar rather than later. Does that make sense?

Norman: Yes, it does.

Windy: So would it make sense to speak up in the first twenty minutes of the seminar?

Norman: Yes, that makes sense.

Windy: Will you do it?

Norman: Yes.

Unit 91: Elicit a Firm Commitment That Your Client Will Carry Out the Homework Assignment

It is important to get a firm commitment from your client to do the assignment rather than a vague commitment such as 'I think I can do that' or 'I'll try'. When your client makes a definite commitment to do the homework assignment, she is more likely to do it than if she makes a vague commitment.

Windy: So would it make sense to speak up in the first twenty minutes of the seminar?

Norman: OK. I'll try to do that.

Windy: Let me show you the difference between 'do' and 'try'. Snap your fingers...(Norman snaps his fingers)...Now try to snap your fingers, but don't actually snap them...(Norman makes the relevant movement but doesn't actually snap his fingers). Can you see the difference between 'try' and 'do'?

Norman: When you do something you do it. But when you try, it doesn't mean that you will do it.

Windy: So will you commit yourself to speak up in the first twenty minutes or will you commit yourself to trying?

Norman: I'll do it.

Unit 92: Encourage Your Client To Keep a Written Note of His Homework Assignment and Relevant Details

Experienced General Practitioners know that one way of increasing the chances that patients will follow medical advice is to provide them with a written summary of that advice. There are several reasons why a patient may not remember medical advice. First, she may simply forget the advice. Second, the advice may be too complex to be processed properly at the time. Third, the patient may be anxious during the medical consultation and this anxiety may affect her cognitive functioning during and after that consultation.

The same factors may operate during the psychotherapeutic interview and having your client write down the homework assignment or providing her with a written summary of the assignment will increase the chances that she will carry out the assignment. Some REBT therapists keep a supply of 'No Carbon Required' (NCR) paper on which they write or have their clients write down the homework assignment. NCR paper provides an automatic copy for the therapist to keep in his or her files to be retrieved at the beginning of the next session when the therapist will check the client's assignment (see Module 22).

What information should be put on the written record? My practice is to have my client record the following information:

(i)   The nature of the assignment.
(ii)   The purpose of the assignment.
(iii)   How often the client will carry out the assignment.
(iv)   Where the client will carry out the assignment.
(v)   When the client will carry out the assignment.
(vi)   Possible obstacles to carrying out the assignment.
(vii)   How these obstacles can be overcome.

The above seven sections can be completed by the client at the end of the therapy session in which the homework task has been negotiated. The following three sections are to be completed by the client between therapy sessions:

(viii) What the client actually did.
(ix)   Actual obstacles to carrying out the assignment.
(x)   What the client actually learned from carrying out the assignment.

Here is how Norman completed the first seven sections of the homework form at the end of the therapy session in which the assignment was negotiated.

(i)   The nature of the assignment.

I will speak up in class while showing myself that I don't need to be certain that I won't say anything stupid and that I can accept myself as a fallible human being if I do.

(ii)   The purpose of the assignment.

Doing this will help me to be able to speak up in class whenever I want to say something, without feeling anxious.

(iii) How often the client will carry out the assignment.

Three times.

(iv) Where the client will carry out the assignment.

    (a) Monday seminar at 3 pm;

    (b) Wednesday seminar at noon;

    (c) Friday seminar at 10 am.

(v) When the client will carry out the assignment.

During the first twenty minutes of each seminar.

(vi) Possible obstacles to carrying out the assignment.

Feeling very uncomfortable.

(vii) How these obstacles can be overcome.

I can show myself that I can speak up even though I am feeling very uncomfortable and that if I do speak up the discomfort will probably subside.

Unit 93: Troubleshoot Any Obstacles That Will Stop Your Client From Carrying Out the Homework Assignment

It has been my experience that when I have helped my clients to identify potential obstacles to homework completion and to find ways of dealing with these obstacles, then they are more likely to do the homework than when I have not instituted such troubleshooting. What may serve as potential obstacles to homework completion? Golden (1989) has provided a comprehensive list of such obstacles and I refer the reader to his excellent discussion of the subject. Given this, I will only consider here the most common obstacle which is a philosophy of low frustration tolerance (LFT). Clients often provide many rationalisations in their explanations of why they did not do their homework (e.g. 'I didn't have the time' or 'I forgot') when the real reason can be attributed to LFT (e.g. 'I didn't do the task because I thought I would feel too uncomfortable doing it'). It is thus worthwhile raising LFT as a potential obstacle to homework completion even though your client doesn't mention it. This is what I did with Norman.

Windy: Now, Norman, it is often useful in therapy to troubleshoot any reasons why you might not do what you have agreed to do for homework. Can you think of any reason why you might not do yours?

Norman: No, I'm pretty sure that I will do it.

Windy: But what if you begin to feel very uncomfortable in the moments before you have decided to speak up?

Norman: Good point. If that happened I might well duck out of doing it.

Windy: What do you think you would need to tell yourself to speak up even though you are feeling uncomfortable?

Norman: That I can speak up even though I am feeling very uncomfortable and that if I do speak up the discomfort will probably subside.

Windy: Would that work?

Norman: Yes, it would.

Windy: So why not imagine yourself feeling very uncomfortable in the seminar situation and show yourself that you can speak up anyway.

Norman: That's a good idea.

Unit 94: Rehearse the Homework Assignment in the Therapy Room

It is often a good idea to rehearse the assignment in the therapy session if this is practicable. If not you can use imagery rehearsal as a plausible substitute. Rehearsing your client's homework assignment in the session serves both to increase his sense that he will be able to do the assignment in reality and to identify potential obstacles to homework completion that haven't been identified through verbal discussion of this issue.

Windy: Let's rehearse the assignment briefly. OK?

Norman: OK.

Windy: Shall I play your tutor and perhaps one other student and we can imagine that there are other students present too? Your task is to speak up while practicing the two rational beliefs that we discussed. OK?

Norman: Fine.

Windy (as tutor): So this week we are discussing the role of Catholicism in Evelyn Waugh's novel *Brideshead Revisited*. Who would like to kick off?

[I first discovered that this was to be the topic for one of Norman's forthcoming seminars.]

Windy (as student): I think that Waugh shows his deep ambivalence about Catholicism in this novel because several of the characters are at one time scornful of it and at another time drawn towards it.

Norman: I would agree with that. For example, who would have thought that Sebastian would have ended up as he did, as a kind of unpaid janitor in a religious order. And his father ended his life by making the sign of the cross, even though he spent most of his life being openly scornful of Catholicism....

Windy (as therapist): How did that go?

Norman: I did feel a bit anxious, but that went as I got into my stride.

Windy: Do you think this will help you to speak up in the seminar?

Norman: Well, I think I'll be more uncomfortable then, but I'm sure now that I'll be able to do it.

Unit 95: Use the Principle of Rewards and Penalties To Encourage Your Client To Do the Homework Assignment

Sometimes it is helpful to suggest to your client that he can use the principle of rewards and penalties to encourage him to do his homework assignment. Basically this involves your client rewarding himself when he does the assignment and penalising (but not condemning) himself if he fails to do it. This principle can be applied by your client particularly when he may not do the assignment owing to a philosophy of LFT, as in the following example.

Windy: So you still think that you might not do the assignment if you experience a lot of discomfort. Is that right?

Norman: I think so.

Windy: If that happens you can use the principle of rewards and penalties as an added incentive. Here is how it works. What do you like doing every day that you would be very reluctant to give up?

Norman: Reading the newspaper.

Windy: And what do you really dislike doing?

Norman: Cleaning the oven.

Windy: OK. If you speak up in class you can read the newspaper and you won't have to clean the oven. However, if you don't speak up then you have to clean the oven and no reading the newspaper. Agreed?

Norman: Wow, that's tough.

Windy: That's right. Tough measures for tough problems.

Norman: OK. I doubt whether I'll need to use this principle, but I'll do it if I need what you call an added incentive.

[If your client is going to use the principle of rewards and penalties then have him write this agreement on his homework form.]

Unit 96: Monitor Your Skills at Negotiating Homework Assignments

I strongly suggest that you monitor your skills at negotiating homework assignments with the purpose of improving these skills. You can do this by tape recording your therapy sessions routinely and using the scale given in Appendix 1 to evaluate your performance. Before you do so, please note that very few therapists will score highly on all of the scale's items. Indeed, some items will not be relevant and there is an opportunity to indicate this on the scale. However, if you do answer 'No' to any item (as opposed to 'Not Appropriate') then write down what you would have done differently given hindsight and what you would have needed to change in order to have answered 'Yes'. As I have suggested throughout this book, take any enduring problems in negotiating homework assignments to your REBT supervisor or trainer.

Module 22
Reviewing Homework Assignments

In this final module, I will discuss the issues that arise when you come to review your client's homework. To give you an idea of the important role that reviewing homework assignments plays in the REBT therapeutic process consider the following view of the structure of REBT sessions put forward by Ray DiGiuseppe (personal communication), the Director of Professional Education at the Albert Ellis Institute for Rational Emotive Behavior Therapy in New York:

Review Homework
Carry Out Session Work
Negotiate Homework

Reviewing homework when therapy is under way, then, is often the first therapeutic task that you have to perform in a session as an REBT therapist and has a decided bearing on the rest of that session. Let me begin the discussion by outlining the most central principle of reviewing homework.

Unit 97: Put Reviewing Your Client's Homework Assignment on the Session Agenda

Reviewing your client's homework conveys to him or her two things. First it shows her that you consider homework assignments to be an integral part of the therapeutic process. If you, as a client, had agreed to carry out a homework assignment and had actually done so, how would you respond if your therapist did not ask for a report on what you did and what you learned from doing the assignment? My guess is that you would not be pleased. Being human, you would also be less likely to carry out future homework assignments than you would be if your therapist had reviewed the homework with you. For that is what I have found as an REBT therapist and supervisor: clients are more likely to do homework assignments when their therapists initiate regular reviews of their previous assignments than when their therapists do not do so. Consequently, the first and perhaps the most important principle of reviewing your client's homework assignments is actually to review them!

The second point that you convey to your client when you review his or her homework is that you are genuinely interested in the therapeutic progress. Earlier in the process of REBT, you will have helped your client to see that homework assignments are an important vehicle for stimulating therapeutic progress by helping him or her to deepen conviction in his or her rational beliefs. In other words doing homework assignments helps your client to go from intellectual to emotional insight. Asking your client about his or her homework assignments shows that you are taking a regular interest in his or her progress on this issue. Failing to review assignments may convey the opposite: that you are indifferent to his or her therapeutic progress.

Unit 98: When Is It Best To Review Homework Assignments?

Having put reviewing homework assignments on the therapeutic agenda, when is the best time to initiate such a review? In my opinion, the best time to review your client's homework assignments is to do so at the beginning of the next therapy session. If you set a formal, structured agenda for each therapy session with your client as many cognitive therapists do (see Beck et al., 1979), you will put the item 'previous homework' on the agenda for every session. You will also want to suggest placing this item early on the agenda. The reason for this is that what your client did or did not do for homework and what he or she learned or did not learn from doing it will have an important influence on the content of the current session.

On the other hand, if your practice is not to set a formal agenda at the beginning of every session, you will still want to initiate the homework review early in the session. Indeed, some REBT therapists routinely begin each therapy session with an enquiry about their client's previous week's homework. For example, Ed Garcia has a tape in the Institute for RET's professional tape library which begins with him asking his client, 'What did you do for homework?'

There are, of course, exceptions to this principle. For example, if your client comes into the therapy session in a very agitated or even suicidal state, I hope that you would deal with this crisis rather than attempt to review his last homework task! Here, as elsewhere, it is important to practice REBT in a humane, flexible manner.

In the following units, I will outline and discuss several points that you need to consider as you review your client's homework assignment.

Unit 99: When Your Client States That He Did the Homework Assignment, Check Whether or Not He Did It As Negotiated

When your client reports that he carried out the homework assignment, the first point to check when you review the homework assignment is whether or not the client did it as negotiated. It may well happen that your client has changed the nature of the assignment and in doing so has lessened the therapeutic potency of the assignment.

You will recall that the homework assignment I negotiated with Norman was as follows:

'I will speak up in three different seminars while showing myself that I don't need to be certain that I won't say something stupid before I speak and that if I do say something stupid I can still accept myself as a fallible human being even if others laugh at me.'

There are a variety of ways in which Norman could have modified the assignment. Here is a selection of the large number of ways in which Norman might have changed the nature of his homework assignment:

(i)   Norman could have done the assignment as agreed, but only on one or two occasions rather than the three we negotiated.

(ii) He could have spoken up on three separate occasions, but without practicing the new rational beliefs or making any changes to his other distorted cognitions such as his inferences.

(iii) He could have spoken up on three separate occasions while changing his distorted inferences or other unrealistic thoughts rather than practicing his new rational beliefs. For example, while speaking up he might have told himself that there was little chance of him saying anything stupid or, if he did, that people would be on his side rather than against him.

(iv) He could have spoken up on three separate occasions while thinking positive, Pollyanna-ish thoughts such as: 'Every time I speak up I'm getting better and better' or defensive thoughts such as 'It doesn't matter if I say something stupid' or 'It doesn't matter if the people in the seminar group laugh at me if I do something stupid.'

One common way in which your client may change the nature of his negotiated homework assignment is when he does not face the situation that he has agreed to face. In REBT parlance, he has not faced the actual A. For example let's suppose that your client has a fear of being rejected by women when he asks them to dance. In the session you work carefully to identify, challenge and help him to change the irrational belief that underpins his anxiety. Following on from this work you negotiate with him an assignment which involves him practicing his new rational belief in the face of actual rejection by a woman. You stress to him that the important aspect of this assignment is not so much asking women to dance, but being rejected by them. Because the client is afraid of rejection, it is important that he faces rejection. At the next session, your client is pleased with the results of his homework. He asked a woman to dance, she accepted his invitation, they spent an enjoyable evening together and they have begun to date. The important point to note from a therapeutic point of view is that the client has not faced the A that he agreed to face. As I will show you below, it is important that you help your client to see that whatever the outcome of his pleasant evening with the aforementioned woman, he has not confronted the source of his problem.

How do you respond when it becomes clear that your client has changed the nature of his homework? I suggest that you do the following:

Step 1: Encourage your client by saying that you were pleased that he did the assignment.

Step 2: Explain how, in your opinion, he changed the assignment and remind him of the exact nature of the task as it was negotiated by the two of you in the previous session. In doing so, if indicated, remind your client of the purpose of the assignment which dictated its precise form.

Step 3: If your client made a genuine mistake in changing the nature of the assignment, invite him to re-do the assignment, but this time as it was previously negotiated. If he agrees, ensure that he keeps a written reminder of the assignment and ask him to guard against making further changes to it. Don't forget to review the assignment in the following session. If he doesn't agree to do the assignment, explore and deal with his reluctance.

Step 4: If it appears that the change that your client made to the assignment was motivated by the presence of an implicit irrational belief, identify and deal with this belief and again invite your client to re-do the assignment as it was previously negotiated, urging him once again to guard against making further change to the assignment. Alternatively, modify the assignment in a way that takes into account the newly discovered obstacle.

Here is an example of how to put this into practice.

Windy: Let's begin by reviewing your homework. How did it go?

Norman: It went fairly well. I managed to speak up on two occasions.

Windy: I'm pleased to hear that. Did you practice the two rational beliefs at the same time?

[See step 1 above]

Norman: Yes, I made sure I did that.

Windy: Good. I'll check what you learned from doing the homework in a moment. But, first, are you aware that you didn't quite do all the homework?

[See step 2 above]

Norman: You mean that I didn't speak up on three occasions?

Windy: Yes, it's important for me to understand what happened on the occasion that you didn't speak up. Can you help me to understand that?

Norman: Well, it was at the Friday morning seminar. I remember feeling quite uncomfortable...but er...I guess I thought that as I'd done quite well I would give myself a break and not speak up on that day.

Windy: I see. You said that you were feeling quite uncomfortable. What exactly was the nature of that feeling?

[Here I am seeking to clarify the client's emotional C. My hunch is that the client did not do the third part of his assignment because he was thinking irrationally at the time and this led to avoidance — see step 4.]

Norman: I was anxious....

I then proceeded to use inference chaining to discover that Norman was anxious about saying something stupid in front of a female student whom he found attractive and who rarely attended seminars. I then identified and challenged Norman's new irrational belief: 'I must speak well in front of Joanna' and we negotiated a new homework assignment where he would seek out Joanna and have an intellectual discussion with her while practicing his new rational belief: 'I'd like to speak well in front of Joanna, but I don't have to do so.' The second assignment that I negotiated with Norman concerned asking Joanna to attend the next seminar and, if she did, he would do the third part of his original homework task. I suggested that Norman ask Joanna to attend the next seminar because, left to her own devices, Joanna would probably not attend another seminar for quite a while.

Unit 100: Review What Your Client Learned From Doing the Assignment

The next step in the homework-reviewing process concerns asking your client what he learned from doing the homework. If your client learned what you hoped he would learn, acknowledge that he did well and move on. If your client did not learn what you hoped he would learn, then you need to address this issue. Let me show how I dealt with this latter situation with Norman.

Windy: So, Norman, you managed to speak up on the three occasions as we agreed and you were also able to practice strengthening your new rational beliefs. Is that right?

Norman: Yes, that's right.

Windy: Good. Now what did you learn from doing the assignment?

Norman: I learned that it is very unlikely that I will say something stupid in a seminar setting.

Windy: Did you learn anything else?

Norman: No, that's about it.

[The purpose of the homework assignment was to help Norman over his anxiety about speaking up in class. The way Norman and I chose to do this was to have him challenge his irrational beliefs about being certain that he would not say anything stupid before he spoke and about how others viewed him and to have him practice the rational alternatives while speaking up. Ideally, what I would have liked Norman to have learned was that he didn't need to be certain before he spoke and that if others laughed at him if he did say something stupid then he could accept himself as a fallible human being in this situation. However, he did not mention either of these two beliefs in what he learned. Rather, he said that he learned that it was now unlikely that he would say something stupid in class. Whilst this is an important learning, it is based on an inferential change which in REBT theory is considered to lead to less enduring results than belief change as we saw in Module 2.

Consequently, my task is to explain this to Norman and encourage him to focus on making a change in belief, while not undermining what for him was likely to be a significant piece of learning.]

Windy: I think the fact that you learned that it is unlikely that you will say something stupid in class is important for you and by saying what I am about to say I do not mean to detract from this. OK?

Norman: OK.

Windy: Good. Now when you focused on the idea that you were unlikely to say something stupid how did this help you?

Norman: It got rid of the anxiety and helped me to speak up.

Windy: But how do you know for sure that you won't say something stupid?

Norman: I guess I don't.

Windy: Right, And let's suppose that you do say something stupid and people laugh at you, will the idea that you are unlikely to say something stupid help you to deal productively with that situation?

Norman: No, it won't.

Windy: Now, again, learning that you are unlikely to say something stupid in class is important and note that you did speak up without having a guarantee that you wouldn't say something stupid.

Norman: Right, but as we talk about it, I can see that I wasn't really telling myself that it was unlikely that I would say something stupid. I was telling myself that I definitely wouldn't say something stupid.

Windy: I see. Now that means that if you are to speak up without such guarantees and if you are to cope with people laughing at you then it would be really useful if you could speak up regularly in class and deliberately say something stupid on one or two occasions.

Norman: So that I introduce some uncertainty into the situation you mean?

Windy: Exactly. And so you can deal with the possibility or even actuality of people laughing at you.

Norman: Wow, that's a tough assignment.

Windy: Well, let's see if we can negotiate something challenging, but not overwhelming. The main thing though is for you to learn (1) that you can speak up even when there is the possibility that you may say something stupid and (2) that you can accept yourself as a fallible human being when you do say something stupid and there is a chance that people will laugh at you.

[Norman and I then proceeded to negotiate an assignment using the guidelines discussed in Module 21.]

Unit 101: Capitalize on Your Client's Success

How do you respond when your client has successfully done his homework and has learned what you hoped he would learn? I recommend that you reinforce him for achievement and suggest that he build on his success.

Windy: So, Norman, you were able to speak up on three separate occasions while practicing your rational beliefs. and you say that you are beginning to really believe that you don't need certainty that you won't say anything stupid before you speak up and that even if you do say something stupid and people laugh at you, you can accept yourself as a fallible human being in the face of ridicule. Is that right?

Norman: Yes, that's right.

Windy: How do you feel about what you have achieved and what you are learning?

Norman: I feel really good about it.

Windy: I'm pleased. I think you are doing really well...(humorously) Of course that doesn't mean that you are a more worthwhile person!

Norman:...(laughs) Ha, Ha, Ha.

Windy: Seriously though, you are doing well, so let's talk about how you can capitalise on your success. OK?

Norman: OK.

Windy: What do you think you can do between now and next week to extend this?

Norman: Well, I guess I can undertake to speak up at every seminar.

Windy: Good. How about undertaking to speak up at least twice at every seminar you attend?

Norman: (humorously) You're a real taskmaster, aren't you?

Windy: Does that mean yes or no?

Norman: OK, I'll do it.

Windy: Excellent. Let's make a written note of what you're going to do and where and when you are going to do it (see Module 21, Unit 92).

Unit 102: Responding to Your Client's Homework "Failure"

Let's suppose that your client has done her homework, but it turned out poorly. When this happens, clients often say that they did the assignment, but 'it didn't work'. I have put the word 'failure' in inverted commas here because although clients regard the assignment as a 'failure', as shown in Module 21, Unit 84, there is much to learn from this situation. So, when you encounter this so-called 'failure', remind your client of the 'no-lose' nature of homework assignments and begin to investigate the factors involved. But first ask for a factual account about what happened. Then, once you have identified the factors that accounted for the 'failure', help your client to deal with them and endeavour to re-negotiate the same or similar assignment.

While you are investigating the factors which accounted for your client's homework 'failure', it is useful to keep in mind a number of such factors. Here is an illustrative list of some of the more common reasons for homework 'failure'.

* Your client implemented certain, but not all the elements of the negotiated assignment (see this module, Unit 99). For example, your client may have done the behavioral aspect of the assignment, but did not practice new rational beliefs with the result that he experienced the same unhealthy negative emotions associated with the target problem.
* The assignment was 'overwhelming, rather than challenging' for your client at this time.
* Your client began to do the assignment but stopped doing it because he began to experience discomfort which he believed he could not tolerate.
* Your client practiced the wrong rational beliefs during the assignment.
* Your client practiced the right rational beliefs, but did so in a overly weak manner with the result that his unhealthy negative emotions predominated.
* Your client began to do the assignment, but forgot what he was to do after he had begun.
* Your client began the assignment, but gave up because he did not experience immediate benefit from it.
* Your client began the assignment, but gave up soon after when he realized that he did not know what to do. This happens particularly with written ABC homework assignments.
* Your client began the assignment, but encountered a critical A which triggered a new undiscovered irrational belief which led him to abandon the assignment.

Let's look at how I responded to Norman when he reported a homework 'failure'.

Windy: Let's start by considering your homework. How did it go?

Norman: Not very well.

Windy: I'm sorry to hear that. Tell me what happened.

[Here, I begin by asking for a factual account of Norman's experience with the assignment.]

Norman: Well, before the first seminar, I practiced the rational beliefs that we discussed and was all geared up to speak up. So after about ten minutes I spoke up, but it didn't go too well. So I didn't do it again.

Windy: Now, do you remember the concept of the 'no-lose' homework assignment?

Norman: I think so. it means that if I do the assignment and it works out, that's fine. And it is also valuable if I do it and it doesn't work out well; that's also valuable because we can discover why.

Windy: Good. Now, let's see if we can discover why in your case. Let me start by asking you what rational beliefs you practiced before speaking up at the first seminar.

[Norman's report indicated that he practiced the correct rational beliefs and did so with sufficient force.]

Windy: Well that seems fine. Now let's look closely at what happened when you spoke up at the first seminar.

Norman: Well, there was a gap in the conversation so I went over the rational beliefs again and took the plunge and spoke up.

Windy: And what happened?

Norman: Well, I wasn't too anxious while I was speaking. But when I stopped I got a bit depressed.

Windy: What were you most depressed about?

[Here I am attempting to identify Norman's critical A. It transpired that Norman was depressed about not saying something particularly noteworthy. His irrational belief was 'When I speak up in class, I must say something noteworthy and if I don't then I am something of a failure.' I then helped Norman to challenge and change this irrational belief.]

Windy: So, Norman, can you now see why you got depressed about what you said and why you didn't speak up in the subsequent two seminars?

Norman: Yes, I can. That's really helpful. I can now really see what you meant by the 'no-lose' homework assignment.

Windy: That's really good. Now let me suggest that you do the same homework between now and next week, but this time how about practicing the new rational belief as well, namely: 'I would like to say something noteworthy every time I speak up in class, but I don't have to do so. If I don't, I'm not a failure. Rather I am a fallible human being who says noteworthy and mundane things at times?'

Norman: That's a good idea.

[I then take Norman through an imagery assignment to give him some practice at the new rational belief, after which we both make a written note of his new assignment.]

Unit 103: Dealing With the Situation When Your Client Has Not Done the Homework Assignment

Despite the fact that you may have taken the utmost care in negotiating a homework assignment with your client and instituted all the safeguards that I discussed in Module 21, your client may still not carry it out. When this happens, I suggest that you follow a similar procedure that I discussed in the previous unit; that is, ask your client for a factual account of the situation where she contracted to do the assignment but didn't do it, remind him of the 'no-lose' concept of homework assignments, identify and deal with the factors that accounted for him not doing the assignment and then re-negotiate the same or similar assignment. As you investigate the aforementioned factors, be particularly aware of the fact that you may have failed to institute one or more of the safeguards reviewed in the previous module. If this is the case and your failure to do so accounts for your client not carrying out the assignment, then take responsibility for this omission, disclose this to your client, institute the safeguard and re-negotiate the assignment.

On the other hand, if the reason why your client did not do the assignment can be attributed to a factor in the client that you could not have foreseen, help him to deal with it and again re-negotiate the same or similar assignment.

In investigating the reason why Norman did not carry out his homework, it transpired that he did not do so because he believed that he had to feel comfortable before speaking up. Team up with a trainee colleague, play the role of therapist and have him or her play Norman and see if you can help your 'client' over the obstacle and then re-negotiate the same homework assignment. Tape record the interchange and play the recording to your REBT trainer or supervisor for feedback.

Appendix 2 contains a form that I recommend you use with your clients when they consistently fail to initiate negotiated homework assignments. I suggest that you use this form in training as well. Again pair up with a trainee colleague and have him or her play the role of a client who doesn't do homework assignments for each of the reasons shown on the form and gain practice at helping your 'client' over the obstacle. Tape record the interchanges and once again seek feedback from your REBT trainer or supervisor.

We have now reached the end of this training manual. I hope that you have found it useful and I wish you well in your career as an REBT therapist.

Appendix 1

Homework Skills Monitoring Form

Listen to the audiotape of your therapy session and circle 'Yes', 'No' or 'N/A' (Not Appropriate) for each item. For every item circled 'No', write down in the space provided what you would have done differently given hindsight and what you would have needed to change in order to have circled the item "Yes".

1. Did I use a term for homework assignments that was acceptable to the client?

Yes   No   N/A

2. Did I properly negotiate the homework assignment with the client (as opposed to telling him/her what to do or accepting uncritically his/her suggestion)?

Yes   No   N/A

3. Was the homework assignment expressed clearly?

Yes   No   N/A

4. Did I ensure that the client understood the homework assignment?

Yes   No   N/A

5. Was the homework assignment relevant to my client's therapy goals?

Yes   No   N/A

6. Did I help the client understand the relevance of the homework assignment to his/her therapy goals?

Yes   No   N/A

7. Did the homework assignment follow logically from the work I did with the client in the session?

Yes   No   N/A

8. Was the type of homework assignment I negotiated with the client relevant to the stage reached by the two of us on his/her target problem?

Yes   No   N/A

9. Did I employ the 'challenging, but not overwhelming' principle in negotiating the homework assignment?

Yes   No   N/A

10. Did I introduce and explain the 'no lose' concept of homework assignments?

Yes   No   N/A

11. Did I ensure that the client had the necessary skills to carry out the homework assignment?

Yes   No   N/A

12. Did I ensure that the client believed that he/she could do the homework assignment?

Yes   No   N/A

13. Did I allow sufficient time in the session to negotiate the homework assignment properly?

Yes   No   N/A

14. Did I elicit a firm commitment from the client that he/she would carry out the homework assignment?

Yes   No   N/A

15. Did I help the client to specify when, where and how often he/she would carry out the homework assignment?

Yes   No   N/A

16. Did I encourage my client to make a written note of the homework assignment and its relevant details?

Yes   No   N/A

17. Did the client and I both retain a copy of this written note?

                        Yes   No   N/A

18. Did I elicit from the client potential obstacles to homework completion?

                        Yes   No   N/A

19. Did I help the client to deal in advance with any potential obstacles that he/she disclosed?

                        Yes   No   N/A

20. Did I help the client to rehearse the homework assignment in the session?

                        Yes   No   N/A

21. Did I use the principle of rewards and penalties with the client?

                        Yes   No   N/A

Appendix 2

Possible Reasons for Not Doing Self-help Assignments

(To be Completed by Clients)

The following is a list of reasons that various clients have given for not doing their self-help assignments during the course of counseling. Because the speed of improvement depends primarily on the amount of self-help assignments that you are willing to do, it is of great importance to pinpoint any reasons that you may have for not doing this work. It is important to look for these reasons at the time that you feel a reluctance to do your assignment or a desire to put off doing it. Hence, it is best to fill out this questionnaire at that time. If you have any difficulty filling out this form and returning it to the counselor, it might be best to do it together during a counseling session. (Rate each statement by ringing 'T' (True) 'F' (False). 'T' indicates that you agree with it; 'F' means the statement does not apply at this time.)

1. It seems that nothing can help me so there is no point in trying.   T/F
2. It wasn't clear, I didn't understand what I had to do.   T/F
3. I thought that the particular method the counselor had suggested would not be helpful. I didn't really see the value of it.   T/F
4. It seemed too hard.   T/F
5. I am willing to do self-help assignments, but I keep forgetting.   T/F
6. I did not have enough time. I was too busy.   T/F
7. If I do something the counselor suggests I do it's not as good as if I come up with my own ideas.   T/F
8. I don't really believe I can do anything to help myself.   T/F
9. I have the impression the counselor is trying to boss me around or control me.   T/F
10. I worry about the counselor's disapproval. I believe that what I do just won't be good enough for him/her.   T/F
11. I felt too bad, sad, nervous, upset (underline the appropriate word(s)) to do it.   T/F
12. I would have found doing the homework assignment too upsetting.   T/F
13. It was too much to do.   T/F
14. It's too much like going back to school again.   T/F
15. It seemed to be mainly for the counselor's benefit.   T/F
16. Self-help assignments have no place in counseling.   T/F
17. Because of the progress I've made these assignments are likely to be of no further benefit to me.   T/F
18. Because these assignments have not been helpful in the past, I couldn't see the point of doing this one.   T/F
19. I don't agree with this particular approach to counseling.   T/F
20. OTHER REASONS (please write them).

Appendix 3

Training in Rational Emotive Behavior Therapy

1. For further details of training courses in REBT worldwide, contact:
   Director of Professional Education
   Albert Ellis Institute for REBT
   45 East 65th Street
   New York
   NY 10021
   USA
   Tel: 212 535 0822

References

Bandura, A. (1977). *Social Learning Theory*. Englewood Cliffs, NJ: Prentice-Hall.

Beck, A.T. (1976). *Cognitive Therapy and the Emotional Disorders*. New York: International Universities Press.

Beck, A.T., Rush, A.J., Shaw, B.F. & Emery, G. (1979). *Cognitive Therapy of Depression*. New York: Guilford.

Blackburn, I. and Davidson, K. (1990). *Cognitive Therapy for Depression and Anxiety: A practitioner's guide*. Oxford: Blackwell Scientific.

Bordin, E. (1979). The generalizability of the concept of the working alliance. *Psychotherapy: Theory, Research and Practice* **16**, 252-260.

DiGiuseppe, R. (1991a). A rational–emotive model of assessment. In: M.E. Bernard (Ed.), *Using rational–emotive therapy effectively*. New York: Plenum.

DiGiuseppe, R. (1991b). Comprehensive cognitive disputing in rational emotive therapy. In M. Bernard (Ed.), *Using Rational-emotive Therapy Effectively*. New York: Plenum.

DiGiuseppe, R., Leaf, R. and Linscott, J. (1993). The therapeutic relationship in rational–emotive therapy: Some preliminary data. *Journal of Rational–Emotive and Cognitive-Behavior Therapy*, **11**, 223-233.

Dryden, W. (1985). Dilemmas in giving warmth or love to clients: An interview with Albert Ellis. In: W. Dryden, *Therapists' Dilemmas*. London: Harper & Row.

Dryden, W. (1986). Vivid RET. In: A. Ellis and R. Grieger (Eds), *Handbook of Rational-Emotive therapy*, volume 2. New York: Springer.

Dryden, W. (1987). *Current Issues in Rational-emotive Therapy*. Beckenham, Kent: Croom Helm.

Dryden, W. (1988). Language and meaning in rational-emotive therapy. In W. Dryden & P. Trower (Eds), *Developments in Rational-emotive Therapy*. Milton Keynes: Open University Press.

Dryden, W. (Ed.) (1989). *Howard Young – Rational Therapist: Seminal papers in rational-emotive therapy*. Loughton, Essex: Gale Centre Publications.

Dryden, W. (Ed.) (1990a). *The Essential Albert Ellis*. New York: Springer.

Dryden, W. (1990b). *Rational-Emotive Counseling in Action*. London: Sage.

Dryden, W. (1991). *Reason and Therapeutic Change*. London: Whurr.

Dryden, W. (1994a). *10 Steps to Positive Living*. London: Sheldon Press.

Dryden, W. (1994b). *Invitation to Rational-Emotive Psychology*. London: Whurr.

Dryden, W. (1994c). *Overcoming Guilt*. London: Sheldon.

Dryden, W. (1994d). *Progress in Rational Emotive Behavior Therapy*. London: Whurr.

Dryden, W. (1996). *Overcoming Anger: When Anger Helps and When It Hurts*. London: Sheldon.

Dryden, W. (1997). *Overcoming Shame*. London: Sheldon.

Dryden, W., Ferguson, J. and Clark, A. (1989). Beliefs and inferences – a test of a rational-emotive hypothesis: 2. On the prospect of seeing a spider. *Psychological Reports* **64**, 115–123.

Dryden, W. & Gordon, J. (1990). Think Your Way to Happiness. London: Sheldon.

Dryden, W. & Gordon, J. (1992). *Think Rationally: A Brief Guide to Overcoming your Emotional Problems*. London: Centre for Rational Emotive Therapy.

Dryden, W. & Gordon, J. (1993). Beating the Comfort Trap. London: Sheldon.

Dryden, W. and Trower, P. (Eds). (1989). *Cognitive Psychotherapy: Stasis and change*. London: Cassell.

Ellis, A. (1959). Requisite conditions for basic personality change. *Journal of Consulting Psychology* **23**, 538–540.

Ellis, A. (1963). Toward a more precise definition of 'emotional' and 'intellectual' insight. *Psychological Reports*, **23**, 538–540.

Ellis, A. (1976). The biological basis of human irrationality. *Journal of Individual Psychology*, **32**, 145–168.

Ellis, A. (1983). The philosophic implications and dangers of some popular behavior therapy techniques. In M. Rosenbaum, C.M. Franks & Y. Jaffe (Eds), *Perspectives in Behavior Therapy in the Eighties*. New York: Springer.

Ellis, A. (1985). *Overcoming Resistance: Rational-emotive therapy with difficult clients*. New York: Springer.

Ellis, A. (1991). The revised ABCs of rational-emotive therapy. *Journal of Rational-Emotive and Cognitive-Behavior Therapy* **9**(3), 139–172.

Ellis, A. and Dryden, W. (1997). *The Practice of Rational Emotive Behavior Therapy*. 2nd edition. New York: Springer.

Ellis, A. & Harper, R.A. (1975). A New Guide to Rational Living. Hollywood, CA: Wilshire.

Gandy, G.L. (1985). Frequent misperceptions of rational-emotive therapy: An overview for the rehabilitation counselor. *Journal of Applied Rehabilitation Counseling* **16**(4), 31–35.

Gilmore, I. (1986). An exposition and development of the debate on the nature of the distinction between appropriate and inappropriate beliefs in rational-emotive therapy. *Journal of Rational-Emotive Therapy* **4**(2), 155–165.

Golden, W.L. (1989). Resistance and change in cognitive-behavior therapy. In W. Dryden & P. Trower (Eds), *Cognitive Psychotherapy: Stasis and Change*. London: Cassell.

Hauck, P. (1974). *Depression: Why it Happens and How to Overcome it*. London: Sheldon.

Hauck, P. (1980). Calm Down: How to Cope with Frustration and Anger. London: Sheldon.

Hauck, P. (1981a). *How to Stand up for Yourself*. London: Sheldon.

Hauck, P. (1981b). *Why be Afraid?* London: Sheldon.

Hauck. P. (1991). *Hold your Head up High*. London: Sheldon.

Knaus, W.J. and Haberstroh, N. (1993). A rational-emotive education program to help disruptive mentally retarded clients develop self-control. In: W. Dryden and L.K. Hill (Eds), *Innovations in Rational-Emotive Therapy*. Newbury Park, CA: Sage.

Mahrer, A.R. (Ed.). (1967). *The Goals of Psychotherapy*. New York: Appleton-Century-Crofts.

Maluccio, A.N. (1979). *Learning from Clients: Interpersonal Helping as Viewed by Clients and Social Workers*. New York: Free Press.

Moore, R.H. (1988). Inference as 'A' in RET. In: W. Dryden and P. Trower (Eds), *Developments in Rational-Emotive therapy*. Milton Keynes: Open University Press.

Rogers, C.R. (1957). The necessary and sufficient conditions of therapeutic personality change. *Journal of Consulting Psychology* **21**, 95-103.

Sacco, W.P. (1981). Cognitive therapy in vivo. In: G. Emery, S.D. Hollon and R.C. Bedrosian (Eds), *New Directions in Cognitive Therapy*. New York: Guilford.

Saltzberg, L. and Elkins, G.R. (1980). An examination of common concerns about rational-emotive therapy. *Professional Psychology* **11**, 324-330.

Segal, J. (1993). *Against self-disclosure. In W. Dryden (Ed.)*, Questions and Answers on Counseling in Action. London: Sage.

Walen, S.R., DiGiuseppe, R. & Dryden, W. (1992). *A Practitioner's Guide to Rational-emotive Therapy*, second edition. New York: Oxford University Press.

Yankura. J. & Dryden, W. (1990). *Doing RET: Albert Ellis in Action*. New York: Springer.

Young, H.S. (1974). *A Rational Counseling Primer*. New York: Institute for Rational-Emotive Therapy.

Young, H.S. (1979). Is it RET? *Rational Living* **14**(2), 9-17.

Index